SHOWDOWN

Also by Richard J. Krickus

The Superpowers in Crisis: Implications of Domestic Discord

SHOWDOWN

The Lithuanian Rebellion and the
Breakup of the Soviet Empire

Richard J. Krickus

BRASSEY'S
Washington • London

Designed by Margaret Nelling Schmidt, Appalachian Prepress

First Edition

Library of Congress Cataloging-in-Publication Data

Krickus, Richard J.
    Showdown: the Lithuanian rebellion and the breakup of the Soviet Empire / Richard Krickus. — 1st ed.
        p.   cm.
    Includes bibliographical references and index.
    ISBN 1-57488-058-6
    1. Lithuania—Politics and government—1991– 2. Lithuania—History—Autonomy and independence movements. 3. Krickus, Richard J.—Journeys—Lithuania. I. Title.
DK505.8.K75 1996
947'.5086—dc20   96-26870
                                                                                            CIP

10 9 8 7 6 5 4 3 2 1

Printed in the United States of America

For
Anthony and Alexandra

CONTENTS

Acknowledgments ix

1 Showdown 1

2 A Turbulent History 4

3 Lithuanian Nationalism Endures 30

4 Popular Front Revolutionaries 47

5 Free Elections 71

6 Independence 94

7 America's Response 118

8 Bloody Sunday 136

9 The Empire Collapses 165

10 An Uncertain Future 191

Notes 211

Appendix 1: Chronology Of Major Events 222

Appendix 2: Biographical Guide 226

Index 230

ACKNOWLEDGMENTS

In addition to those who granted me interviews, I am indebted to many people in both Lithuania and the United States who contributed to this book. In Lithuania they are Gintautas Alksninis, Lucija Baskauskaite, Algimantas Cekuolis, Rita Dapkus, Algirdas Deguitis, Arvydas Juozaitis, Vladys Gadys, Andrius Kubilius, Mecys Laurinkus, Arvydas Matulionas, Arturas Racas, Ignas Stankovicius, Egle Taurinskaite, Lionginas Vasiliauskas, Romas Vastukas, and Emmanuelis Zingeris.

In the United States, the following people shared with me their knowledge about the Lithuanian rebellion and the reaction of the United States to it: Asta Banionis, Ginte Damusis, Al Gecys, Paul Goble, Ambassador Daryll Johnson, Linas Kojelis, Romas Sakadolskis, Yuri Urbanovich, and Vaiva Verba. Members of the Lithuanian embassy also graciously responded to requests for information: the ambassador, Alfonsas Eidintas, Stasys Sakalauskas, Kerry Stromberg, Edvardas Tuskensis, and Vytautas Zalys. Father Casimer Pugevicius and Victor Nakas deserve special mention because they first encouraged me to write about developments in Lithuania and later provided me with critical insights and information about the Lithuanian rebellion. Both significantly contributed to the ultimate restoration of an independent Lithuania.

My colleagues Joe Bozicevic, Lew Fickett, Vic Fingerhut, Jack Kramer, Dora Minor, Margaret Mock, Ron Singleton, and Paul Slayton facilitated completion of this book as did our academic home, Mary Washington College, which provided me funding to conduct research and deliver lectures in Lithuania during the course of this project.

Once again, both Frank Margiotta and Don McKeon at Brassey's made helpful recommendations about making this book more readable.

Finally, my son, Anthony, and daughter, Alexandra, sustained me during the most difficult phases of this undertaking, and at a time when they were embarking upon new educational challenges of their own.

The Baltic States

Legend
- International boundary
- ★ National capital
- Railroad
- Road

0 50 100 Kilometers
0 50 100 Miles

FINLAND

Kouvola
Vyborg
Sosnovo
Lake Ladoga
Kotka
Primorsk
Porvoo
Helsinki
St. Petersburg
Gulf of Finland
Gatchina
Hanko
Tallinn
Paldiski
Kohtla-Järve
Narva
Tapa
Rakvere
Slantsy
Haapsalu
Hiiumaa
Gdov
Luga
Batetskiy
ESTONIA
Viljandi
Lake Peipus
Ozero Il'man'
Saaremaa
Pärnu
Tartu
Kuressaare
Lake Pskov
Valga
Võru
Dno
Gulf of Riga
Kolka
Valmiera
Pskov
RUSSIA
Gotland (SWEDEN)
Ventspils
Alūksne
Ostrov
Mērsrags
Cēsis
Gulbene
Velikaya
Sushchëvo
Stende
Riga
Pytalovo
Baltic Sea
Tukums
Jūrmala
Ogre
LATVIA
Velikiye Luki
Liepāja
Saldus
Jelgava
Rēzekne
Novosokol'niki
Jēkabpils
Pustoshka
Mažeikiai
Daugava
Nevel'
Šiauliai
Panevėžys
Daugavpils
Kretinga
Rietavas
Navapolatsk
Polatsk
Klaipėda
Utena
Vitsyebsk
Šilutė
LITHUANIA
Pastavy
Hlybokaye
Orsha
Tauragė
Kėdainiai
Ukmergė
Jonava
Švenčionėliai
Zelenogradsk
Nemunas
Neris
BELARUS
Kaliningrad
Kaunas
Vilnius
Viliya
Pregolya
Chernyakhovsk
RUSSIA
Alytus
Maladzyechna
Barysaw
Byarezina
Mahilyow
POLAND
Suwałki
Druskininkai
Ełk
Lida
Minsk
Olsztyn
Hrodna
Nyoman

SHOWDOWN

1 SHOWDOWN

On the morning of August 19, 1991, I retrieved the *Washington Post* from outside my front door and was shocked by the headline "Close Aides Oust Gorbachev; Hard-Line Group Takes Over." I dashed to my TV and turned to CNN. For the next four days I joined an audience of billions and watched the drama that was unfolding in the world's largest empire. Recall the images that appeared before our eyes as we witnessed events occurring thousands of miles away from the comfort of our living rooms:

We saw tanks lumbering ominously through the streets of Moscow as bystanders watched with grim foreboding.

Then we saw the putschists at a press conference, where Gennady Yanayev, the vice-president who had replaced the "ill" Gorbachev, presided. Doubts about the coup's success were confirmed when the camera zoomed in for a close-up of Yanayev's hands, they were shaking uncontrollably. Later we would learn he had an alcohol problem.

We saw Boris Yeltsin, the maverick Russian president, standing tall on a T-72 tank denouncing the coup. In his finest hour, he called Muscovites to the White House—the building where he shared offices with members of the Russian legislature—to help him resist the coup.

We watched in anticipation as crowds around the White House built barricades and pelted tanks with Molotov cocktails as they approached the democrats' redoubt. We sadly observed the bodies of three young men who were killed as they tried to disrupt tank movements.[1]

As the tension mounted, we asked ourselves if the courageous people who had bravely joined Yeltsin could possibly succeed in resisting the neo-Stalinists who commanded the vast armed might of the Soviet state. But the assault never materialized. We learned that the commanders of the USSR's airborne units and air force wings—Generals Pavel Grachev and Yevgeni Shaposhnikov—had warned their colleagues that they would use their forces to defend the

White House. By Thursday the headlines of the *Post* proclaimed: "Coup Fails; Gorbachev Returns." The campaign to restore Stalinism to the USSR was over. Later, on TV, we saw Gorbachev descending from an airplane upon his return to Moscow. He was tired and disoriented. From his brief remarks it was apparent that he had returned from his vacation retreat in the Crimea, Cape Foros, without a clue to just how fundamentally his country and people had changed.

The next day, when Gorbachev appeared before a gathering of the Russian parliament, the world witnessed the transfer of power from the Soviet president to Yeltsin, the Russian president. Yeltsin acted with dispatch as he outlawed the Communist Party and placed people loyal to him in the country's power ministries, the KGB, army, and militia. Gorbachev tried desperately to keep the union intact but he failed, and on December 25, 1991, the Soviet empire faded into history.

For older Americans, who had experienced the Cold War for a lifetime, the collapse of the Soviet empire was a miracle. After all, the leaders of that empire had an awesome nuclear strike force capable of destroying the United States in a matter of hours. Indeed, they could do that with just one component of their nuclear triad, the 304 SS-18s armed with ten warheads each. If the full complement of SS-18s were launched, over three thousand nuclear-tipped reentry vehicles would come raining down on the United States, killing tens of millions of Americans. What's more, in Europe, the Red Army was deemed capable of launching a conventional blitzkrieg attack across the plains of central Germany and rolling over the NATO defenders until the Communist legions stopped at the English Channel.

With such awesome power, how could the USSR have collapsed? Why did Stalin's successors not put up a real fight to retain the reins of power? We had read for years about reports from journalists and academics that the Soviet Union was faced with desperate economic problems; that Moscow was worried about the loyalties of non-Russians in the USSR itself, the "inner empire"; and that the Eastern European satellites in the "outer empire" were restless. But in the past, the men in the Kremlin and their puppets in the satellite states had crushed resistance to communism—Hungary in 1956, Czechoslovakia in 1968, Poland in 1981.

Something had happened within the Soviet Union itself which spread like a cancer through the vast empire. Since the demise of the Soviet Union we have been preoccupied with Russia's struggle to build a democratic society, and we have forgotten what it was that precipitated the breakup of this largest empire in modern history. Even the historians who are rummaging through the archives of the former Soviet Union have failed to identify the force that set events in motion.

When asked why the Soviet security forces and the Red Army did not move against Yeltsin in August 1991, a KGB colonel responded: "Vilnius was the last straw, and our patience ran out. . . . Honestly, had it not been for Vilnius, we would not have refused to storm the White House." He was speaking of the Lithuanian capital. This observation and other clues have been lost in the vast outpouring of postmortem explanations of why the Soviet empire collapsed. Few witnesses among the hundreds of millions of people who were mesmerized by the TV images that recorded the events of those amazing days in 1991 could fathom the significance of the colonel's words. The world didn't understand that this final drama began when the Lithuanians restored their independent state in March 1990 and when they thwarted Gorbachev's attempt to crush them on "Bloody Sunday," January 13, 1991.

The Lithuanian rebellion precipitated the coup against Gorbachev and the subsequent breakup of the Soviet empire. Because thousands of Lithuanians stood their ground and, with their bodies as their only weapons, resisted Soviet tanks and a KGB shock force, the world is a much different place today. If the Lithuanians on Bloody Sunday had bolted in the face of Soviet might, it is likely that the Soviet empire would exist today. Gorbachev might not be at the helm and the system almost certainly would be in grave difficulty. But the Union of Soviet Socialist Republics might still be intact, in command of a vast nuclear arsenal, and in control of strategically vital territory running from the Baltic Sea to the Pacific Ocean.

As an American scholar of Lithuanian ancestry, I was privileged to be present at these earthshaking events and to be a small part of them. Hundreds of other Lithuanian-Americans aided their old homeland as it struggled to bolt from the Soviet empire. But this is only incidentally our story. Instead, it is the story of those courageous people who led the fight to restore an independent Lithuania after a long, turbulent history. For centuries, generations of their ancestors had been pawns of the larger powers that pressed against their small country on the Baltic Sea. In the modern era, Lithuanians would endure czarist autocracy and, after breathing the air of freedom from 1918 to 1940, would be forced back into Stalin's gulag. There, for a half century, they were subjugated by a cruel dictatorship, but they endured—and eventually prevailed.

This book is the fascinating story of the events leading up to the showdown in Vilnius and how that showdown led to the disintegration of the Soviet Union. It is the story of how unarmed, brave men and women struggled for freedom and, in the struggle, brought down an empire.

2 A TURBULENT HISTORY

There . . . stacked like cordwood were the bodies of many parti-
sans who had been killed by Soviet troops. They were being dis-
played in this awful fashion to teach Lithuanian schoolchildren
that it was hopeless to resist"

—*Ausra Jurasas, literary critic*

When the Lithuanians boldly challenged Soviet leader Gorbachev in March 1990, few Americans could locate Lithuania on the map, and fewer still knew anything about its history. This was not surprising, since U. S. schools devote little or no attention to Eastern Europe, even though many Americans trace their heritage to this part of the world and it has contributed significantly to the richness of Western civilization.

When developments in Lithuania forced pundits and policymakers to consider the Baltic region, few of them could answer basic questions about it. What were the historical factors that sustained Lithuanian nationalism? Why did this small republic and not larger ones like the Ukrainian SSR, challenge the mighty Soviet empire? And finally, why was it a mistake on Gorbachev's part to think that offering the Lithuanians greater economic opportunities would induce them to surrender their primary goal—the restoration of a free and independent Lithuania? To answer these questions, a brief glance at Lithuania's history is warranted.

On March 23, 1939, Adolf Hitler boarded the German battleship *Deutsch-land,* which immediately steamed for the Lithuanian port city of Klaipeda. The Germans called it Memel, but Germany had lost legal control over it in 1919 after World War I, when the League of Nations placed it under French jurisdiction. (The Prussians, a Baltic-speaking people who were cousins to the Lithuanians, had lived in the area before they were slaughtered by the Teutonic Knights. Germans then settled in what would become known as Lithuania Minor and ruled this rump part of Lithuania until World War I.) In

January 1923, the Lithuanians occupied the East Prussian city and acquired a much-needed port facility for their newly independent country. They had embarked upon the adventure believing that Germany was too weak and pre-occupied to prevent them from reclaiming a city that they claimed belonged to Lithuania.

At the time the Lithuanians took Memel in 1923, its mostly German population numbered 141,840, and the Germans bridled at their minority status. After the Nazis took power in Berlin, the Germans in Memel looked toward Hitler to release them from Lithuanian control. But not wishing to drive the Lithuanians into the arms of the Poles or Russians, Hitler did not press the issue as rapidly as the Germans there wished. After the British and French allowed Hitler to grab Czechoslovakia, however, it was clear to Baltic-watchers that Memel would be Hitler's next target. The Lithuanians' presumption that the defeated Germany would remain powerless for a long time had been sadly incorrect.[1]

Hitler was not a good sailor, but he was intent on demonstrating his personal ire over Germany's loss of the ancient Baltic port. He had presented the Lithuanians with an ultimatum three days earlier, at a time when the world was still shocked by his March 15 invasion of Czechoslovakia. As he had calculated, the French and British had no stomach to oppose his coup, and he had little reason to fear that his occupation of Klaipeda would provoke a response from the democracies or the Soviet Union.

Impatient, Hitler did not wait for a response from the Lithuanian government but boarded the warship determined to take the city by force if the Lithuanians were recalcitrant. The German foreign minister, Joachim von Ribbentrop, presented the Lithuanians with that ultimatum, and they capitulated. This was not a new experience for the Lithuanians, for over the centuries their ancestors had been subjugated by their larger, more powerful neighbors—Germans, Poles, and Russians.[2]

Since Lithuania was a hub connecting the three largest nations in northeastern Europe, its people had been victims of geography throughout Lithuania's turbulent history. Using current designations, the Baltic lies to its west, Latvia to its north, Belarus to its east, and Poland to its south. In their southwest the Lithuanians also share a border with Kaliningrad, formerly East Prussia. Today, that triangle of territory belongs to Russia and is home for about 800,000 people, many of them military personnel.

In spite of their location and relatively small numbers, the Lithuanians established their own state in the thirteenth century, and that fact goes a long way toward explaining a historical conundrum: how did the Lithuanians, unlike similarly situated small nationalities such as the Tyrolians, the Basques, and the Catalans, establish a sovereign state in the twentieth century?

Lithuania in the Middle Ages was one of the largest countries in Europe. At one point it consisted of present-day Belarus, parts of Latvia, Estonia, and Russia, and much of Ukraine, spreading as far south as the Black Sea. Nonetheless, Lithuania's perennial problem was coping with threats from more populous peoples who resided in the region. Indeed, it was the last country in Europe to shed its pagan traditions, and it embraced Christianity primarily for reasons of national security.

In 1237, after defeating the Teutonic "Brothers of the Sword," King Mindaugas sought additional protection against the marauding Germans by converting to Christianity. He then consolidated Lithuanian lands under a grand duchy, but in 1263 he was assassinated, and his successors returned to paganism. But not for long. In 1386, the Lithuanian grand prince Jogaila married the Polish heiress, princess Jadvyga. A condition of the betrothal was returning to Catholicism, and once again the dictates of realpolitik forced the Lithuanians' hand. The stage was set for a long union between Poland and Lithuania.

In 1569, the Polish-Lithuanian Commonwealth was established with the Treaty of Lublin, and the partnership lasted until the "third" partition of Poland in 1795. (With the Tripartite Alliance of that year, Austria, Prussia, and Russia absorbed the commonwealth's territory. The Russians occupied most areas where Lithuanians lived.) The word "partnership" is inappropriate, because the more numerous Poles were decidedly the senior party in the relationship as members of the Lithuanian aristocracy—such as the Radziwills—shed their language and national values and became culturally Polish. The Lithuanians' dependence on the Poles grew not long after the commonwealth was forged as the Russian czars turned their sights westward. Previously they had been preoccupied with the Tatar hordes that had controlled much of Russia for centuries. But once this ancient enemy was crushed, the imperialist ambitions of the czars expanded, and as they acquired more land their appetite grew as well. In keeping with the imperialistic ambitions of the czarist, and later Soviet, leaders, the Kremlin rulers saw the Baltic region as a gateway to the West and a buffer against European ambition.

As the threat of Russian hegemony grew, the commonwealth served as a mutual defense pact to thwart the spread of Russian domination. Together, the Lithuanians and Poles hoped to hold off the Russians in much the same fashion as they had checked the German threat at the battle of Grunwald in 1410. They were successful for a long time.

With the third partition, the problem of Polish cultural hegemony subsided, but afterward Lithuanians faced an even more dangerous and daunting challenge to their national existence from the Germans and Russians. By the nineteenth century, the Germans had replaced the Scandinavians in Latvia and Estonia and Lithuania Minor, a landmass on the Baltic where Lithuanians had always resided. The Russians absorbed "Lithuania Major," so named because historically most Lithuanians lived in this much larger chunk of their ancestral territory, which was deeper in the hinterland of Eastern Europe. The Lithuanian peoples would remain divided and stateless until February 1918, when they gained their independence with Kaiser Wilhelm's military defeat and the Romanov empire's disintegration.

The resurrection of a Lithuanian state was the culmination of a nationalistic movement that began early in the nineteenth century. At that time, as the ideology of nationalism spread across Europe, conditions for a Lithuanian national revival were unfavorable. In contrast to Estonia and Latvia, where an urban bourgeoisie would develop, the cities of Lithuania were largely populated by Poles and Jews. Since most Lithuanians were peasants, there was neither a sizable urban intelligentsia nor an educated middle class that could provide the masses with a Lithuanian national identity and forge them into a nationalist movement. Furthermore, most of the gentry had become Polonized or Russified and did not speak Lithuanian, and the Lithuanian clergy remained under the influence of the far larger and more powerful Polish Catholic hierarchy.

In spite of these obstacles, the Lithuanian national reawakening began early in the nineteenth century, at a time when the romantic celebration of language and folk culture was enthralling European society. Johann Gottfried Herder, who served as a pastor and teacher in Riga between 1764 and 1769, had encouraged the Balts to resurrect and celebrate their folklore. Indeed, it was under goading by German philologists that some Lithuanians began to study their mother tongue and their country's history and culture. Later, Russian philologists would become mentors to a new generation of Lithuanians seeking to resurrect their ancient traditions. Foreigners were attracted to the Lithuanian revival by the uniqueness of the Lithuanian language, an ancient tongue that, it was believed, faced extinction. The resurrection of the Lithuanian language among a growing segment of society would have an important influence on the rebirth of Lithuanian nationalism.

The "Polish insurrections" of the 1830s and 1860s helped reignite Lithuanian consciousness as well. Following past practices, large numbers of Lithuanians fought alongside Poles against Russian oppression, and in the crucible of combat a Lithuanian national consciousness was advanced. The insurrection was abortive, but the authorities in Moscow sought to prevent a recurrence of a Polish-Lithuanian alliance by reducing the influence of Polonia over the less numerous Lithuanians. Among other things, provisions were made for Lithuanians to study in Russian universities. Jonas Basanavicius, a founding father of the Lithuanian reawakening and the publisher of *Ausra* ("Dawn"), the first Lithuanian newspaper, would be lured to the University of Moscow with a scholarship. Basanavicius lived much of his life practicing medicine in Bulgaria, but from that distant country he helped promote the cause of Lithuanian nationalism.[3]

The czarist Russification campaign was heavy-handed. Lithuanian materials published in Latin script were banned; it was dictated that Cyrillic script be used instead. This change of script alarmed the Lithuanian Catholic clergy, because they rightly saw it as part of a campaign on Moscow's part to convert the Lithuanians to the Russian Orthodox faith. The Russian campaign, in turn, helped forge the link between the Lithuanians' language and their dominant religion. Henceforth, Latinized Lithuanian publications were smuggled from East Prussia into areas dominated by the Russians. Among the Lithuanian nationalists orchestrating this campaign was the linguist Jonas Jablonskis, who was the maternal grandfather of Lithuania's future president Vytautas Landsbergis (whose paternal grandfather, Gabrielus Landsbergis, published an underground Lithuanian newspaper and was deported for his troubles).

Throughout history, the Lithuanian language had been both a curse and a blessing to the people speaking it. In denying Lithuanians easy access to intellectual developments elsewhere in Europe, such as political and economic liberalism, it was a curse. Yet, it was a blessing because it sustained a profound sense of national identity and solidarity even in face of German, Polish, and Russian political and cultural hegemony.

Along with Latvian, Lithuanian is the last of a line of Indo-European languages that once thrived in the Baltic region. Prussian, a related language, has vanished as a spoken tongue; the last person known to use it died in 1677.[4] Had Lithuanian been cousin to German or Russian, the language and the people speaking it probably would have been absorbed centuries ago.

By the second half of the nineteenth century, Lithuanian had fallen into disuse by the educated classes, but on the eve of the twentieth century it was from the common folk that a new wave of intellectuals appeared. Often the first in their families to attend university, they would provide the leadership needed to mobilize the peasants, who had been the repositories of Lithuanian national life. It was also among this segment of society that one found the most devout Catholics.

The Lithuanians were the last people of Europe to become Christians, but after their conversion they earned a reputation for their unshakable Roman Catholicism. By the time of the modern national revival, however, much of the clergy had shed their Lithuanian identity. While the peasants spoke Lithuanian at home and their children used Russian in school, all Catholics attended mass, where Polish was the primary language. Given the Polish cast of the Church, many secular nationalists like Jonas Sliupis saw the Church as a barrier to the national revival. Some even argued that a true Lithuanian was a pagan and Christianity was anathema to his nature. Perhaps such views better reflected the contrary nature of the Lithuanians and not their naturalistic impulses. But clearly, pagan symbols were integrated into Lithuanian Catholicism. Even today, important pagan symbols such as the moon, sun rays, and serpents are often found in wood carvings, paintings, and sculptures depicting traditional Christian subjects. Wood and metal sculptures of the "suffering Christ," which one encounters throughout Lithuania, are a replica of a figure that has its origins in pagan folklore.

From the very outset of Russian rule, however, Roman Catholicism stood as a bulwark against the czarist campaign to crush the Lithuanians' national identity by forcing them to embrace the Orthodox faith. In the modern era, Lithuanian nationalism and Roman Catholicism developed symbiotically. In 1908, for example, devout Catholics established the Ateitis (Futurist) movement. Its members embraced an ideology that merged Catholicism with nationalism. Composed of students, clergy, and former priests, the movement secured a devoted following in Lithuania after independence. Ateitis was later outlawed in Lithuania as the country fell to authoritarian rule between the two world wars, but it was resurrected in North America, where the association between Catholicism and Lithuanian nationalism became firmly fixed.

In the United States, masses and religious instruction were conducted in Lithuanian, and through Church-affiliated social and cultural associations Lithuanian-Catholic youngsters learned about their national history and culture. As immigrants in a foreign land, the Lithuanian-American community could ill afford the secular/religious schism that divided their relatives in the old country. Moreover, those Lithuanians who resided outside homogeneous Lithuanian neighborhoods saw the Catholic Church as a positive affiliation, conferring status upon poorly educated working people with low self-esteem. Along with organized labor and urban political machines, the Church was a vital part of the trinity of Catholic, white ethnic power for much of the twentieth century. But that trinity eventually attenuated the impact of nationalism among the first wave of Lithuanian immigrants.

The Lithuanian diaspora—people of Lithuanian heritage living outside of

Lithuania—first appeared after the 1863 insurrection, when many Lithuanians left their homeland in search of new economic opportunities abroad. Most of them emigrated to the United States, with an estimated 500,000 emigrating between 1867 and 1914. According to some accounts, among an additional 200,000 to 300,000 immigrants who identified themselves as Poles or Russians a large number were conceivably ethnic Lithuanians.[5] Chicago became a magnet for Lithuanian immigrants, and by the turn of the century about 100,000 Lithuanians resided there, making it the largest Lithuanian city in the world. In his book *The Jungle,* Upton Sinclair tells a riveting story about the fate of a Lithuanian family in Chicago's stockyards. It was through this novel that most Americans would first learn about these Baltic peoples.

Although their numbers in America were small, the American Lithuanians would play a significant role in the Lithuanian revival. The United States was a refuge for many nationalist leaders who were hounded from the Russian empire, and they continued their work in the New World until the collapse of the Romanov dynasty and the emergence of an independent Lithuania in 1918. With American funds gleaned from the slim earnings of working people, the Lithuanian language and culture were sustained in the diaspora. Books and other publications in Lithuanian were published in the United States and transported back home. Indeed, this small, financially strapped community even produced its own encyclopedia.

In 1905, American representatives attended the Grand Vilnius Congress (Seimas), which attracted two thousand Lithuanians from all corners of the globe. It passed resolutions supporting the Lithuanian language and culture and called for an independent Lithuanian state. In 1915, Lithuanian Americans would establish an information center in Geneva to lobby the Allies for Lithuanian national self-determination.

After Lithuania achieved independence, Americans provided economic assistance, arms, and manpower as Lithuanians fought Polish, Russian Soviet, and Lithuanian Bolshevik enemies. An estimated twenty to thirty thousand Lithuanians returned to an independent homeland between the two world wars. It is not clear whether they carried American values with them and had a discernible impact upon Lithuanian society. Probably not, since they were few in numbers among the total population and had returned to a country that had never been exposed to a democratic political culture.[6]

With the twentieth century under way, some leaders of the Lithuanian renaissance realized that their national existence was at risk as long as they did not live in a sovereign state of their own. On the eve of the century, the Lithuanians had concluded that the best they could hope for politically was autonomy within a Russian federation. After the Russian Revolution and Germany's defeat (the Kaiser's armies had occupied Lithuania in 1915), they believed that an independent Lithuania was within their grasp. The Germans had established a Lithuanian state council, the Taryba, hoping one day to absorb Lithuania, but instead the Taryba provided the Lithuanians with a semi-independent political institution. It proclaimed Lithuanian independence on February 16, 1918.

The western Allies remained skeptical about the viability of a Lithuanian state and feared it would become a puppet of Germany, but the Lithuanian nationalists demonstrated their resolve by rebuffing the Germans, Russians, Poles, and Lithuanian Bolsheviks who tried to subjugate them. In 1919, Britain provided de facto recognition and strengthened Lithuania's bid for sovereignty. A year later, Lenin signed a treaty with Lithuania, renouncing, forever, any claims on Lithuanian territory. In 1922, the United States extended diplomatic recognition, and Lithuania was admitted to the League of Nations that same year.

From the outset, the new state was confronted with serious minority problems. About 20 percent of the population—totaling about 2.4 million in 1923—was not ethnic Lithuanian. The largest minority were the Jews, who accounted for 7.1 percent of the population, or 170,400 people. Many lived in Kaunas, which had become the nation's capital after a rogue Polish general, Lucijian Zeligowski, occupied the Vilnius region in 1920—where a sizable Jewish population also resided. It has been estimated that by the time of the 1940 Soviet annexation, over 200,000 Jews lived in Lithuania.

Ezra Mendelsohn has observed that the Lithuanian Jews were the most "Jewish" of their brethren in Eastern Europe largely because the mainstream culture was poorly defined; the indigenous intelligentsia was small and most Lithuanians were peasants. By contrast, many Jews had become secularized in Poland and Russia as they were attracted to large and viable cultures in both societies. For these reasons, and because anti-Semitism was less virulent than in other East European countries, the Jewish leadership supported an independent Lithuania and through their international contacts actively fought for its establishment. Fearful of Polish control of Vilnius, the Jews also had supported the Lithuanians in their quest to regain their ancient capital, where a large and vibrant Jewish community lived.[7]

In return, Istvan Deak writes, "the new democratic regime granted special rights to all ethnic minorities, and thus also the Jews. A ministry of Jewish affairs was set up in Kovno (Kaunas) as well as a Jewish national council." Moreover, "Jews served in the Lithuanian administration, in parliament (where they were free to address their audience in Yiddish), and as officers in the army." But after Zeligowski's forces seized Vilnius in 1920, the Lithuanians lost a large number of what they assumed would be their Jewish population. That year the government began to restrict Jewish rights, and the Jews suffered economically as the authorities subsidized their Lithuanian competitors.[8]

The second-largest minority were the Germans, who amounted to 4.1 percent of the population, or close to 100,000 people, most of whom lived in the Memel area. Many would leave when the Soviets occupied Lithuania, and others would flee the advancing Red Army in the last years of World War II. Few of them remained in Lithuania after the war.

Before 1939, the Poles accounted for 3 percent of the population, or about 60,000 people, with a far larger number living in eastern Lithuania, which was under the control of Poland. Lithuanian-Polish relations were strained during the independence period from 1918 to 1940. In 1918, Poles in Lithuania, preferring association with Poland, refused to join the Taryba, and a year later, fearful of Polish fifth columnists, the Lithuanians denied the Poles a place in the government. After Zeligowski's units seized Vilnius, the Lithuanians established a "provisional" capital in Kaunas. Ethnically it was more Lithuanian than the cosmopolitan Vilnius, but Vilnius was the country's ancient capital, and the Polish occupation of that city and the Polonization campaign conducted by the Polish authorities there fed Lithuanian enmity toward the Poles. For much of the interwar period, Polish-Lithuanian relations did not exist, and the two countries were on the brink of war on more than one occasion.[9] Ironically, Lithuania would get Vilnius back in 1939, as a result of the very treaty that would seal its fate as an independent country, the Molotov-Ribbentrop Pact.

The Lithuanians' minority problems aside, they lost their democracy on December 17, 1926, in a military coup. Earlier that year, "[a] Populist–Social Democratic coalition took power, dependent for support on the ethnic minorities, including the Poles. Concessions to the Poles in the field of education, at a time when Poland was closing Lithuanian schools in the Vilnius area, allowed the Right to allege treason."[10] Some Catholic activists supported the army, and the nationalist party, Tautininkai, would form a ruling coalition with the Christian Democrats. Antanas Smetona and Augustinas Voldemaras, who had been leaders in the country's fight for independence but later had been excluded from power, were appointed president and prime minister. A year later, Smetona broke with the Christian Democrats, dissolved parliament, and wrote a new constitution that provided for a strong presidency. He also had a falling-out with the Vatican in 1931 as the latent secular-clerical fissures among Lithuanian nationalists became manifest.

In 1934, Voldemaras, who led an ultranationalist organization called Iron Wolf, was arrested when he led a coup against the government. Smetona himself had autocratic tendencies, and he characterized the Tautininkai as the country's "ruling party"; aping both Germany and Italy, he formed a nationalist youth group, Young Lithuania. But Lithuanian autocracy was benign and did not rest on a police state and the oppression of ethnic minorities as was typical of Europe's fascist states.

In face of mounting economic problems, religious/secular and ethnic divisions, powerful enemies on its borders, and a society barren of a pluralistic political culture, Lithuanian democracy was doomed. A decade later, Adolf Hitler and Joseph Stalin would sign an agreement that denied the Lithuanians their independence.

The news that Hitler had "taken Memel" back from the Lithuanians set off alarm bells in Moscow. Hitler's appetite would not be satisfied by Memel, and Stalin feared that his German nemesis meant to annex all of Lithuania along with Latvia and Estonia which shared a border with the USSR. These fears, and the hope of reincorporating the Baltic countries within the Soviet empire, led to the signing of the Molotov-Ribbentrop Pact.

In secret protocols to the pact, Estonia and Latvia were given to Moscow and Lithuania was awarded to Berlin. Stalin was unhappy with the arrangement, because he believed that Lithuania was vital to the Soviet Union's security. But he decided to bide his time before opening up negotiations for the prize. Security considerations aside, Stalin was determined to restore all of the boundaries of the former czarist empire.

The Nazi invasion of Poland, precipitated by Stalin's nonaggression pact with Hitler, provided him with that opportunity. The Soviet Union had received some Polish territory under provisions of the pact, and Stalin intended to retain those areas inhabited primarily by Belorussians and Ukrainians. Not unmindful of traditional Polish resistance to foreign occupation, Stalin did not relish keeping those areas that were populated primarily by ethnic Poles. Immediately after the Nazis overran Poland, Stalin contacted the German ambassador in Moscow, Friedrich Werner von der Schulenburg, and said that to avoid friction between their two countries, he "considered it wrong to leave an independent (divided) residual Poland."[11] He suggested Germany take all of the areas of Poland that were predominantly inhabited by ethnic Poles, including territory previously awarded to the USSR, and the USSR, in turn, would receive Lithuania.

The proposition displeased Hitler, but Stalin was in the room when von Ribbentrop took a call from Berlin in which Hitler agreed to the trade. Later, Stalin was overheard telling Molotov that by accepting an offer he opposed,

Hitler, in effect, had declared a future war with the Soviet Union. Hitler accepted the proposal simply because he could get what he wanted, Lithuania, when he invaded the USSR in the future. Since Stalin was so prescient, it is puzzling why when confronted with overwhelming evidence that the Germans were poised to attack the USSR in June 1941, Stalin refused to acknowledge the warnings.

On October 3, 1939, Juozas Urbsys, the Lithuanian foreign minister, was called to Moscow to meet with Molotov and Stalin. He received the same harsh treatment as his Estonian and Latvian colleagues had earlier suffered. Urbsys was told that his country had to accept the deployment of 75,000 Soviet troops on Lithuania's soil. "It is in your best interests to accept our proposition," Stalin said.[12] Part of Lithuanian territory around the city of Suwalki would be annexed by Germany, but Stalin would return Vilnius to Lithuania. One of Stalin's motives for this last move was to de-Polonize Lithuania, and he undertook this campaign with alacrity.

Late on October 10, Urbsys and his colleagues met with Stalin to sign the agreement that returned Vilnius to the Lithuanians but compelled them also to sign a mutual assistance treaty, which involved the stationing of Soviet troops in their country. While the papers were being prepared, Stalin offered the despondent Lithuanian diplomats drinks, and they watched several films with the Soviet dictator until early in the morning of October 11.[13] Estonia and Latvia had been forced into a similar treaty with Stalin and were overcome with the same grim foreboding that they soon would be absorbed by their rapacious neighbor.

But wanting to build a legal case for his ultimate reannexation of Estonia, Latvia, and Lithuania, Stalin did not immediately replace the governments in all three capitals with his puppets. His strategy and rationale for eventually doing so, however, was revealed in the Latvian Communist newspaper, *CINA*. In referring to the Baltic-Soviet defense treaty it announced: "The treaty has released the revolutionary dynamic forces of the people that had been held in check for twenty years. These forces have started moving and there is nothing that can stop them anymore."[14]

In the spring of 1940, when Hitler's forces overwhelmed Allied resistance to the Wehrmacht's invasion of France, Stalin moved to subjugate the Baltics. On May 25, the Lithuanian minister in Moscow was dressed down by Molotov for provocative anti-Soviet actions in Lithuania. Other complaints were made by Moscow to the three Baltic governments, including charges that Lithuanian authorities had been involved in the "disappearance" of Soviet soldiers in the country.[15] On June 15, Soviet troops occupied the Baltic states without resistance. The Soviets had given the Lithuanians an ultimatum before they moved, and some Lithuanian leaders, including Smetona, had recommended the country's military forces resist, but they were overruled.[16] Later many Lithuanians felt shame that they had not offered armed opposition to Soviet occupation, even though there was no hope of victory. Soviet troops were already stationed within the country, and large numbers of them were situated on its borders.

The same day that the Lithuanians heard broadcasts announcing German troops were entering Paris, they looked from their homes and apartments in Vilnius to observe Soviet troops entering their newly reclaimed capital. For decades afterward, Americans would remember the pictures of weeping Parisians watching the conquering Germans moving under the Arc de Triomphe as they marched arrogantly down the Champs Éylsée. Few ever knew about the terrible fate that befell the residents of Vilnius that very same day as Soviet troops marched triumphantly down Gedimino Street. The new authorities would give it a new name: Lenin Prospect.

The previous evening, Vladimir Georgievich Dekanozov, the NKVD (precursor to the KGB) foreign department head, told several officials who were being sent to the Baltic capitals on diplomatic missions: "At the decision of the Politburo and at the request of Comrade Stalin, the security problem along our northwest frontier is now to be solved." One of Stalin's Georgian cronies, Dekanozov noted that "the bourgeois governments of the three Baltic states . . . on the instructions of the stock exchanges of Paris and London" had done "everything possible to sabotage the treaties that they signed with the Soviet Union."[17]

Dekanozov himself went to Vilnius but was confronted with a legal difficulty: President Smetona had fled the county without appointing a replacement as required under the Lithuanian constitution. (Smetona died in Cleveland in 1944.) The Georgian resolved the problem by declaring that Smetona's flight constituted his resignation, and he appointed Justas Paleckis, a left-wing journalist, president. Vincas Kreve-Mickevicius, a widely known writer and scholar, was selected prime minister.

In July new deputies were elected in rigged parliamentary elections and the Baltic countries were "legally" annexed by Stalin. Henceforth, Moscow would contend that a "people's revolution" had precipitated the Balts' annexation into the USSR. The United States, and all the other democracies except Sweden, Finland, and New Zealand, refused to recognize this action, but to no avail. Molotov, in a conversation with Kreve-Mickevicius, indicated that the absorption of Lithuania into the USSR was final. "You must take a good look at reality," he told the Lithuanian, "and understand that in the future small nations will have to disappear. Your Lithuania along with the other Baltic nations, including Finland, will have to join the glorious family of the Soviet Union."[18]

In Lithuania, Stalin suppressed resistance to Soviet rule by liquidating and arresting the political, intellectual, and religious elite. Early in June 1941, just prior to the Wehrmacht's invasion of the USSR, 35,000 Lithuanian leaders were rounded up and shipped to concentration camps in northern Russia and Siberia. Others, escaping Soviet security forces seeking to incarcerate them, fled to the West.

Three days after the June 21, 1941, German attack, Soviet troops were pushed from Lithuania. Initially, some Lithuanians greeted the German occupation with favor. The harsh experience of Soviet rule and the realization that Stalin was bent on destroying Lithuania's national existence accounted for such behavior. But the Germans soon demonstrated that they intended to impose their rule upon the Lithuanians and had no intention of allowing them a voice in their country's future. The provisional Lithuanian government that had been established on August 1940 with the Soviets' departure from the country was disbanded. Lithuania was to be incorporated into the Third Reich.[19]

The Baltic-German Alfred Rosenberg, Hitler's authority on racial matters, was appointed Reich minister of the occupied eastern territories. His office had plans to deport about two-thirds of the existing Lithuanian inhabitants and to replace them with German immigrants. The massive deportation of Lithuanians was to be postponed, however, until the Third Reich won its final victory on the battlefield against Bolshevism.

During the German occupation some twenty thousand Lithuanians, who had been compelled to fight with the Red Army but surrendered en masse with the German invasion, were given the option of entering PW camps or fighting with German-led units. Most chose the latter option. Also, the Germans allowed the Lithuanians to organize local units to fight Soviet partisans, but the primary rationale for their formation in the minds of Lithuanian nationalists was to have military units in place in the event the Soviets returned.[20]

Lithuanians, who had expected decent treatment from the Germans, had their hopes dashed further after some 75,000 Lithuanians were sent to Germany to fill compulsory labor drafts. Others deemed anti-Nazi were placed in concentration camps. Vytautas Landsbergis's father and brother were among those Lithuanians incarcerated in Germany. The Jewish community in Lithuania, of course, suffered an even more comprehensive and deadly fate.

Unfortunately, the Holocaust in Lithuania was not a strictly German operation. Some Lithuanians eagerly joined the Nazis in their extermination of the country's Jewish population. An estimated 140,000 to 143,000 were slaughtered.[21] For most Lithuanians, this was an unspeakable act of murder, but others—in seeking to explain without justifying this monstrous crime—noted that after the Soviets invaded Lithuania, many Jews collaborated with the new authorities. In this connection, Mendelsohn has written:

> The coming of communism, a calamity for Lithuanian nationalists, was welcomed by the left-wing elements within Lithuanian Jewry, whose importance within the small Lithuanian Community Party has already been described. Having little support among the Lithuanian population, the new regime encouraged, at first, Jewish support, and a sizable number of Jewish leftists rose to positions of prominence in areas previously closed to them—the state apparatus, the army, the judiciary, and so forth. The Soviets therefore established a pattern which would be followed, after World War II, in the satellite states of Eastern Europe. The prominence of some Jews in the communist regime . . . was a disaster for the entire Jewish community.[22]

Anatol Lieven notes that few Jews belonged to the Lithuanian Communist Party, but their numbers were proportionally high. Whereas about 7 percent of the Lithuanian population in 1940 was Jewish, about 15 percent of the members of the Lithuanian Communist Party were Jewish. Moreover, many of their brethren took comfort in the Soviet occupation (less because of their love for the Russians or attachment to Marxism, than out of fear and hate of the Nazis), and "Jews were also prominent in the NKVD, whose activity in Lithuania reached its height on 14 June 1941, with the deportation of thousands of Lithuanian citizens to Siberia."[23]

Perhaps the most authoritative voice among those debating the source of the Lithuanian Holocaust is that of a survivor, Aleksandras Shtromas. Out of a family of a hundred people, he was one of four who were not killed; after he fled the infamous Ninth Fort in Kaunas (when Jews from that area were incarcerated and systematically murdered) he was sheltered by a "righteous Christian" family, the Macenaviciuses. He was about to leave Lithuania with a group of Russian youngsters when members of that family, who did not know anyone in his own family, said: "Wait, you cannot go. You speak Lithuanian. You will be killed. We can't keep that on our conscience." They harbored him and saved his life. Another Lithuanian family did the same for his sister.[24]

Shtromas says that other Lithuanians provided protection to Jews—not many, but the Lithuanians were no better nor worse in this respect than

Christians in Western Europe. Some individual Lithuanians blamed Jews for the suffering of Lithuanians under Soviet rule. Shtromas reports:

> A very nice, timid and well-educated Lithuanian lady once confessed to me that, although very much ashamed of that feeling, she was unable to suppress her hatred for Jews. This hatred, she told me, originated in the spring of 1941 when an NKVD squad, consisting of three Jewish men and one woman, came to arrest her parents, whom she never saw again. The head of this squad was a Jew whom the family had considered a friend.[25]

Shtromas continues: "These explanations are based on the false assumption that what some Jews have done wrongly makes the rest of the Jews automatically guilty for those wrongdoings." Most Jews were Orthodox Jews. "Only a handful of assimilation-oriented Lithuanian Jews became Communists or Communist sympathizers." Moreover, Shtromas reminds Lithuanians that what they deem their Holocaust—the forced migration of Lithuanians to Siberia and northern Russia—was actually the salvation of the Jews who were among the deportees. "Not less than 20 percent of the Lithuanians brutally deported in June 1941 to Siberia (altogether 34,200 people) were Jewish; that is two and a half times more than their proportion in Lithuania's population. . . ."

But Shtromas reminds all of us that it is a mistake to collectively blame all Lithuanians for the Holocaust or to impose upon them norms of behavior that most of us, from any background, do not have the courage to honor.

> I sometimes wonder how the Jews would have behaved if they had changed places with the Lithuanians after the holocaust. Would there have been fewer Jewish Lithuanian-killers than there were Lithuanian Jew-killers? Would there have been as many Jews ready to risk their lives and the lives of their families in order to save Lithuanians as there were Lithuanians who did so for the Jews? I doubt it.[26]

None of us can refute this observation, but it would be a mistake for Lithuanians to interpret it as a pretext to remain silent about the fact that some of their number participated in one of the greatest crimes in history. Collective guilt no, but a collective understanding that a truly monstrous crime was committed in their country must be a lesson taught schoolchildren forever after.

The underground organizations the Lithuanians had organized to oppose the Nazis had limited capacity to challenge them in an armed confrontation. The Germans possessed an overwhelming military advantage, and those who resisted were treated brutally. For example, 191 Lithuanian peasants were burned to death by the Nazis after a Soviet partisan attack near the village of

Pincinpis on June 3, 1944. Few Lithuanians fought the Germans, however, because they did not want to do anything to help the Soviet cause.[27]

In the final analysis, the Lithuanians under German occupation had placed their hope in help from the West. A Lithuanian underground newspaper published on the anniversary of Lithuanian independence day noted on February 16, 1944: "We are convinced that the Western nations who have formed the Atlantic Charter . . . will help us, at the right time, to secure and to defend from National Socialism as well as from Communism that for which we are prepared to sacrifice all."[28]

When the Russians returned to Lithuania in 1944, Stalin had resumed his campaign to cleanse the country of any potential resistance to his rule. Many Lithuanian leaders were executed or forced into exile, and a six-year-long deportation of an estimated 350,000 people began. In spite of overwhelming odds, a large number of Lithuanians, believing that the West would come to help them shed Soviet rule, took to the forests and bravely fought the Red Army until 1953. Exactly how many Lithuanians lost their lives fighting the Soviets during the second occupation is not known, but an estimated thirty to fifty thousand Lithuanians died resisting the two Soviet occupations. Ausra Jurasas, a literary critic who would be exiled in the mid-1970s after her husband, Jonas—a Kaunas theater director—was fired for his "anti-Soviet" activities, recalled that as a girl she and her classmates one day were ordered to the schoolyard. "There . . . stacked like cordwood were the bodies of many partisans who had been killed by Soviet troops. They were being displayed in this awful fashion to teach Lithuanian schoolchildren that it was hopeless to resist."[29]

In the aftermath of the second Soviet occupation, several hundred thousand Lithuanians (out of a population of slightly less than three million) were imprisoned in labor camps, where many perished. Included among the "deportees" were families who had been sent to Siberia simply because they owned farms and were deemed kulaks by Soviet authorities. Others, like the mother of Mecys Laurinkus, head of Lithuanian security during Bloody Sunday, was deported because she was an avid stamp collector and belonged to the international Philatelist Society. Stalin had deemed any Lithuanian belonging to an "international organization" a threat to the Soviet Union and ordered they be placed on his list for deportation.

Even those Lithuanians who escaped Stalin's terror directly were traumatized by the brutal Soviet occupation of their country. Dr. Danute Bieliauskas recalled a half century after the event: "I was a young medical student studying in Kaunas. I remember standing on Freedom Alley"—the main street in the city—"watching Soviet tanks rolling slowly down the street. I've had recurring nightmares of that incident ever since . . . over fifty years of my life."[30]

President Franklin Roosevelt had refused to recognize Stalin's annexation of the Baltic countries, but the old Georgian ignored the snub. In face of Moscow's drive to liquidate political, intellectual, and religious leaders, thousands of Lithuanians had fled the country. A second migration occurred with the Nazis occupation of Lithuania in 1941, and a third with the return of the Red Army and Soviet occupation several years later.

Those Lithuanians who remained behind were watched closely by Soviet authorities. Indeed, it was because Moscow knew that the three Baltic nations had been forced into the Soviet empire that travel to the Baltic republics was restricted long after foreigners could move freely around much of the rest of the USSR.[31] Over time, the Soviet leaders reasoned, the Balts would lose their national identity and adopt a new Soviet consciousness. Toward this end, the Bolsheviks looked to Marxist theory to drive their policy of "Soviet pluralism."

Karl Marx had claimed nationalism—the ultimate expression of ethnic-group self-consciousness—was a product of the modern world that capitalism had helped promulgate. When it contributed to feudalism's demise it was a positive impulse. But when the bourgeoisie exploited nationalism to divide the proletariat and avoid a socialist revolution, nationalism was a reactionary force. While Marx, and his benefactor and collaborator Frederick Engels, acknowledged nationalism could enhance or forestall the advent of socialism, there was no doubt in their minds about the final outcome; under socialism, parochial ethnic impulses would be superseded by a new international consciousness.

This conviction was bolstered by the claims of Western social science, which predicted ethnic ties and values associated with traditional society would be destroyed in the crucible of modern life—industrialization, urbanization, and secularization. Like their Marxist opponents, liberal theorists believed economic factors best explained human behavior in the modern world. But they had proclaimed that free-market imperatives and not universalistic, socialist policies would destroy traditional ethnic values and loyalties. For all intents and purposes, then, mainstream social theory, whether Marxist or liberal in origin, evaluated human behavior in terms of class rather than ethnic criteria, in terms of interests rather than values.

It is amusing to speculate how this area of agreement between Marxist and Western social theory had encouraged the Soviet elite to continue policies that were fatally flawed and certain to disrupt the regime they fought so hard to preserve. One could speculate that among other things, had Western social theorists written that ethnicity is vital to a person's self-esteem and group identity and is deeply imbedded in one's psyche and not just a peripheral impulse, Soviet policymakers might have realized that their nationalities policies were flawed—though this is not really likely. Instead, Western thinkers agreed with their Soviet counterparts that ethnonationalism was doomed in the modern world. One of the best testaments to this observation is that after World War II, American political science and international relations courses ignored ethnic politics and nationalism in the industrialized societies. Like their Marxist brethren, most Western intellectuals deemed class and not ethnicity the driving force behind politics in the twentieth century, at least in the advanced countries.

By the turn of the twentieth century, setting the record straight on the intellectual origins of nationalism was not merely an abstract theoretical issue confronting Marx's disciples but a practical political problem. It was a hot topic, since many "mininations" in Europe were demanding the right of national self-determination. Should Marxists oppose or assist ethnic nationalists in the Russian and Austro-Hungarian empires in their independence drives? Otto Bauer, an Austrian Marxist, argued in favor of the radical left siding with the nationalists of Eastern and Central Europe. More orthodox comrades, such as the Pole Rosa Luxembourg, disagreed. She had contended that support for national self-determination would encourage ethnic chauvinism and undermine proletarian solidarity. To legitimize the nationalists' cause was to set loose forces of reaction that were hostile to socialism. Of course, she was a Jew, and ethnicity might have had something to do with her position. Even though she was secularized and not religious, she could not be unmindful of the fact that historically, the czar and his agents had manipulated anti-Semitism in the empire to deflect criticism of imperial rule. Furthermore, many of the most fervent exponents of nationalism in Europe were unabashed Jew-baiters.[32]

V. I. Lenin supported Bauer's line. Unlike the founding fathers of "scientific socialism," Marx and Engels, he had to confront nationalism directly in his drive for power. By demonstrating solidarity with oppressed minorities in the Russian empire, Lenin had hoped to enlist their help in overthrowing the czar. He had characterized the Romanovs' empire as a "prison of nations" and attacked Russian chauvinism for denying the myriads of people in it a proletarian consciousness. Joseph Stalin would later attribute the Bolsheviks' victory in the civil war (1918–1921) to Lenin's enlightened policy toward the non-Russians.

In power, Lenin had courted their loyalty by adopting a federal system that recognized their uniqueness. In 1922, representatives of Russia, Ukraine,

Byelorussia, and the Transcaucasian Federation had signed an agreement creating the USSR. Later, Armenia, Azerbaijan, and Georgia evolved from the Transcaucasian Federation and the five Central Asian states, Kazakhstan, Uzbekistan, Turkmenistan, Kyrgyzstan, and Tajikistan, from the Russian Soviet Federated Socialist Republics (RSFSR). After the Balts and Moldavians were incorporated into the USSR, there would be fifteen national republics and many autonomous republics and lesser political entities that paid homage to the national principle. But Lenin's courting of the non-Russians as manifested in his adopting a federal system, rather than a unitarian one as he favored, was only a tactical move. He had remained confident that ultimately all national differences would vanish as a new Soviet consciousness evolved.

Left-wing thinkers elsewhere in Europe and North America had hoped fervently that the Bolsheviks would be successful in their quest to build a universalistic consciousness—in the Soviet context, Homo Sovieticus, "Soviet man." Men and women of every race, nation, and creed would be blended into a new society, one where the narrow, parochial, and hostile impulses that had precipitated World War I would be swept into the ash heap of history. How could any progressive-minded person not look favorably upon such a society?

However, Lenin's first commissar for nationalities, Joseph Stalin, was skeptical about a rapid solution to the nationalities question. As a Georgian, he knew that the non-Russians remained firmly wedded to their languages, cultures, and national homelands. He had posited a definition of a nation that would be far superior to the one Soviet ethnographers favored, which linked nationalism to economic impulses. Stalin wrote that, "a nation is a historically constituted, stable community of people, formed on the basis of a common language, territory, economic life, and psychological makeup manifested in a common culture."[33] It is noteworthy that Stalin contends that "economic life" is merely one of several factors that forge a national consciousness.

Here, in the campaign to denationalize the USSR's ethnic minorities, we witness a fundamental difference between Lenin and Stalin. The former postulates, in effect, that ethnic group identity has its roots in a capitalist social system that will disappear in a socialist society. From Stalin's perspective, ethnicity has much more complicated origins; ethnonationalism is multidemensional, not unidimensional, and there is no easy way to suppress it whatever the economic circumstances that exist in society.

Stalin's campaign to eliminate the scourge of ethnonationalism rested on three initiatives, which he carried out ruthlessly and single-mindedly. First, those who displayed overt nationalistic tendencies were to be liquidated, even if they had fought alongside Stalin in the Bolshevik revolution. Many comrades from the Central Asian republics would die at the hands of Stalin's agents for allowing their national proclivities to supersede their Bolshevik loyalties. For example, by 1919 the Mujahidin of Central Asia had organized twenty thousand Basmachi fighters to wrest control of the territory from the Russian Bolsheviks with whom they were once allied. Second, Stalin sought to prevent the centrifugal forces of ethnonationalism from emasculating Soviet power through a campaign to Russify all peoples in the USSR. Third, to marginalize the non-Russians living outside of the Russian Federation, Stalin had forced millions of Russians through massive economic development programs to relocate in the Caucasus and, Central Asia and, after World War II, in the Baltic countries.

The collaboration of some ethnic minorities with the Germans during World War II, such as the Crimean Tatars and Chechens, reconfirmed Stalin's worst fears, and in the war's aftermath, he took measures to expedite his Russification campaign. He proclaimed in the spring of 1945 that the Russians had "won the right to be recognized as the guide for the whole nation." Practically, this meant that everyone in the USSR would accept Russian political, economic, and cultural hegemony.[34]

After Stalin died, his successors persisted in his Russification campaign because they realized that latent ethnonationalistic tendencies could become manifest and place the very survival of the Soviet regime at risk. Indeed, the "Beria incident" demonstrated to the ruling elite in the Kremlin just how dangerous the nationalities question could be if not handled correctly. In 1952, Lavrenti Beria, the Georgian chief of the secret police, gave a speech at the Nineteenth Party Congress which "was at variance with the official line of the day."

> Scarcely mentioning "bourgeois nationalism," Beria was the only speaker to refer to "great-power chauvinism" and "national oppression." He also avoided the standard phrase "great Russian people," alluded to the sovereignty of the Soviet republics, and emphasized the importance of safeguarding the native languages and relying on native cadres in non-Russian republics.[35]

These words pretty much describe how Nikita Khrushchev and his allies perceived Beria's behavior. After Stalin's death, Beria, who was head of the ministry of internal affairs courted local Communists in the republics in what his comrades perceived as a crude attempt to manipulate national sentiment to advance Beria's political ambitions. In the end of June 1953, Beria was machine gunned to death in the bowels of the Lubyanka prison for his treasonous behavior. "On 10 July, *Pravda* announced his removal and declared him a 'vicious enemy of the Party and the Soviet people.'" In particular it was charged that Beria "tried to sow discord among the peoples of the USSR, to intensify the activity of bourgeois nationalist elements in the Union republics. . . ." The Lithuanian Communist leader Antanas Snieckus would assert that Beria's agents had attempted to foster friction among Russians and Lithuanians in his republic.[36]

Amy Knight, in her biography *Beria: Stalin's First Lieutenant,* provides another interpretation of his position on the nationalities question. Without dismissing his lust for personal power, she notes that Beria realized that if the post-Stalinist leadership was to acquire political legitimacy it had to solicit support from the people voluntarily, not through brutal oppressive policies Stalin had favored. De-Stalinization meant, among other things, transferring power from the party to the state, and this shift in power was deemed intolerable by his colleagues. He also got into trouble with the Russian elite by attacking the regime's policies on the nationalities question. In his speech at Stalin's funeral he shocked the mourners by indicating he favored a change in direction on this vital issue. Later, by selecting indigenous people to fill important slots in the republican MVD branches and encouraging the use of the indigenous language, such as in the Ukrainian SSR, he indicated that he was opposed to "Great Russian chauvinism." All the Soviet leaders, following the lead of the great Lenin, consistently make similar statements while coveting the privileges Russians enjoyed in Soviet society.

In summary, Knight remarks:

> It hardly needs to be pointed out that Beria's radical approach to nationalities policy marked a sharp departure from the Stalinist line. The implications for center-periphery relations were far-reaching, to say the least. For the first time since the creation of the Soviet Union non-Russian nationalities were encouraged to assert their own cultural and political identities and the traditional policy of Russification was thrown into question. Western historians have generally considered Beria's appeal for support from non-Russians to be a sort of desperate, foolhardy gambit. Now, with the hindsight gained by seeing the strength of nationalist sentiment in the former Soviet Union, it appears as a promising, though risky, strategy for consolidating political power. Stalinism represented not only despotism, but also domination by Great Russians over other national groups. As Beria realized, an attempt to gain credibility by de-Stalinization required some recognition of national rights.[37]

In part to prevent another Beria from manipulating ethnonationalism, but also because they deemed Stalin's policies too harsh, his successors were less brutal in their treatment of nationalistic displays and adopted a more accommodating line toward the non-Russians. Khrushchev, and later Brezhnev, allowed them to publish in their native tongues and to depict their disparate cultures in novels, plays, and films. But when they became too enthusiastic in celebrating national achievements, they were silenced. A case in point was the treatment of Petro Schelest, the first secretary of the Ukrainian Communist Party. Schelest was allegedly removed from office because he was opposed to détente. His real crime, however, was publishing the book *Our Soviet Ukraine,* which his Russian comrades deemed a celebration of the Ukrainian nation.[38]

But such exceptions aside, the Russian ruling elite had concluded that the denationalization drive was producing results, and some of them really believed in a form of Soviet pluralism that was not merely a cover for Russian domination. Confusing wishful thinking with fact, they had rejected accusations that Russians enjoyed a privileged position in Soviet life. And many others seemingly accepted the party line that the denationalization drive was working when in fact they had grave doubts about how much progress was being made.

In a 1977 speech celebrating the fiftieth anniversary of the Russian Revolution, Leonid Brezhnev said, "We have every reason to say that the nationality question . . . has been resolved. . . ." But later in the address he conceded that "distorted manifestations of national feeling are extremely tenacious phenomena that are deeply embedded in the psychology of people with insufficient political maturity."[39]

Meanwhile, the consensus among Western students of Soviet nationality policy was that the Russification drive was working. Younger and better-educated minorities living in urban areas spoke Russian and associated their material advancement with the adoption of "universalistic" Soviet and not "particularistic" ethnic values. The most ambitious young people in the Soviet Union were the ones being exposed to Russian language and culture at school, in the military, in top-level party posts, government ministries, or industry, and in the liberal professions. Like the Soviet nationalities theorists, the American experts reasoned that as the non-Russian elites secured careers and advanced socially and economically they would shed outmoded ethnic sensibilities for a Soviet mind-set. Over time, their less-gifted brethren would follow them.[40]

The Russian settlers who had migrated to the cities in the Baltic countries, the Caucasus, and Central Asia were playing a vital role in the denationalization process. They were the avant-garde in the quest to achieve an international Soviet identity throughout the USSR. Of course, they had access to resources, promotions, and perks that the non-Russian minorities envied. On the other hand, indigenous peoples, who displayed "Soviet" sensibilities, were favored by their Russian superiors, and many voluntarily adopted Russian values to enhance their careers. The "best and the brightest" among the ethnic minorities realized—without blatant pressure—that they had a stake in the "system" too. And yes, as we now know, it was the gifted person who wished to actualize his or her potential who faced the greatest compulsion to accept the system. It was a unique individual who preferred, after excelling at the university, to drive a bus or to run a lathe rather than take a position as college professor, laboratory researcher, or journalist—even if it entailed "compromises."

In spite of social and economic affirmative action programs, which were designed to woo the ethnic minorities, Stalin's successors continued to favor the Russians. As Rasma Karklins wrote while the Soviet Union still existed, "Soviet nationality policy . . . while granting concessions to a few native claims, keeps a strict rein on the politically most crucial structures and processes."[41] Since Russians typically dominated the all-union institutions, the words "Soviet" and "Center" suggested to ethnic minorities "Russia" and "Russian hegemony."

Soviet scholars attending international academic gatherings in the West, however, could take comfort in the fact that most of their American colleagues had paid little attention to the non-Russian population in the USSR. Indeed, when traveling to the Soviet Union, most Western scholars limited their visits to Russia, and then to Leningrad and Moscow and not the smaller provincial towns. And the people they spoke to were academics, government officials, and maybe even some dissidents, but hardly ever ordinary folk. Not surprisingly, since most prominent academic observers simply wrote about developments in Russia and focused on the elites and not the masses, the information they provided foreign policy practitioners was profoundly flawed.

The Lithuanians, however, had advantages not shared by their Baltic cousins. In contrast to Estonia and Latvia, Lithuania enjoyed a relatively large and homogeneous population. After Armenia, it was the second most homogeneous of the USSR's republics, and after the Georgians and Armenians, the Lithuanians were the third least likely to change their ethnic identity.[42]

With postwar industrialization, Lithuania's labor requirements were met primarily with indigenous manpower. (And because Lithuania was not pacified for years, Russian workers were not transported in large numbers the way they were in Estonia and Latvia.) As Lithuanians left the countryside for the city and more of them attended university, they acquired skills to fill positions that Russians had occupied in other republics where rates of urbanization and university training were lower. The number of Russians who found employment in the republic grew, but contrary to the expectations of Soviet planners and many American academics, intermarriage between the local population and the Russian migrants did not promote Russification. In mixed Russian-Lithuanian marriages, children generally identified with the Lithuanian parent. This phenomenon reflected ethnic homogeneity and the strength of Lithuanian nationalism.[43]

Unlike Estonia and Latvia, Lithuania was not afflicted by a large number of Russified Balts who had lived in the USSR between the wars and returned with the Red Army. Two Latvians who fit this description of unrepentant Leninists were Boris Pugo, whom Gorbachev would turn to in the winter of 1990 as he sought to crush the Baltic independence movements, and Colonel Viktor Alksnis, a leader of the hard-line Soyuz faction in the USSR Congress of People's Deputies, who opposed any effort to reform the Soviet system.

Longevity in office allowed the Lithuanian party chief Antanas Snieckus (1940–74) to build his own personal machine and to manipulate strong nationalist sentiments to his advantage. According to Shtromas, who was adopted by Snieckus, the man "was an outstandingly strong, inveterate and autocratic leader who, without interruption from the end of 1926, had practically been in sole charge of the Lithuanian Communist Party and in full control of everybody in it." Snieckus and the Lithuanian Communists, unlike their counterparts in Estonia and Latvia, were allowed to conduct their affairs without close scrutiny from Moscow. "Stalin was personally extremely impressed with Snieckus's performance and even used to say that the two of them were the only real communists left in the whole of the Soviet Union."[44] One reason why Stalin was so impressed with Snieckus was that the Lithuanian leader carried out Moscow's order to deport Lithuanians with great alacrity. But ultimately, according to Shtromas, even this faithful tool of the Soviet Union became disillusioned with the ideology that legitimized Soviet rule.[45]

An unimaginative party bureaucrat, Petras Griskevicius, replaced Snieckus in 1974, but the Lithuanian Communist Party continued to enjoy a degree of autonomy from Moscow that its Baltic cousins could only envy. What's more, although the Lithuanian party would grow at a faster pace than the CPSU as a whole, by "1984 the percentage of party members in the population of Lithuania (5.25%) was still below the corresponding USSR average (6.75%)."[46] Many Lithuanians were opportunists and joined the party to acquire privileges associated with membership, much as American politicians in the Bible Belt join the Baptist Church. But they retained a strong sense of being Lithuanian and rejected the designation "Soviet." The impulse was powerful and organic; if it had not been, the Lithuanians, like many other "mininations" of Europe, might have vanished as a people.

Also, members of the Lithuanian Communist establishment had a greater opportunity to appreciate just how corrupt the Soviet system was than ordinary citizens. According to Algimantas Cekuolis, a former Soviet apparatchik who would become a Sajudis activist:

> Anyone who achieved any prominence in this society knew that the Soviet system was rotten and corrupt. In my travels throughout the USSR, I always carried two suitcases—one with my clothes and personal things, and a second with gifts for the party leaders I intended to meet. The bigger the official, the bigger the gift. Surprisingly, it was the little people who kept believing in the system long after the rest of us knew that it was a giant pool of shit![47]

But few intellectuals resisted. Even those, a minority, who did not join the Communist Party remained silent. Vytautas Landsbergis said that the intellectuals of his generation "were concerned to last until" the system eventually collapsed.[48] But in the interim they would remain on the sidelines and not overtly challenge Soviet rule. This, of course, included Landsbergis, who later would display great courage in leading the country out from under the heel of the Red Bear. But for years at the Vilnius Conservatory on Lenin Prospect, Landsbergis had preoccupied himself with his musical studies. The pianist and composer Mikalojus Ciurlionis was his passion. For many like-minded Lithuanian intellectuals, the celebration of pre-Soviet Lithuanian culture had provided a psychological retreat from the crude, materialistic aesthetics of "socialist realism." But while composing at his piano at the conservatory, Landsbergis could not lose sight of the fact that Lithuanian culture was at risk. For how could he forget that KGB headquarters was situated in the building adjacent to the one he was occupying and that in the park across the street a giant statue of Lenin stood with right hand pointing, some in Vilnius claimed, toward the cells that held prisoners in the building's basement?

Of course, some intellectuals had maintained their belief in communism in spite of evidence which indicated that it could provide Lithuanians neither bread nor freedom. Since the Soviet Union's demise, few of them have had the courage to admit that they ever believed in Marxism-Leninism, but clearly many did. How could it be otherwise for those who had been born during the Soviet era and attended Soviet schools and were denied information that enabled them to challenge the dogma to which they were constantly exposed in school, at work, and through the media?

Algirdas Degutis, now a libertarian who believes government has no business interfering in private affairs under any circumstances, recalls that when he was a boy he believed in the rightness of Marxism even though his family had been deported to Siberia, where he was born. "We were deemed kulaks, a threat to the Soviets, even though my father was not involved in politics." One would surmise that a young man whose family had been so mistreated by the system would have nothing but contempt for it. But for years he was a true believer, a steadfast Marxist-Leninist. "I'll tell you how bad I was," he told me. "I almost had convinced my father that it was a good thing that we had been deported, because driving Lithuanians from their homeland would destroy bourgeois society and set the stage for building a new, Soviet society in its place."[49]

3 LITHUANIAN NATIONALISM ENDURES

We're not afraid anymore!
—*Jonas Jurasas, Lithuanian theater director*

"Dick, Sajudis wants some foreign observers to witness the February elections. Would you like to go?"

The caller was Victor Nakas, who ran the Washington office of the Lithuanian Information Center. Sajudis was the Lithuanian popular front movement that had been formed in 1988, following the examples of similar movements in Estonia and Latvia. In February 1990, elections would be held to select deputies to the Lithuanian Supreme Soviet, the parliament of the Lithuanian Republic, which would choose a chairman who would form a government. It would be the first truly free and democratic election in the history of the Soviet Union.

Without hesitation, I answered in the affirmative, because what happened in Lithuania could have profound consequences for the future of the Soviet empire, and, in turn, for the world.

It was believed that if the Sajudis slate of delegates won a majority its leader, Vytautas Landsbergis, would be selected chairman of the Supreme Lithuanian Soviet. American journalists used the term "president" to describe the post, because that term made sense to readers unfamiliar with a parliamentary system. Landsbergis, a musicologist, came from a prominent family. His father and grandfathers had played a major role in forming a modern Lithuanian state, and his wife had been deported to Siberia during the Stalin era. The election of a nationalist to the highest post in Lithuania would be news indeed, especially since it was rumored that Landsbergis would restore Lithuanian independence if the Sajudis slate supporters secured control of the parliament.

Soon the American media would be depicting the Lithuanians as David locked in mortal combat with the Soviet Goliath. The confrontation was astonishing. How had it come to pass? Most scholars, who had devoted their careers to the study of the Soviet Union, were baffled, for they had assumed that the flame of Lithuanian nationalism had been extinguished.

It almost had been, but it was sustained in the New World by the Lithuanian diaspora, which included people who had left Lithuania in the nineteenth century and those who had fled the advancing Red Army after World War II. Both communities (by 1990 they would number 800,000 strong) would nourish the idea of Lithuanian independence until their loved ones broke free of the Soviet Empire.

When the Soviets occupied Lithuania in 1940, people belonging to the first Lithuanian migration played a pivotal role in lobbying Washington not to recognize the USSR's annexation of the Baltic countries.

On June 15, 1940, a day after 300,000 Soviet troops occupied Lithuania, Anthony Olis, a Chicago attorney, invited representatives of several Lithuanian-American newspapers and organizations to his residence. Shocked by the news from Europe, the group pondered how they could help their old homeland. By the end of the meeting they had formed an ad hoc committee. They wrote President Franklin D. Roosevelt to protest the Soviet Union's occupation of Lithuania. They waited five weeks before they received a response. On July 23, 1940 Acting Secretary of State Sumner Wells provided a statement that was gravely disappointing. It merely repeated the obvious, that the Baltic states had lost their independence, and in a weak attempt to placate Baltic-Americans it added that, "the people of the United States have watched their [the Baltic countries] admirable progress in self-government with deep and sympathetic interest."[1] That was it. Wells in his patronizing brush-off did not bother to condemn the Soviet Union's subjugation of the three small Baltic countries.

Though disappointed, Olis and his colleagues remained resolute in seeking a meeting with FDR. They tried to arrange one throughout the summer and early fall, but without success. Then they got a lucky break. The private secretary to FDR's adviser Harry Hopkins was a Lithuanian, and she helped arrange a meeting with FDR through her boss. At the meeting, one of the delegation remarked that Lithuanian independence had been lost. The president responded: "The independence of Lithuania is not lost but put temporarily aside. The time will come when Lithuania will be free again." FDR promised that he would do everything in his power to restore Lithuania's independence. According to the historian Antanas J. Van Reenan, "As a result, Roosevelt's action provided the foundation for United States de jure recognition of a Lithuanian government in exile at a time of de facto occupation."[2]

In the wake of the fateful meeting, the ad hoc group was joined by leaders of other Lithuanian organizations, and together they formed the Lithuanian American Council or LAC. It would lobby to sustain the policy of nonrecognition even after the United States became a World War II combatant and relied heavily upon the USSR to help defeat the Nazis in Europe. Later, LAC played an important role in preventing the forced repatriation of Lithuanians to the Soviet Union. As the Red Army returned to Lithuania, as many as 65,000 people fled west in the summer of 1945.

Fear among Lithuanian-Americans about the fate of the Lithuanian displaced persons (DPs) was real. Refugees, prisoners of war, and other former citizens of the USSR were being sent back to Stalin's gulag even if they desperately wished to remain in the West. The forced repatriation of hundreds of thousands of "Soviet citizens" to the USSR was one of the most shameful incidents of World War II. And this was done with the complicity of the Western powers; in one instance, refugees who resisted repatriation were shot dead by American guards. Others took their own lives rather than return to the Soviet Union and face slow but certain death as slave laborers.

In a secret agreement to the 1943 Tehran Conference, according to Van Reenan, "presidential interpreter Charles E. Bohlen recorded point 2 of a secret Roosevelt-Stalin agreement in which '. . . the President also disclaims interest in the political integrity of Lithuania, Estonia and Latvia in favor of the Soviet Union.'"[3] At the 1945 Yalta Conference, the Allies conceded Moscow's right to determine the fate of Soviet citizens who were scattered over the European continent. If Allied authorities honored this pledge, most if not all of the Lithuanians could have been returned to Soviet-occupied Lithuania.

But Lithuanians on both sides of the Atlantic mobilized to oppose forced repatriation of Lithuanian DPs to the USSR. In the United States, LAC led the fight to spare the Lithuanians living in camps the fate of tens of thousands of Russians and Ukrainians who were forced onto cattle cars and returned home, where many of them perished. On the continent, leaders of the Supreme Committee for Liberation of Lithuania (Vyriausias Lietuvos Islaisvinimo Komitetas, or VLIK) lobbied Western officials to save their fellow Lithuanians from a similar fate. Several underground Lithuanian political organizations had formed VLIK in November 1943 as the German authorities tightened control of the country in the face of the advancing Red Army. On April 26, 1946, VLIK wrote General Dwight David Eisenhower:

> . . . the independent state of Lithuania exists to this day de jure, as was also authoritatively affirmed by the late President of the United States, Franklin D. Roosevelt. . . . No Lithuanian considers himself a citizen of the Soviet Union, nor will he agree to avail himself of the rights of a

citizen of the Soviet Union, nor to take upon himself the duties devolving from such citizenship.[4]

In the spring of 1946, Fiorello La Guardia, the newly appointed director general of UNRRA (the United Nations Relief and Rehabilitation Administration) ended the practice of forced repatriation as opposition to the sadistic policy reached critical mass among American authorities.

Subsequently, Lithuanians in America continued to help their brethren, who had fled Nazi and Soviet tyranny, at pivotal points in their great odyssey: first by sustaining FDR's policy of nonrecognition and second by saving Lithuanian refugees from certain incarceration in the Soviet gulag. Later, they helped those living in German and Austrian DP camps to develop schools to sustain their Lithuanian consciousness. And still later, Lithuanian-American organizations helped the refugees relocate in Western countries, primarily in North America. Most, about thirty thousand, moved to the United States, favoring areas where Lithuanian communities already thrived, such as Chicago, Detroit, and Philadelphia.

But in contrast to those who had arrived earlier, the second-wave migrants created "exile" organizations, since they deemed their residence in the United States only a temporary refuge. They ultimately hoped to return home. Over time, the two communities would go their separate ways, but on occasion—when the plight of a Lithuanian dissident materialized or there were rumors the U.S. government might adopt measures weakening the policy of nonrecognition—they would collaborate. Most first-wave Lithuanians identified themselves as Americans and like their parents were concentrated in the working class or were newcomers to the middle class. The DPs proudly proclaimed their Lithuanian identity, and many came from the ranks of the privileged classes back home.

Ateitis would become one of the most important émigré organizations in the diaspora, and it would produce some of the most energetic fighters for Lithuanian independence. In the crucial years preceding and during the independence struggle, men and women who had once belonged to the youth wing of Ateitis would play an important role in sustaining political support for nonrecognition, provide information about conditions in Soviet Lithuania, report growing resistance to Soviet rule there, and lobby the media and authorities in Washington.

After Lithuania's occupation, Stasys Lozoraitis, who had served as the country's foreign minister until 1938—and was Lithuania's envoy in Italy at the time—functioned as the chief diplomatic representative of the former government, although no "government in exile" was formally established. After his death in 1983, his son Stasys would serve in the same capacity. The younger Lozoraitis told me that the diaspora sustained him during the "darkest hours" when the cause of Lithuania independence seemed hopeless. "During the early years, I was quite optimistic. I believed after the war that Lithuania would regain its independence with the West's help. But by 1948, I began to realize that things were very bad," and at one point Lozoraitis believed that Stalin's Russification campaign might lead to the extinction of the Lithuanian nation. By the 1950s, "the West Europeans were so preoccupied with economic development that they scarcely paid any attention to Lithuania." It appeared to many that the Soviet Union would remain a permanent fixture in world affairs and Lithuania had disappeared forever. In 1958, Pope John XXIII, in an attempt to improve relations with Khrushchev, sought to close the Lithuanian legation in Rome, which was Lozoraitis's base of operations. This move would have further undermined Lozoraitis's diplomatic status and the notion that there was a Lithuanian government in exile. "But the diaspora saved us when it put so much pressure on the papacy that the pope had to back down."[5]

When he shared this story with me, I thought in particular of the little old ladies from the first wave of immigrants who lived in working-class neighborhoods in America's Rust Belt cities where they and their parents had struck roots upon leaving the old country. Adorned with babushkas, they faithfully attended mass throughout their lives and placed cash earned through menial hard labor in the collection box to support the "Holy Mother Church." One hardly thought of them as revolutionaries, but they too played a role in facilitating the events that led to Lithuania's restoration of independence in March 1990, which, in turn, helped destroy the mighty Soviet empire.

I first became interested in the Lithuanian struggle for independence in the early 1970s when I began to receive underground publications—samizdats— from a Lithuanian-American priest, Father Casimer Pugevicius. We had met after I founded the National Center for Urban Ethnic Affairs with Geno Baroni, an Italian-American priest whom the *Washington Post* called, "the most relevant white man in Washington."[6] We had organized the center to direct national attention to the largely Catholic working-class neighborhoods in the country's Rust Belt. They and their residents had been neglected in America's campaign to revitalize the country's most troubled cities. Products of such neighborhoods, Geno and I knew that there was ethnic dimension to them. It had to be acknowledged if these troubled communities were to develop the organizational capacity to meet the needs of their residents and to cooperate with their minority neighbors. But when we mentioned the ethnic factor, we encountered stiff resistance. The assumption was that ethnic ties and values had been eradicated in the American melting pot, and to the extent that such ties and values persisted they were deemed pernicious by the activists we worked with in government agencies, the foundations, academia, and the religious community.

It was through the center's work that I became interested in ethnicity in the United States, and after writing a book about the American white ethnic subculture, I shifted my focus to the Soviet Union. Beginning in the early 1970s, Father Cas had provided me information about developments in Lithuania that contradicted the conventional wisdom among most American scholars—which is to say that Moscow's effort to submerge Lithuanian nationalism through a campaign of suppression and Russification had succeeded.

Born in Baltimore in 1928 and ordained as a Roman Catholic priest in 1953, Father Cas had served as the chaplain for the Knights of Lithuania, organized to serve Lithuanian immigrants who had first arrived in United States in the last quarter of the nineteenth century. He also functioned in a similar capacity for the youth wing of Ateitis, the Lithuanian Catholic organization, which attracted the children of the Lithuanian DPs who had fled Nazi and Soviet oppression. In 1976 he became the director of Lithuanian Catholic Religious Aid (LCRA), whose primary function was to help sustain Catholicism in Lithuania by sending Bibles, books, and religious materials to the homeland. Having earlier served as a media specialist for the Church in Baltimore, Cas appreciated the power of the press, and he formed the Lithuanian Information Center (LIC) as a subsidiary of LCRA.

By providing American media representatives and other persons interested in "Soviet affairs" with information about Lithuania, Father Cas hoped to remind American opinion-molders that the U.S. government had never recognized Stalin's annexation of Lithuania. As long as the world's most powerful democracy held to that policy, Lithuania might one day regain its independence. He urged me to meet and lecture before several organizations formed by Lithuanian DPs. I began to read about this second wave of Lithuanian immigrants who by courage, foresight, or luck had escaped the fate of their friends and relatives who were living in Soviet-occupied Lithuania. In meeting members of the DP community, I noted that some looked upon the old Lithuanian migrants, because of their humble origins, with condescension. I reminded them that they would not have found refuge in North America had they not been helped by Lithuanians who had first arrived in the United States a century ago.

Father Cas faced formidable obstacles in conducting this public information campaign. His superiors deemed LIC a secondary operation, and they cautioned him not to forget that his "real" job was to provide religious, not political, assistance to the Lithuanian faithful.

A second obstacle was securing funding for his small operation—a difficult task, since there was not much of any significance happening in Lithuania. Indeed, it was conventional wisdom, even among Lithuanian-Americans, that there was little reason to hope that Lithuania would soon be free of the Soviet yoke. He persevered nonetheless and received donations from Lithuanian-Americans of both migrations.

But American journalists saw little reason to write about the small republic on the Baltic, and those who eventually were posted to the Soviet Union reported from Russia, usually Moscow or Leningrad, and only occasionally from the USSR's hinterland. When they did write about the non-Russian republics, their articles often were shaped by biases or misinformation they culled from the Russian press and Soviet authorities. They could excuse their restricted reporting by citing the fact that Soviet authorities made it difficult to travel to the Baltic republics.

Consequently, if the good father had not been a stubborn man, committed to the independence of his ancestor's homeland, the information center would never have materialized. In the early 1970s, Father Cas was conducting media affairs for the Catholic Church in Baltimore, and noticing my Lithuanian name (which somehow had remained intact in spite of the long trek from the Old World to the New One), he began giving me information about developments in Lithuania.

After leaving the National Center for Urban Ethnic Affairs for an academic career, I turned to the USSR, the "nationalities question" in particular, which dealt with Soviet policy toward the non-Russians in the empire.[7] Like their Soviet colleagues, American scholars of the Soviet Union conceded that many "minority peoples" continued to cling to their traditional values and identities but believed their ranks were shrinking. Moscow was succeeding in creating a "Soviet" identity among the most gifted non-Russians as they shed their parochial, ethnic loyalties for a universalist, Soviet mind-set.

In research that I had conducted for government agencies, such as the Department of State and the Department of Defense, I discovered that this view prevailed among policymakers and analysts in the U.S. government. This was not surprising, since government officials attended universities where the non-Russians in the USSR were neglected in classroom lectures and the texts students read. They could not ignore resistance to Soviet rule in the Soviet "outer empire"—the satellite countries of Eastern Europe—but they did not properly conclude that it represented a threat to the viability of the Warsaw

Treaty Organization (WTO). Consequently, during the Cold War, Pentagon analysts in their threat assessments dismissed the fact that many of the soldiers belonging to the WTO were both anti-Russian and anti-Soviet, and many of them would not fight well, or at all, in a war with NATO.

Nor did defense analysts think much of those who argued that there were serious ethnic cleavages in Soviet society, which, although latent during peacetime, might become manifest if the Red Army fought a major war with the West. Zbigniew Brzezinski, the Polish-born political scientist, baffled SIOP officials (the acronym stands for Single Integrated Operational Plan, and the people associated with SIOP determine U.S. nuclear targeting doctrine) when he became President Jimmy Carter's national security adviser and asked whether they discriminated between Russian and non-Russian areas. Brzezinski reasoned that we should spare the latter, if possible, to enhance their prospects of achieving power in an event of a war between the superpowers.[8] But as to most educated Americans in and out of government, Russia and the Soviet Union were synonymous in the minds of the SIOP planners.

One day, Cas called and said that he was receiving an underground publication, that lay Lithuanian Catholics and clerics had begun to publish: the *Chronicle of the Catholic Church in Lithuania.* The first issues appeared in 1972, and in spite of a massive KGB campaign to stop publication they continued to appear until 1988, when in the period of glasnost ("openness") they no longer were needed. Until his arrest in 1983, a Jesuit priest, Father Sigitas Tamkevicius, would be its principal editor. After he was incarcerated, another Jesuit, Father Jonas Boruta, and nuns of the Congregation of the Eucharist would take his place.[9]

Through the *Chronicle,* Catholic activists were providing detailed information about religious persecution in Lithuania in violation of both the Soviet and Lithuanian constitutions not to mention the UN Declaration on Human Rights. Children were scolded by their teachers for attending mass and told that if they persisted they would not get into the university. Their parents were warned that if they adhered to Catholic dogma their jobs were at risk, and, of course, open protest was deemed "anti-Soviet behavior" and could result in a long jail term. But the Catholic faithful refused to be intimidated, and in spite of real cause to fear for their freedom they openly resisted. The following "Letter to the Teacher of My Child" is a moving example of what one found in samizdat.

> I have been trying from the very beginning to instill in my children those principles which would help them all their lives to remain honest, decent and resolute persons. These principles I received from my own parents. That which I hold good and necessary I am duty-bound in con-

science to hand on to my children also. . . . No one has the right to forbid me or to stop me from handing on to my children those mental and moral principles which it is my conviction are the most necessary for human beings. I know that, if one wishes to remain an honorable person, it is necessary to struggle against one's weaknesses, vices and temptations from without. For this struggle I prepared my children. From my experience of life I am convinced that such a struggle is most successful when the person feels a responsibility not only in the eyes of human beings, but also in the sight of God, when one is convinced that one's actions and deeds have not only a temporary, transient value, but also an eternal worth, when one obeys not only the law but also the voice of one's own conscience.[10]

It was only after their superiors refused to resist Soviet antireligious policies that the Catholic militants had decided to publish the samizdat. It spite of persistent KGB attempts to stop its publication, including numerous arrests, the incarceration of people in mental institutions, and mysterious deaths, the Soviets never succeeded in their campaign.

As I read copies of the *Chronicle* throughout the 1970s and interviewed Lithuanians who had openly opposed the Soviet system, it was evident that Moscow's campaign to destroy the Lithuanian national ideal had failed. When I shared such views with colleagues, their response was that my evidence was anecdotal, whereas those scholars who proclaimed that the Soviet drive to Russify the more than one hundred ethnic groups in the USSR was producing concrete results had mustered "hard data" in reaching their conclusions. The data in question involved crude correlations, such as drawing relationships between rising levels of urbanization and industrialization and the propensity to speak Russian.

The *Chronicles* and the testimony of those Lithuanians who fled or were expelled from the Soviet Union for their anti-Soviet activities strongly suggested that Lithuanian nationalism had survived the Soviet campaign to crush it. And if Moscow had failed to destroy Lithuanian nationalism, what about the nationalistic impulses of other non-Russian peoples—the Ukrainians, Georgians and millions of other "minority peoples" in the USSR who had not surrendered their national identity? It was among those students of the USSR who realized that Soviet nationalities policy had failed that a small band of academics and policymakers began to look at other flaws in the Soviet system. Although the mainstream community of Soviet-watchers would ignore their work, they would be the first ones to reach a startling conclusion: the Soviet empire was in danger of imploding.

Through the *Chronicles,* the Catholics human rights activists provided detailed information about religious persecution in Lithuania. In addition to hostile actions taken against devout lay Catholics, priests and nuns were assaulted, imprisoned, and even murdered for their religious work. Religious guarantees provided under the Soviet and Lithuanian constitutions, as well as international human rights accords—which Moscow had signed—were blatantly ignored by Soviet authorities.

Under Stalin, the Soviets' anti-Catholic campaign was most brutal and deadly. By exiling and executing Catholic clergy and lay activists, he had sought to crush Catholicism in Lithuania. As noted earlier, like its counterpart in Poland, the Church historically had been closely associated with Lithuanian nationalism—at least in modern times. Stalin outlawed all religious orders, and closed and demolished churches, and those priests who escaped execution or arrest were exiled or denied the opportunity to perform their pastoral duties. In the face of Stalin's draconian policies the Catholic Church was driven underground.

It fared somewhat better under the old Georgian's successors, but by the late 1960s, many Catholics concluded that if they did not actively resist the Soviet drive the very existence of the Church was at risk. They were encouraged by the Prague Spring of 1968, the activities of Russian activists like Andrei Sakharov, and protests by Jewish refuseniks and other ethnic activists. Simas Kudirka, the first Lithuanian "dissident" to capture the attention of the West, said: "When I was sent to prison I was amazed to see how many people had resisted the Soviets from all parts of the USSR, people from Asia, the Caucasus, the Ukraine." Sitting in the kitchen of Father Cas's Brooklyn rectory, he added, "It was in prison that all of us learned that we were not alone in our struggle against the Soviets and Russian imperialism."[11]

Kudirka gained fame as a result of an incident that began in November 1970 and later became a *cause célèbre.* On November 23, 1970, Kudirka was a radio operator on the *Sovetskaya Litva,* a factory ship that served the Soviet fishing fleet. The Soviet vessel was situated alongside the American Coast Guard cutter *Vigilant* a half mile off the island of Martha's Vineyard. The ships had gathered there for a meeting between American fisherman and Soviet authorities. The Americans were angry because the Soviet fleet was harvesting a vast supply of fish off New England waters. Kudirka, a Lithuanian, had been refused the right to enjoy shore leave in foreign ports because his loyalty was suspect, but in spite of long-smoldering resentments toward the Soviet authorities it was on an impulse that he jumped onto the *Vigilant* in hope of achieving political asylum. After the American cutter's commander, Ralph Eustis, who was on the *Sovetskaya Litva,* was told that a Soviet sailor was on board his ship, Eustis contacted his superior, Captain Fletcher W. Brown, Jr., on shore and informed him of the request. Brown then contacted his superior officer, Rear Admiral William B. Ellis, who was at home. Ellis took little time making a decision, and he instructed Brown as follows:

> First, don't take any action that would indicate the *Vigilant* condones defection. Do nothing to indicate to the man that refuge will be granted. Second, if the man jumps into the water, we should give the Russians the opportunity to pick him up.[12]

Even after it was learned that Kudirka was a Lithuanian, it made no difference to Ellis, who called him a "coward" and "traitor" who therefore should be returned to his ship. This display of appalling political illiteracy resulted in the American crew's standing aside in shame as the Soviet officers sent several sailors from their vessel to the *Vigilant* where Kurdirka was beaten into submission and forced back on the factory ship. Upon his return to Lithuania, Kudirka was tried and imprisoned for his anti-Soviet activities.

During his trial, Kudirka informed his Soviet prosecutors: "My decision to go abroad does not even contradict your Soviet constitution, which guarantees the freedom as you seem to have conveniently forgotten. I say your constitution. It is not mine. If my country, Lithuania, were sovereign and free, I would not be standing here before you. I am innocent, completely."[13]

Soon after the scandalous incident became public, Lithuanians in American began a campaign to secure Kurdika's release through marches and lobbying in Washington and an effort to arouse the media. Four years after he was imprisoned, Kudirka was released and allowed to emigrate to the United States when it was learned that his mother was an American citizen. The fact that the shameful incident occurred within the territorial waters of the United States and was reported in the American print and electric media did not hurt either. Indeed, the incident received so much publicity that Hollywood eventually produced a made-for-TV movie, staring Alan Arkin, to dramatize Kudirka's brush with history. Because of Kudirka's highly publicized tale, the issue of Lithuania's subjugation was aired, but only briefly. Most members of the American Soviet studies community did not give it much thought; Kudirka was an anomaly. The assumption was that most Lithuanians were quietly accepting Soviet subjugation and through Russification were shedding their Lithuanian identity.

There were, however, other Lithuanian nationalists who bravely resisted Soviet subjugation throughout the Soviet era, though few in the West knew about their exploits. The case of Viktoras Petkus is illustrative because it testifies to the power of the Lithuanian national ideal, to the fact that human beings are prepared to endure cruel punishment and risk their lives to sustain their language and culture.

As a seventeen-year-old, Petkus was arrested for his activities in the anti-Soviet Catholic youth organization Ateitis. He received a ten-year sentence at hard labor, but was released in 1953 in a post-Stalinist amnesty. Upon returning home, he graduated from high school and attended Vilnius University as a major in Lithuanian literature. He was convinced that "the preservation of [Lithuania's] national culture [and] spiritual values" represented another way to struggle against Soviet subjugation.

He collected and distributed the works of Lithuanian writers, including those who had fled their homeland rather than endure Soviet rule. In 1957, he was arrested and imprisoned for disseminating "anti-Soviet" propaganda. Tomas Venclova, the Lithuanian poet, who would become one of the founders of the Lithuanian Helsinki Watch Group, commented: "It is interesting to note that at that time, in 1957, a collection of the Russian poems of Jurgis Baltrusaitis, published in 1912, that is five years before the Revolution, was included in this 'anti-Soviet literature.' "[14]

After serving his full eight-year term, Petkus returned home but was banned from teaching literature. Instead, he worked at various jobs, among them hospital attendant and sexton in several Roman Catholic churches. His commitment to the preservation of his nation's culture had not cooled in prison; on the contrary, he devoted much of his time to composing a massive bibliography of Lithuanian poets and frequently gathered with young Lithuanians wanting to learn more about aspects of their country's history and culture that were neglected or distorted at school. The KGB kept him under close surveillance and was especially displeased by the assistance he lent Simas Kudirka's mother in her attempt to get her son released from prison.

Despite KGB harassment, Petkus remained free. In 1975, however, the Russian biologist, Sergei Kovalev, who was a charter member of the Moscow chapter of Amnesty International, and one of the editors of the dissident Russian samizdat journal *Chronicle of Current Events,* was arrested. In December he was tried in Vilnius, allegedly because of his association with Lithuanian civil rights activists. He had helped those activists, but as Andrei Sakharov noted, Kovalev was tried in Lithuania to discourage friends and supporters from Russia from attending his trial and to limit publicity about it. This ploy did not deter Sakharov and several other Russian democratic activists from making the trip to the Lithuanian capital. They were joined by Lithuanian protesters outside the courthouse, but all were denied entrance to witness the four-day trial. Petkus was among the Lithuanians who sought access, and it was at this time that he met Sakharov.[15]

The KGB informed Petkus that his association with Kovalev's supporters and his attempt to witness the trial would get him into trouble. In light of his past encounters with Soviet authorities, he could not take this warning as an idle threat. But, undaunted, he helped form the Lithuanian Helsinki Watch Group in November 1976, emulating several sister organizations that had been established in other parts of the Soviet Union to monitor "Basket Three" of the Helsinki Accords guaranteeing freedom of speech, conscience, and travel. In December, Petkus announced the formation of the Lithuanian group in Sakharov's Moscow apartment. The significance of Lithuanians and Russians—traditional enemies—working together in a dangerous undertaking did not escape the authorities' attention. Under the czars and the Soviet rulers alike, interethnic divisions had deterred the formation of opposition movements. Consequently, the Soviet authorities could not be happy about the fact that along with Petkus, Tomas Venclova, the son of a prominent Communist, Father Karolis Garuckas, a Catholic priest, and Eitanas Finkelsteinas, a Jewish scientist, cofounded the Lithuanian Helsinki Group.

While the Lithuanians were encouraged by the brave resistance of dissidents in Eastern Europe and in the USSR itself, they were emboldened by the signing of the Helsinki Accords of 1975, and specifically by Basket Three, which offered them the legal pretext to attack Moscow's human rights violations. At that time, many American critics of détente had denigrated the accords, asserting that the Soviets got what they wanted, legal recognition of the USSR's "outer empire" in Eastern Europe. In return, the West received worthless human rights guarantees. In fact, the accords were welcomed by opponents of Soviet rule both in the USSR and in Eastern Europe, since they provided a legal basis to resist prohibitions on free speech, the right to travel, and the freedom of religious worship.

As I read the *Chronicle* throughout the 1970s and 1980s, I was struck by one really big difference between the Russian intellectuals and the Lithuanian human rights activists. In contrast to the Russian opponents of Soviet autocracy, who represented primarily an intellectual elite, the Lithuanian Catholic activists had attracted mass support for their cause. Ordinary Lithuanians, young and old, rural and urban, were supporting it. In a two-year period in the early 1970s, over fifty thousand people courageously signed petitions protesting the government's religious persecution.[16] On several occasions, militant Catholics, workers and students, had taken to the streets, and in the spring of 1972 several protest suicides had occurred.

The self-immolation of Romas Kalanta, the son of a Communist, who had expressed a desire to enter the Catholic seminary, had a particularly profound impact upon Lithuanians in all parts of the country. The nineteen-year-old worker had set fire to himself to protest Soviet rule in the center of Kaunas, in a park across the street from the central committee of the Lithuanian Communist Party. It was not surprising that the anti-Soviet demonstrations, which would occur in the wake of his death, took place in Kaunas. Unlike Vilnius, Kaunas after World War II had become a city where the vast majority of residents were ethnic Lithuanian, and they frequently displayed their hatred of the Soviet system. In 1960, during a state-sponsored celebration of Lithuania's twentieth year in the USSR, a riot erupted after militia fired into a crowd of counterdemonstrators. Several people were killed and wounded.

On May 18, the day of the young man's funeral, KGB agents arrived at the Kalanta home and took a series of measures to prevent the funeral from being exploited by "anti-Soviet demonstrators." For example, the procession started four hours before the funeral's announced schedule. Then the small group of family members were put on a bus. "The funeral cortege moved at eighty kilometers per hour. There were militiamen at every crossing, all traffic lights were green. Thus only a few passersby bid farewell" to the young martyr. Later that day, however, thousands of people arrived in the area surrounding Kalanta's house shouting: "Communists are liars, murderers and cheats! Freedom for Lithuania! Russians go home!"[17] The crowd then moved to downtown Kaunas and continued the protest. Among the throng were young workers, hippies, and actors from a local theater group. Outraged, and seeking some way to vent their anger, elements of the crowd began tossing stones at shop windows that proclaimed "The fiftieth anniversary of the USSR."

At that very time, Lithuanian Communist apparatchiks and KGB generals were celebrating the success of their operation in a famous restaurant, the Tulpe Café, on Laisves Aleja (Freedom Avenue). When militia and troops arrived, the young people started building barricades to protect themselves. The rioting carried over until the next day, when it was squelched.

After the incident, muted discontent was channeled into purposeful public resistance to state oppression. The anniversary of Kalanta's death precipitated annual public protests conducted by Catholics and non-Catholics alike. He had become a symbol for both groups, and his martyrdom had linked people who previously thought that they had little in common. For example, Father Cas told me that some of the first copies of the *Chronicle* to reach the West were carried out of the country by Lithuanian Jews. And Father Tamkevicius is unstinting in his praise of Russian dissidents who helped him transmit the samizdat to the West—in addition to Kovalev they included the Russian orthodox priest Gleb Yankunin, and the democratic activists Aleksandr Lavut and Tatiana Velykanova.[18]

The *Chronicle* and interviews I conducted with people who had been forced into exile indicated that something else of great significance existed among the USSR's non-Russians. There were people who had meekly accepted the system who no longer would remain silent in the face of the slow strangulation of their national life. This was first revealed to me by Jonas Jurasas, a theatrical director from Kaunas. He had been expelled after a confrontation with Lithuania's minister of culture.

Jurasas had gained considerable fame in his homeland for producing plays that were deemed controversial by the artistic community. There were several reasons, he said, why he had been allowed unusually broad artistic latitude. He was deemed politically reliable because when he was a boy, his parents were killed by Lithuanian fascists. Second, because he attended the University of Moscow, and thereby had been exposed to the best and brightest segment of the Russian population, he presumably had become Russified. Finally, he was a person of real talent, someone whom the authorities could cite as evidence that gifted Soviet citizens were rewarded even if they were not Russians.

But by the early 1970s, Jurasas wanted to direct bolder, more innovative plays; in every instance he was denied permission. Finally, out of frustration and in the name of artistic freedom, he wrote a letter of protest on August 16, 1972, to the Lithuanian minister of culture.[19] He was fired immediately. The minister scolded him for his impetuous behavior and said that Jurasas should have followed the example of a Polish play he had once directed. In the play, the lead character appeared onstage wearing a long overcoat that covered his shoe tops. Periodically, his conscience would appear in the form of an actor, on his knees under the long garment, who peaked through the coat and expressed doubts about the hero's thoughts and actions. The minister suggested, "You must do the same thing. Keep your most provocative thoughts to yourself. You don't always have to repeat out loud what's on your mind."

Then Jurasas recounted his first experience with the KGB. He was taken to a large room where his interrogator sat in a chair at the end of a long table. Flipping through the director's file, the agent finally exclaimed somewhat philosophically: "How did we allow you to get away with all of this shit?"

He then answered his own question. "The problem is that the KGB is like a big tank, with tiny eye slits making it difficult to see the road. The tank moves along it slowly and sometimes fails to see flowers—like you—growing on the side. But eventually we see, and then do you know what we do? We roll over them. That's what we're going to do to you."

The authorities threatened to put him in a psychiatric hospital, imprison his wife, Ausra, and make his son a ward of the state. He was, however, given a chance to repent. The minister of culture told him, "Look. We know you're young and headstrong. Wait six months and then write a letter retracting your criticisms of the state and its so-called suppression of art. Then we'll bring you back."

Jurasas refused to recant. When I indicated that I doubted that if faced with a similar situation I would have had the courage to refuse, Jurasas responded: "That's what everyone in the West says. But you fail to realize something very important. We're not afraid anymore!"[20] More than a decade passed before I realized that he spoke for tens of thousands of Lithuanians and not only for himself and a small band of men and women who openly resisted Moscow's subjugation of their country.

At first, Jurasas was despondent because many of his old friends, members of the Kaunas intellectual community, avoided him when he appeared in public. "They even crossed the street when they saw me moving in their direction." But he was welcomed by what he called "invisible people," ordinary men and women who persisted in their resistance to Moscow. Indeed, the Catholic protest movement that produced the *Chronicle* never was squashed because many working men and women had risked their freedom to publish and circulate it.

The formation of the Lithuanian Helsinki Watch Group was an important new development in protest against Soviet rule, because it involved a more cosmopolitan membership than the Catholic human rights movement. It "collected considerable evidence of violations of civil rights," but did not dwell upon developments in Lithuania alone. It drew "attention to the separation of families, denial of the right of emigration for the Volga Germans," and "harassment of Estonian political prisoners," according to V. Stanley Vardas. Its first statement "dated April 10 1977, however, concerned the situation of the Catholic Church and believers in Lithuania. This document on institutionalized religious persecution was cosigned by the Russian Helsinki Group of Moscow."[21]

Russian dissidents like Andrei Sakharov and Sergei Kovalev had provided important assistance to the Lithuanians. Many Western observers would have ignored protest in Lithuania altogether had not Sakharov's name been associated with it. Sakharov, in particular, legitimized the claim that Lithuania had been illegally incorporated into the USSR when he joined Baltic activists in Moscow protesting the Molotov-Ribbentrop Pact. Sakharov signed "A Statement of Russian Democrats," which proclaimed, "Lithuania, Estonia and

Latvia have been annexed into the Soviet Union…as a result of the occupation of the Baltic States by the Red Army." The Helsinki Group, however, declined in effectiveness as a result of the arrest, death, and emigration of its leading members.[22]

Nonetheless, it was noteworthy because it represented the first indication that intellectuals, who had been silent during the Soviet era, were prepared to protest Soviet rule overtly, and its activities emboldened fainter-hearted colleagues. Until the late 1980s, aside from occasional protests from people like Jurasas and Thomas Venclova, intellectuals and academics remained silent, some fantasizing that the Soviet Union would be destroyed in a war with the West or, faced with mounting internal contradictions, self-destruct.

The Lithuanian national idea was sustained by the diaspora and the brave few in Soviet Lithuania who openly resisted foreign occupation of their country. But organized resistance to Soviet imperialism and the mobilization of thousands of new Lithuanian activists would not materialize until Gorbachev concluded that the only way to save the Leninist political system and the Soviet empire was to "restructure" it, and henceforth the word "perestroika" came into vogue. Perestroika, Gorbachev's naive belief that he could encourage and then channel protest at the grassroots level to revitalize Leninism and sustain the Russian-dominated empire, clearly provided a change in objective circumstances and helped make the Lithuanian protest movement viable. Gorbachev's reforms provided the energy, and like Dr. Frankenstein he would be destroyed by the "monster" that he had created.

4 POPULAR FRONT REVOLUTIONARIES

*Aleksandr Yakovlev came to Lithuania to determine whether
Sajudis was a reformist or nationalist movement. He thought it
was a perestroika movement and made a big mistake!*
—*Arvydas Juozaitis, early Sajudis leader*

Growing but diffuse resistance to Soviet rule did not become organized until
1988, with the founding of Sajudis, the Lithuanian Reconstruction Movement
(Lietuvos Persitvakymo Sajudis). With the exception of diehard Bolsheviks,
most Lithuanians were unhappy about their country's subject status and had
been for years. They included disenchanted Communists like Algimantas
Cekuolis, who believed the system was corrupt and irredeemable and feared
Moscow's Russification campaign eventually would destroy the Lithuanian
nation. They also included Lithuanians who refused to join the party but
never openly challenged the system. An example was Vytautas Landsbergis.
Everyone knew that the authorities would not tolerate even minor displays of
dissent without punishment and so it was foolhardy to protest Soviet oppression. What then emboldened Lithuanians in the late 1980s to challenge the
system that had cowed them into silence for decades?

Perestroika provided a change in objective circumstances that made the
Lithuanian protest movement viable. But Sajudis would not have developed as
rapidly (and radically) as it did without a change in the national consciousness
that had kept most Lithuanians mute during the Soviet occupation. At noted
previously, this change in consciousness had its origins in a band of fearless
people who never stopped resisting foreign domination of their country and
openly defied their Soviet masters before the Helsinki Watch Group and
Sajudis were formed. Although proportionately small in number, the Catholic
human rights activists, deportees, and former "forest brothers"—who risked
careers, freedom, and even their lives—sustained the will to resist. Like their
counterparts in Estonia and Latvia, their irrational (in light of the overwhelming odds against them, this is the proper adjective) opposition to Soviet rule

kept the spark of resistance alive. Over time, the rallies they conducted goaded more fainthearted Lithuanians to actively rebuke the Soviet leviathan, to openly support perestroika, and eventually to go beyond Gorbachev's liberalization drive. Without their physical courage and moral force, the March 11 restoration of Lithuanian independence might never have occurred, and without that provocation, subsequent events, leading to the demise of the Soviet Union, also might never have occurred.

However, open displays of protest—culminating in the formation of the popular front movements—did not begin in Lithuania, the largest and most ethnically homogeneous Baltic republic, but in Latvia and Estonia. In July 1986, a joint Soviet-American Chautauqua conference was scheduled to be conducted in Jurmala, Latvia. In response, some workers in Liepaja formed an organization called Defense of Human Rights Helsinki–86 to submit documents to the Jurmala gathering. They demanded that Latvians be allowed human rights proclaimed in the 1975 Helsinki Accords. The group never reached Jurmala, as their members were harassed and arrested by the KGB. But documents prepared for the Chautauqua conference, the UN, and the CPSU were translated and disseminated in the United States by the American Latvian Association.

The Helsinki–86 dissidents had suffered a setback, but they were not silenced. On June 14, 1987, they gathered at the Freedom Monument in Riga to protest Stalin's 1941 deportations. The demonstrators stood in concentric rings around the monument; long-standing dissidents clustered toward the central point of the gathering, serving as magnets for their more timid brethren. Jan A. Trapans writes, "Among the outer rings of spectators were scattered most of Riga's intellectual elite: writers, artists, professionals, poets— excited, curious, embarrassed not to be at the heart of the demonstration."[1] Such "calendar demonstrations," which marked important dates in Stalin's campaign to oppress the Latvians, soon spread to the sister Baltic countries. Protests, for example, occurred in all three on August 23, the anniversary of the Molotov-Ribbentrop Pact.

In November, demonstrators at the Riga monument would be bloodied in a clash with KGB agents, prompting several American senators to warn Gorbachev that this was a violation of glasnost. But it was the Latvian Greens, the Club for the Defense of the Environment (Vides Aizasardzibas Klubs, or VAK), which ultimately provided the radical leadership and mass base for the creation of a popular front movement there. In 1986, the incipient Green movement demonstrated its clout by halting the construction of a huge hydroelectric project.

One of my students, Tija Karkle, left for Latvia soon after she graduated from college and became a VAK volunteer. Tija and her entire family had been active in Latvian-American affairs for years, and like members of the Lithuanian-American community, Latvians in the diaspora would play a pivotal role in their homeland's drive for independence. After independence their level of participation in governmental affairs was also much higher than that of their Lithuanian cousins. In large part this was the result of a demographic fact: only 52 percent of the population were ethnic Latvian.

In 1987 the Estonians took the lead from their Latvian cousins when they pressed Moscow for wider Estonian autonomy. That spring, through what became known as the Four-Man Proposal, they demanded full control of their economic affairs. According to Lieven, the dialogue that ensued between proponents of economic autonomy and opponents in the Estonian Communist Party, it became clear that Gorbachev's promises aside, the bureaucrats in the Soviet ministries had no intention of sharing power with authorities in the republics.[2]

In April 1988, the Estonians formed a popular front fueled by widespread concern about the country's ecosystem. "In Estonia, opposition to state plans for phosphate mining was motivated by a genuine fear of further wastelands like the oil-shale mining areas of northeast Estonia, but also because the plan involved bringing in thousands of Russian workers."[3] Simultaneously, the National Heritage Society, ostensibly devoted to the protection of national monuments, organized protests against pernicious anti-environmental policies. It was the society that first displayed the pre-Soviet national flag in April 1988 and mobilized Estonians, who no longer could remain silent, against Soviet rule.

Some Lithuanians who traveled frequently to Latvia and Estonia to attend academic conferences and party gatherings and to conduct other business transactions had numerous friends and colleagues in both countries, and they were impressed by developments in Riga and Tallinn. Arvydas Juozaitis said, "I was encouraged by what they were doing in Riga," and he returned to Lithuania confident that his countrymen could organize a similar movement. According to Mecys Laurinkus, it was the Estonian and Latvian examples and not encouragement from Gorbachev that first inspired young academics at Vilnius University to form Sajudis.[4]

Meanwhile, it was the old Lithuanian resistance fighters who would embolden Lithuanians from all walks of life. On August 23, 1987, Antanas Terleckas, a nationalist activist, and Nijole Sadunaite, a nun and Catholic activist, organized a gathering in Vilnius to protest the Molotov-Ribbentrop

Pact in coordination with similar demonstrations in Tallinn and Riga. Few Lithuanians had the courage to join them, and only about three hundred protesters gathered at the monument of the Lithuanian-Polish poet Adam Mickiewicz, adjacent to St. Ann's Church in Old Town.

The demonstration, however, was not altogether a flop. Moscow media portrayed the rally as evidence that democracy was at work in Lithuania, and this emboldened some people to test Gorbachev's pledge that he would welcome open discussion. Henceforth a growing number of artists, writers, philosophers, and historians openly challenged party-dictated policies and interpretations of the country's history under Soviet rule. Grievances previously voiced only in the safety of a friend's kitchen were now being aired in public forums. Emboldened, some intellectuals even signed petitions of protest about scheduled oil drilling in the Baltic. In November 1987, members of the Artists' Union further roiled the waters when they removed that organization's old leadership, which had been imposed upon them by party hacks. That very evening, Petras Griskevicius, the Lithuanian Communist Party leader, suffered a lethal heart attack; he was replaced by Ringaudas Songaila.

Excitement mounted in 1988 as Lithuanian Independence Day, February 16, approached. The Lithuanian dissidents responsible for the August rally had announced that they planned to commemorate the seventieth anniversary of Lithuanian independence in a street demonstration. The authorities reacted by arresting the demonstration leaders prior to the rally, and by intimidating potential protesters they prevented the rally from reaching significant proportions. Consequently Western journalists at the scene found no evidence of protest, but the organizers asserted that isolated protests did occur in Vilnius and Kaunas.

In the spring of 1988, Juozaitis and like-minded colleagues concluded Gorbachev was serious about encouraging wider participation in the political process. Gorbachev's chastising the party leadership, KGB, and police for harassing demonstrators in Estonia and Latvia was clearly a positive sign. For a while, protesters continued to be subjected to arrest, but the arrests were ad hoc and were not part of a systematic campaign of oppression. By late 1989, they would stop altogether.

In Lithuania, many hard-liners witnessed open anti-Soviet protest and Gorbachev's pluralistic reforms with dismay and lost the will to move harshly against the dissidents. Their disarray and flagging courage reflected the general feeling of malaise afflicting apparatchiks throughout vast stretches of the Soviet Empire. The Communist regimes of Eastern Europe would fall like dominos in 1989 because the leaders there had lost the will to retain power by force and were incapable of attracting popular support through free elections.

With encouragement from activists in Estonia and Latvia, young faculty members at the University of Vilnius took the first steps to organize a Lithuanian popular front movement. Among the founders were Mecys Laurinkus and Arvydas Juozaitis in the philosophy department and Alvydas Medalinskas, an economist. "Later, we decided we needed an older man to help us," Laurinkus said, "someone not associated with the Communist Party. . . . That's when we visited Landsbergis."[5]

In the early days, Juozaitis shared leadership status with Landsbergis, who enjoyed good connections among the country's intellectuals and nationalists. The young philosopher had high name recognition in Lithuania among common folk because he had won a bronze medal in swimming at the 1976 Olympics. He captured the attention of the nation's intellectuals in April 1988 when he gave a talk on "political culture." It caused a stir because Juozaitis's analysis was deemed an open assault on the Soviet system, then still a rare event. He enchanted people with his good looks and fostered admiration among them because of his courage. "Juozaitis was the first prominent leader to openly wave the old Lithuanian flag in public gatherings, long before it became legal to do so," the libertarian Algirdas Degutis told me.[6]

Many people believed that ultimately Juozaitis would become the president of Lithuania, but he would clash with Landsbergis and the "Kaunas radicals" over just how fast Sajudis should move toward independence. Later he would earn the enmity of many Lithuanians by attacking Landsbergis for calling him a dictator. To this day, neither man can talk about the other in a civil, or rational, fashion.

Among the original founders of Sajudis were professors at the University of Vilnius and other academic institutions in the country's capital as well as intellectuals and members of the liberal professions living there. Many from this group were Communists, such as Bronius Kuzmickas, a philosopher; Antanas Buracas, an economist; Romualdas Ozolas, a philosopher and adviser to the central committee; Kazimiera Prunskiene, an economist who in July 1989 would become a deputy prime minister in a government led by Communists; and Bronius Genzelis, a philosopher and head of the Communist Party at Vilnius University. Altogether, among the thirty-six founders of the "initiative group," seventeen belonged to the Lithuanian Communist Party.

A member of the Kaunas faction in Sajudis, dominated by people with decidedly more nationalist aspirations, was typically "a technically trained white-collar worker from Kaunas or the provinces: they were engineers, small managers, schoolteachers, lawyers, agronomists and the like." A fault line ran through Sajudis which reflected the cosmopolitan, diverse subculture of Vilnius in contrast to the ethnically homogeneous subculture of Kaunas. Lieven claims there was also a class dimension to the factional split. "The 'Kaunas Faction,' as it was later known, represented the 'intellectual petty bourgeoisie': hating Communism but without access to Western culture, they had steeped themselves in the traditional culture of Lithuania in 1939, or whatever of it had survived. They were passionately ambitious to drive the existing establishment and bureaucracy from its place."[7]

On June 14, 1988, Sajudis and the Terlecka's Freedom League (comprised of nationalists who had resisted Soviet rule even prior to perestroika) although in separate groups, had gathered in Old Town Vilnius's Gedimino (Cathedral) Square, which would become the site for many of the large demonstrations against Soviet rule. From Sajudis headquarters, which looked over the square, one could witness history reaching a critical mass without leaving Landsbergis's crowded office. The two groups were sharing the same space in the square to commemorate the 1941 mass deportations but at that time were separated by a broad ideological chasm. Many of the longtime dissidents viewed Sajudis as a newly formed Communist-dominated organization whose leaders could not be trusted. This view prevailed among leaders of Lithuanian organizations in North America but was revised after several Sajudis activists, including Juozaitis and Landsbergis, conferred with them in the United States.

Young Canadians and Americans of Lithuanian descent would work for Sajudis as translators, press aides, and liaisons with the Western media even before Sajudis was accepted by leaders in the North American diaspora. For years it had been divided over the wisdom of allowing youngsters to participate in programs that were conducted by the Lithuanian government. Some of them argued that as long as the government was Communist, even casual visits to the homeland were forbidden lest they gave legitimacy to the Communists there. Others proclaimed that there was no danger of young Canadians and Americans being brainwashed by their hosts and such visits would actually strengthen their resolve to fight for Lithuanian independence.

Asta Banionis, who later would become the outspoken public affairs director of the Lithuanian-American Community (the major lobbying group among the Lithuanian DPs), recalls when members of the U.S. diaspora remained suspicious of Sajudis. Like Father Cas's energetic and articulate assistants Ginte Damusis and Victor Nakas, Asta's parents had been part of the post–World War II migration, and she too had been brought up in Michigan and participated in émigré community life. When her husband took a job in Washington she found a position on Capitol Hill. In September 1988, a "left-wing" Lithuanian-American organization, Santara Sviesa, had invited three Lithuanian intellectuals to speak before its annual gathering, which met to discuss Lithuanian issues from a highly charged intellectual perspective. The troika included the actor Regimantas Adomaitis, the writer Sigitas Geda, and the geographer Ceslovas Kudaba, all Sajudis activists. Although not officially invited, the irrepressible Algimantas Cekuolis, editor of *Gimtasis Krastas,* a paper published for Lithuanians abroad, also attended, "because he was in the United States anyway." All four were held suspect, but Cekuolis in particular was closely watched, since it was rumored that he was a KGB agent. The four guests, however, impressed the émigrés at the gathering—including representatives from other Lithuanian-American organizations—and concluded that Sajudis was a legitimate anti-Soviet movement.[8]

The following May, Asta met Emmanuelis Zingeris, a young Jewish leader from Vilnius, who was in the United States to study at YIVO (the Jewish Scientific Institute) in New York City. Before the war, the research organization had been located in Vilnius to serve the country's large Jewish community. After he discussed Sajudis policies, Zingeris removed suspicions among American observers that Sajudis was a traditional ultranationalist organization and was racist, as some spindoctors in Moscow had claimed. His being a Jew helped dispel that conclusion. Asta then agreed with Gabija Petrauskas, the Canadian leader, that it would be a good idea to invite Landsbergis and Juozaitis to North America, where they could tour cities with heavy Lithuanian populations. It was after the duo made their tour that the Lithuanian diaspora concluded that they were authentic and that Sajudis deserved all the support the Lithuanians from North America could provide.

The knowledge that the diaspora would help was a morale boost for the Sajudis leaders. Henceforth, Lithuanian organizations in North America (from both migrations) would provide Sajudis with fax machines, computers, and financial assistance. They would lobby Congress and executive agencies to enlist support for the Lithuanian cause. In response, the American quasi-governmental National Endowment for Democracy would provide modest assistance; for example, the Lithuanian Information Center received three grants, not exceeding $35,000, to purchase fax machines and other communications equipment.

Ginte and Victor, under the dogged leadership of Father Cas, kept reporters abreast of the latest developments in Lithuania and adroitly refuted disinformation emanating from Moscow. By computerizing information about developments in Lithuania, Marian Skabeikis enabled the LIC to respond quickly to inquiries from journalists and academics. Later the center's small but talented staff would help plan and advance U.S. trips for Lithuania's first prime minister, Kazimiera Prunskiene, and for President Vytautas Landsbergis, and acted as interpreters for them in meetings with President Bush and members of Congress.

During my first visit to Lithuania, I was surprised that American journalists were ignoring the role that men and women from the diaspora were playing in support of Sajudis. I recall having dinner with Charles Krause, a correspondent for Public TV's *McNeil-Lehrer Hour,* at Stikliai, Lithuania's first private restaurant. I urged him to devote coverage to the Americans and Canadians who were helping Sajudis conduct the election campaign and provide information to the global media gathered in Vilnius. Krause, a first-rate reporter whose journalism I admired, had worked many years in Latin America and was unhappy about his Lithuanian assignment because a presidential election was being conducted in Nicaragua at the time. He dismissed my argument that something truly monumental was occurring in Lithuania and the election in Nicaragua was relatively insignificant. He said, "Why would our viewers want to hear what Canadian housewives had to say about the Soviet Union?"[9]

The Lithuanians struggling to break free of Moscow hoped through émigré organizations and their political and media contacts to exploit the enormous influence that the United States could exert upon Gorbachev. The émigré activists themselves did not possess the clout needed to hold the attention of powerful members of the U.S. political establishment and the media, but they played a pivotal role in encouraging opinion-molders who had such clout to support the Lithuanian cause.

Victor Nakas appeared frequently on American TV answering questions about developments in Lithuania, refuting misinformation emanating from Moscow, and later serving as an interpreter for Landsbergis. And he possessed a much better grasp of how to pitch the independence movement's case to the American media than any other person in the émigré community. To a large degree, his modesty explains why his role in the drama has not received the attention it deserves. The same can be said for Ginte Damusis (whose father was an Ateitis leader) and Father Pugevicius.

Victor had attended Saturday language school in Detroit with Ginte, and she had helped him secure his job at the Lithuanian Information Center. In 1977, Victor had organized a demonstration in Washington protesting human rights violations in Lithuania. "President Carter's human rights campaign provided us a pretext to protest violations in Lithuania," he said. At a time when the diaspora had little cause to be sanguine about developments in Lithuania, "Carter's campaign gave Lithuanians in America a much-needed shot in the arm."[10]

The KGB in Lithuania, which closely followed the émigré community in North America, henceforth identified Victor as an "enemy of the Soviet Union." Years later, in a tour of the pre-independence KGB headquarters in Vilnius, he perused his KGB file and found it amusing that he had been given the code name "the coordinator," because of his efforts in 1977. He also learned that the KGB had assumed that he would become a major leader in VLIK (the Supreme Committee for Liberation of Lithuania), which they erroneously believed had a large membership in North America.

One Lithuanian-American, who helped Sajudis while serving in a quasi-official position, was Victor's friend Romas Sakadolskis. Born in a DP camp in Fulda, Germany, in 1947, Sakadolskis grew up in Chicago, where he worked for the Lithuanian-language Margutis Radio as a staff reporter and announcer. He became a stringer for Voice of America in 1969 and joined VOA's Lithuanian Service full-time in 1973. After returning to graduate school at Kent State University, he worked in VOA's Chicago bureau from 1977 to 1986 as a writer and reporter. In 1988, he returned to Washington to become chief of VOA's Lithuanian Service.

When he visited Lithuania, Sakadolskis was treated as a celebrity. As many Lithuanians have told me, the VOA and other Western radio programs had served as a vital lifeline to the West. They beamed to the Iron Curtain countries objective information about world affairs and developments within the USSR itself while Soviet media continued to engage in a campaign of lies and distortions. Over time, the broadcasts simultaneously bolstered the spirits of people who opposed the Soviet system and undermined the morale of the apparatchiks who controlled it. Indeed, on one occasion Sakadolskis played a small part in a September 1988 Sajudis demonstration.

Sajudis had planned the event in the predominantly ethnic Russian city of Snieckus, to protest the expansion of the Ignalina nuclear power plant, which was built to the specifications of the Chernobyl installation. The authorities refused to issue a permit allowing Sajudis to protest at the site. Undaunted, Sajudis decided to proceed with the demonstration, but the question turned to how this decision would be communicated to the Lithuanian people.

When someone in the audience asked how the group could possibly learn of the final plans with only three days intervening before the action, another voice shouted out 'Sakadolskis will tell us!' The suggestion drew laughter, but [Zigmas] Vaisvila was in fact to use this alternative. Romas Sakadolskis, as the Lithuanian voice of the Voice of America, had his own place in the ferment in Lithuania. Conservatives, reformers, and radicals alike listened to his broadcast and quoted him to make their points in discussion.[11]

Another Ateitis youth group alumni who became an energetic lobbyist for the Lithuanian cause was Linas Kojelis. Linas's father was a high school vice-principal in Klaipeda and was arrested by the Gestapo during the war. Later, as the Red Army was advancing on Lithuania, he escaped. He lived in a DP camp for a while and then migrated to the United States and eventually settled in Los Angeles. The elder Kojelis organized a group of fellow Lithuanian émigrés to publicize the cause of their occupied homeland, and Linas became intrigued with Lithuania and its quest for independence even while in grade school. Like other young Lithuanians who came of age in the 1970s, he was influenced by Father Cas, who was one of the "few Lithuanians in the United States who had a sophisticated grasp of American politics." As a whole, Linas gives the Lithuanian-American organizations poor marks for their political action programs. "The Lithuanian-American community is politically illiterate, he says." [12]

As a result of his work with the Republican Party, Linas was appointed assistant director of ethnic affairs at the Reagan White House. His mission was to serve as liaison with the disparate white ethnic communities that had been ignored by the GOP. Later, as the president of the U.S.–Baltic Foundation, but still retaining his Republican identity, Kojelis applauded both President Jimmy Carter and his national security adviser, Zbigniew Brzezinski, for putting human rights on the American foreign policy agenda. If Ford had won the 1976 presidential election, he said, "I'm afraid that Henry Kissinger would have ignored the human rights issue" and made it difficult for the Lithuanian-Americans to maintain support for their country's independence drive in Congress. While lamenting the failure of the Lithuanian diaspora to build an effective lobbying organization, he says that "they did play an important role in publicizing the fact that the forcible annexation of Lithuania was a violation of international law and that the United States had to maintain a policy of nonrecognition."

Kojelis claims that the United States, by sticking firmly to that policy, provided moral support to the Lithuanians living under Soviet occupation and sustained a strong legal case for Lithuanian independence in the West. "I remember in the late 1980s foreign service officers [who had lobbied for the Baltics in the State Department] stopping me in the halls and remarking with pride that the policy had been 'the right one to take'" and would eventually pave the way for Baltic independence.

In Lithuania, in spite of the positive reception that Sajudis had received among the diaspora, many Freedom League activists remained suspicious of Sajudis and would boycott the 1990 elections to the Lithuanian Supreme

Soviet even though most Lithuanians by that time believed Sajudis was a patriotic movement and was serious about independence. A week before the elections, Petkus told me that he did not "trust Sajudis" and said the elections were "a fraud."[13]

Members of Sajudis, in turn, considered Terleckas and his colleagues to be extremists, cranks, and anachronisms from the past. Close association with such people could play into the hands of the Communist apparat, which was trying to discredit Sajudis in the eyes of moderate Lithuanians and Moscow. At this point, many members were not altogether comfortable cooperating with the Catholic clergy, who, in turn, remained wary of Sajudis. But many Catholics would change there minds about Sajudis on June 24, 1988.

On that day, Sajudis held a rally at Gedimino Square with delegates to the Nineteenth Party Conference of the Communist Party of the Soviet Union on the dais. The cathedral there had been closed to worshipers since the 1950s after it had been converted into a warehouse. Twenty thousand people gathered in a demonstration of solidarity; among them was Algirdas Brazauskas, then a central committee secretary. This gathering would promote the political fortunes of the Sajudis leaders, for it demonstrated that the Lithuanian people were behind them. Among other things it would support Gorbachev's campaign to shift power from the CPSU to governmental bodies, discuss the restoration of Lithuania's sovereignty, and "declare Lithuanian the official language of the republic, guarantee autonomous development of republic education and culture, reestablish constitutional courts at the all-Union and republic levels, and ensure opportunities for 'direct' republic relations with foreign countries."[14]

On July 9, Sajudis held another mass meeting to welcome the delegates upon their return from Moscow and attracted an estimated 100,000 people. Those in attendance saw pre-Soviet flags in abundance and witnessed numerous patriotic speeches, both phenomena still novel, still a source of pride and sheer joy. The old Bolsheviks in the LCP were appalled by such open displays of anti-Soviet sentiment. The growing courage of "counterrevolutionary" elements was deeply troubling to them. They were shocked when Gorbachev released dissidents from prison in Russia who were then given access to the media and other forums to throttle the system, boldly publicizing the flaws of the command economy and the CPSU's shortcomings. Andrei Sakharov's release, in December 1986, was especially unsettling, as was Moscow's toleration of Estonia's popular front movement.

But the worst was yet to come. As Sajudis displayed growing popular support in the summer of 1988, the authorities in Moscow decided that someone of stature had to investigate the situation firsthand. Several weeks later, Aleksandr Yakovlev spent three days in Lithuania, August 11 through 14. Arvydas Juozaitis, with a smile on his face, told me in the summer of 1992, "Aleksandr Yakovlev came to Lithuania to determine whether Sajudis was a reformist or nationalist movement. He thought it was a perestroika movement and made a big mistake."[15]

Yakovlev, an otherwise clear-headed observer, did not understand just how strongly Lithuanians felt about their nation and how deeply they feared that its language and culture would not survive Soviet rule. Days prior to the August 23 fiftieth anniversary of the Molotov-Ribbentrop Pact, Yakovlev had conceded in *Pravda* that the pact was illegal but said that this was insignificant because the Baltic peoples had joined the USSR of their own free will.

Lithuanians branded such claims as boldfaced lies, but many Russians clung to a different interpretation of the Balts' annexation. Perhaps Stalin was crudely inept in his negotiations with Baltic officials, but they could not ignore the logic of his argument that only the Red Army could protect them from Hitler. And who can deny that it was the same army that freed them from German occupation at awful cost in human lives?

At the time Yakovlev visited Lithuania, he was a member of the Politburo and held two powerful central committee posts: secretary for propaganda and secretary for international affairs. Insiders in Moscow claimed that he was the true godfather of perestroika. And he was by no means a fainthearted supporter. In August 1991, when Gorbachev was reportedly being held captive in his Cape Foros compound, Yakovlev demonstrated his commitment to reform by joining Yeltsin at the White House to resist the coup.

Yakovlev was born in 1923 to a humble family in the small Russian village of Korolyovo. But he excelled at school and at the age of eighteen was a lieutenant in the 6th Brigade of the Baltic Marines. He was badly wounded in a battle outside Leningrad and survived only because four of his men dragged him to safety, at the cost of their own lives. In 1956, he was working in the CPSU central committee when he was invited to attend the Twentieth Party Congress in the Kremlin. There he heard Nikita Khrushchev deliver his famous indictment of "Stalin's crimes."

According to David Remnick, Yakovlev and the audience around him were stunned; with the exception of the word "yes," which he heard moving throughout the throng, there was silence. "People went around shaking their heads." The significance of Khrushchev's words did not sink in for a while. "It was hard, very hard. It was especially hard for those of us who had not become hardened by cynicism. . . ."[16] In November 1972, Yakovlev would, in effect, be exiled to Canada for his cavalier attitude toward party dogma. He would serve there for ten years at the Soviet Union's ambassador.

In May 1983, Yakovlev met Gorbachev, already a power in the Politburo, and they traveled together throughout Canada and discovered they shared a compelling conviction that the USSR was on the brink of disaster. "The most important common understanding was . . . that we could not live this way anymore. . . . It was a thrilling experience politically and intellectually." [17]

Gorbachev was impressed by Yakovlev and arranged to have him return to Moscow as the director of the prestigious Institute of World Economy and International Relations. Smart, tough, and favoring reform, Yakovlev was the kind of man that Gorbachev wanted around him as he set upon his formidable and daunting campaign to save the Soviet empire. But when he came to the attention of Western observers of the Soviet scene, he was deemed anti-American, even though he had attended Columbia University in the 1950s and had lived a decade in Canada. This assessment rested largely on the strength of his book, *On the Edge of the Abyss,* which excoriated life in the United States and depicted the government there as a "miserable democracy." [18] In truth, Yakovlev had returned home with the knowledge that his country was falling behind the Americans, Europeans, and Japanese. The Soviet system was corrupt, inefficient, and incapable of improving its performance without fundamental changes in all aspects of Soviet life.

In a lengthy address to Lithuanian Communists and intellectuals, laced with Marxist-Leninist babble, Yakovlev indicated that the time had come to allow dissent, nay to encourage it. In his speech, "In the Interests of the Country and of Every Nationality," he discussed the myriad problems plaguing Soviet society: economic stagnation, Afghanistan, and the like. He also called for an honest accounting of the past and condemned "bureaucratism" as "the greatest impediment to our progress today." He indicated that "national consciousness" was a fact of life and reminded the somber Lithuanian hard-liners about Lenin's position on this vital matter. Moreover, "As far as ethnic and nation-state differences were concerned, they would, according to Lenin, remain for an indefinitely long time after the victory of socialism on a worldwide scale." [19]

Yakovlev then discussed the delicate issue of language and quoted an unidentified "man of letters", who said: "Isn't it paradoxical: I know three ethnic languages and I'm being called a nationalist. The person who calls me this knows only one language, Russian, although he has lived in the republic for several decades. But he calls himself an internationalist!" Most of the audience knew that the unidentified author was the Lithuanian writer Vytautas Petkevicius and the person he directed these words at was the Russian second secretary of the Lithuanian Communist Party, Nikolai Mitkin.

Yakovlev, following standard Soviet procedures, warned against the "dangers" of nationalism but said: "As far as our country is concerned, I do not think there is any danger of national consciousness growing into national egoism, into a feeling of national exclusiveness."[20] Like his boss, Gorbachev, Yakovlev would soon find his words challenged.

The Communist reformers were encouraged by Yakovlev's address but proceeded cautiously, knowing that Ringaudas Songaila and his closest advisers would resist Gorbachev's efforts to democratize the party. Songaila had tried to ignore Gorbachev's recommendation that delegates to the Nineteenth Party Congress receive popular approval for their candidacy Vardys says. The Lithuanian hard-liners further fueled open displays of opposition when the government announced that "central ministry authorities had unilaterally decided to speed up the expansion of giant chemical industries" in several areas that were "already choking from pollution."[21]

But the old Bolsheviks watched in shock and horror as Sajudis continued to grow as a popular national movement. On August 23, 1988, 250,000 gathered at Vingis Park in Vilnius to commemorate the infamous signing of the Molotov-Ribbentrop Pact. The throng was thrilled to hear a tape recording of encouragement from the frail Juozas Urbsys, the last prewar Lithuanian foreign minister who had negotiated with Stalin and Molotov. Other speakers boldly denounced Stalinism, demanded publication of the pact's text, and called for the restoration of Lithuanian sovereignty. At this point, Vardys notes, "Sajudis had shifted its priorities from the needs of perestroika as defined by Moscow to the requirements of reform as defined by the Lithuanians."[22]

The mass demonstrations in the summer of 1988 had a profound impact upon other reformed-minded members of the Lithuanian Communist Party. They were both impressed by Sajudis's popular appeal and emotionally moved by mass displays of Lithuanian nationalism. But at this point they were unsure how they should respond to the powerful tide of nationalism that was sweeping the country. Algirdas Brazauskas was assigned the task to serve as the LCP's liaison with Sajudis. At the June 24 demonstration, he demanded that the tricolor Lithuanian independence flag be lowered before he spoke. Then he did not say much; the one noteworthy remark he made was that the cabinet of ministers had requested that Moscow halt plans to construct an additional reactor at the Ignalina nuclear power plant. But he told me later that for the first time he realized just how widespread support for Lithuanian independence was in the country and how deeply people felt about it. Clearly, more pragmatic elements in the party now knew that they had to reach some kind of accommodation with Sajudis, and if possible to co-opt the energy it was generating.[23]

Reactionaries in the party, however, continued to think in terms of crushing the fledgling national protest movement. Vardys relates that on September 28, 1988, members of the Freedom League organized a meeting "to mark the anniversary of the day on which Hitler 'traded' Lithuania to the Soviet sphere of influence in 1939." Vilnius city officials refused to provide a permit for the meeting, but Terleckas and his supporters were not cowed, and ten thousand people gathered at Gedimino Square. According to Vardys, when he began speaking, "about 500 riot police and troops from the Ministry of the Interior, wearing helmets and plexiglass shields, charged the crowd and began forcibly to disperse it."[24] It took four attacks before the police cleared the square, but the demonstrators reassembled at the shrine of Our Lady of the Dawn, embedded in the old wall that once surrounded the city. This time when the police advanced, the demonstrators pelted them with stones and sticks. The security forces and police under Songaila's command bungled the job, and this incident provoked demands that he be removed from his high office.

In contemporary discussions of those fateful years, many of the key players disagree about the motives of their fellow actors. Brazauskas's opponents claim, for example, that he was forced by the Communist Party to serve as liaison with Sajudis. This task fell to him because of his low status in the party hierarchy, not because of his prominent position in the LCP. Over time, when the fortunes of Sajudis soared and the Communists deemed it in their interest to support the popular front, Brazauskas was the man who was in the right place at the right time.[25]

What we do know is that with the help of Gorbachev, Brazauskas replaced Songaila on October 20, 1988. Nikolai Mitkin, whom Gorbachev two years prior had appointed as the Lithuanian Communist Party's second secretary, was removed as well. He was replaced by an ethnic Russian, Vladimir Beriozov, whose father had taught in Lithuania before World War II, and who lived in the country.

Brazauskas was born in Rokiskis in 1932 and received his engineering degree at the Snieckus Polytechnical Institute in Kaunas. He was active in the Komsomol, and upon graduating he worked as a construction engineer. Later, Senn writes, "he entered the republic's Council of Ministers in 1965 and became deputy chairman of its State Planning Committee. A party member since 1959, he rose to the position of party secretary and member of the LCP's Bureau in 1977."[26]

In contrast to his predecessors, the new Communist leader enjoyed great popularity with the Lithuanian people and clearly convinced many of them that he too was a patriot. Critics who claimed Brazauskas was a Gorbachev plant, however, found concrete evidence for this charge when Brazauskas blocked the Supreme Soviet of the Lithuanian SSR from considering a constitutional amendment in November 1988 that provided Lithuania with the power to nullify Soviet law. This was the authority that the Estonian government would acquire through a revision in Estonia's constitution. Brazauskas could or would not go as far as the Estonians did until May 1989, and his recalcitrance hurt him in his drive to woo popular support. Defenders of Brazauskas conceded that he was cautious—after all, he was a politician who could not ignore the awesome power of Moscow—but would show his true nationalist colors in a December 1989 showdown with the Kremlin.

It may be years before the complete story of these fateful years is told, but Lithuanians and foreign observers of these events agree on one vital matter. The mass demonstrations had a powerful, organic impact upon the vast majority of Lithuanians who participated in them. A dramatic transformation of consciousness took place as people previously intimidated by the oppressive might of the Soviet state became fearless and ignored threats and concrete displays of force that once had cowed them into demeaning silence. Others found that their latent nationalistic sentiments had become manifest after attending one of the Sajudis demonstrations. The compelling sense of national solidarity they displayed, however, would not have materialized had their love of the Lithuanian idea not been deeply imprinted upon their collective consciousness in the first place. Perhaps at the root of their consciousness was something appropriately labeled "primordial"; clearly it was not merely a question of exploiting nationalist sentiment to improve their living standards. As Landsbergis would later exclaim, "people do not lie in front of tanks and risk their lives for better kitchen appliances."[27]

Historians may one day conclude that the final chapter in the collapse of the Soviet order began on October 22, 1988, when Sajudis held a two-day-long founding congress. What would be called the Second Great Vilnius Seimas was attended by supporters from abroad and throughout the Soviet Union, among them leaders from the diaspora like Vytautas Bieliauskas, who was the president of the World Lithuanian Community, (which represents the global Lithuanian diaspora) and Yuri Afanasyev, who represented the Russian democrats. Brazauskas in his speech said that in a meeting with Gorbachev three days earlier, the general secretary sent his greetings to the Lithuanian people and said he considered Sajudis a "positive force."

For two days, Lithuanians throughout the country watched with amazement as the proceedings were televised. What better evidence that Moscow had given its blessings? At one point, Antanas Buracas—an economist, Communist, and Sajudis leader—interrupted the congress and astounded the gathering and TV audience when he announced that the cathedral would be returned to the Catholic Church. Although it was the Catholic civil rights activists who had led this fight for decades, the final victory help assuage doubts about Sajudis on the part of many Catholic clergy and laypeople. The congress was concrete proof that Sajudis was as deeply committed to a Lithuania free of Moscow's domination as most ordinary people were, perhaps more so. What was more, people throughout Lithuania realized something else: the apparat's inability to prevent the gathering was further evidence that its power was in decline.

Lithuanians who had vainly resisted Soviet rule and others who were searching for leaders to mobilize the nation into a powerful opposition movement had found what they were looking for in Sajudis. It provided highly educated, talented, well-connected leaders who could forge popular, but heretofore inchoate, protest into organized opposition. As former, older members of the Lithuanian Communist Party, such as Ozolas, Kuzmickas, and Prunskiene, exerted their influence, Sajudis policy no longer ignored the political realities that existed in Moscow. This did not mean that the Lithuanians would bend to Moscow's will as they always had in the past, but it did mean that Vilnius would approach the Soviet leviathan with greater subtlety then some of the younger and more radical members of Sajudis deemed necessary. In a word, Vilnius would adopt measures that advanced the Lithuanian cause but could be characterized as consistent with perestroika.

By the fall of 1988, however, Moscow was having second thoughts about extending unqualified support to Sajudis. Aleksandr Yakovlev, who in August had done so much to demoralize the old-guard Reds in Lithuania and to encourage Sajudis, now characterized talk about independence among the organization's members as unrealistic. Brazauskas, meanwhile, was saying that Sajudis was moving too quickly.

In a November 18, 1988 session of the Lithuanian Supreme Soviet, Lithuanian was proclaimed the republic's official language and the pre-annexation flag and national anthem were restored. But Sajudis representatives in attendance were outraged, and so were the people who had gathered outside the parliament building, when the body refused to declare Lithuanian law sovereign. The next day, Brazauskas, on Lithuanian TV, tried to minimize the damage that had been done by implying that a declaration of sovereignty would mean the removal of Lithuanian authorities in favor of "outsiders" by Moscow.

The Sajudis activists pressed on, and on November 20, they selected Landsbergis as the organization's president and proclaimed: "Only Lithuania can decide and execute its laws."[28] This declaration in support of sovereignty set Sajudis and the Lithuanian Communist Party on a collision course. And on February 16, 1989, after attempts by party hard-liners to co-opt Sajudis failed, Landsbergis called for the full restoration of Lithuanian sovereignty. In a brief statement, the Sajudis diet council noted that Lithuania had been forcefully incorporated into Germany and the USSR via the Molotov-Ribbentrop Pact and added that "international recognition of Lithuanian independence is still valid."[29] By boldly distinguishing Sajudis from the LCP, Sajudis captured the hearts and votes of the vast majority of Lithuanians who continued to retain strong nationalist feelings.

In March 1989, Sajudis won thirty-six of Lithuania's forty-two seats in the Soviet Union's Congress of People's Deputies (CPD). Not wishing to embarrass Brazauskas or Beriozov—and realizing their support would be helpful—Sajudis decided not to run candidates against the Communist Party leaders. Juozaitis was scheduled to contest the seat that Brazauskas sought, so he never gained elected office. Only one LCP candidate, Kestutis Zaleckas, who was the head of the Vilnius party organization, won a seat without Sajudis's endorsement. Senn agrues:

> Brazauskas concluded that he had to move closer to his Lithuanian constituents, even though this would risk antagonizing both Moscow and also conservatives in his own organization, perhaps even splitting the party. As he told an audience in Klaipeda, 'the party must rethink its tactics and strategy in order to regain people's trust'. . . From Brazauskas's point of view, all this dictated the need to cooperate with Sajudis, and he called on the newly elected CPD deputies to work out a common program in order to have a strong impact in Moscow.[30]

The Sajudis victory was stunning, especially since old Bolsheviks in the LCP had tried to obstruct Sajudis's campaigning by denying its candidates access to the media and printing materials. Their inability to prevent the first expression of popular will for almost fifty years and the appearance of Sajudis and reformed Communist delegates at the CPD further emboldened the people and disheartened the apparat.

The Lithuanians' behavior in the congress, moreover, infuriated Gorbachev, because he had perceived it as his instrument to shift his power base from the party to the government. By attenuating the party's power, he could reduce the influence of the deadwood in the CPSU and with pro-reform appointees in the government ministries move forcefully toward restructuring the

USSR. At the same time, he hoped the Baltic republics would serve as test cases demonstrating the wisdom of his reforms.

Although the Lithuanians supported Gorbachev in his election to the CPD chairmanship on the first day of the proceedings, they later proved obstreperous. They objected to the ban on demonstrations, which the Soviet government had imposed, and on May 26, 1989, Landsbergis said that he could not take part in the CPD proceedings under existing voting arrangements. On June 8, fifty Lithuanian deputies walked out when the formation of a constitutional commission was being discussed—lest their participation place Lithuanian sovereignty at risk. Senn writes:

> Gorbachev met with the Lithuanians for a half hour on the morning of June 9, and for many this constituted their first opportunity to meet the Soviet leader in person. He sat down beside Prunskiene and declared his readiness to defend the rights of the republics. The Lithuanians raised other issues concerning the republics' rights, but Gorbachev insisted that the state had to be centralized—all confederations were unstable and doomed.[31]

Gorbachev did agree to postpone the formation of the constitutional commission, and on June 11 an upbeat Landsbergis told a gathering at Vingis Park: "We have progressed from relations between a great all-powerful center and poor subjects into a new, honorable relationship of partners."[32]

But while the CPD provided the Sajudis activists with a forum in Moscow and their behavior impressed separatists in other republics, they did not enjoy governmental power at home. The Communists—including Moscow loyalists—maintained control of the Lithuanian government and made policies that keenly affected the Lithuanian people. The Sajudis slate, elected to the USSR's CPD, enjoyed personal prestige and privileges in Moscow but not Vilnius. For example, in February 1990, Antanas Buracas, as a delegate to the CPD, had a room at a first-class hotel in Moscow that was made available to all deputies. But in Vilnius, he had very little influence. At one point he tried and failed to secure a room for me at the Hotel Lietuva. The managers of the hotel were unimpressed by his credentials, because the people who wielded real power in Vilnius belonged to the Communist Party hierarchy and the Lithuanian Supreme Soviet, not the all-union parliament in Moscow.

By the summer of 1989, Gorbachev had grown impatient with both Sajudis and the reformers in the LCP. Sajudis had infuriated him by demanding that the findings of a commission Yakovlev chaired be made public. It revealed that secret protocols to the Molotov-Ribbentrop Pact, which resulted in the Balts' annexation by the USSR, did exist. Gorbachev continued to insist that there was no documentary evidence to that effect.

Meanwhile, relations between the CPSU and the Lithuanian Communists deteriorated according to Senn. "In June 1989 the CPSU Control Commission demanded that the LCP dismiss" a number of comrades who had joined Sajudis—such as Ozolas and Genzelis—or who had taken "anti-Soviet" positions—such as the party's chief of ideology, Justas Paleckis. (His father, of the same name, had been appointed president of Lithuania in 1940 by the Soviets.) In August he would join with Landsbergis and Terleckas in supporting the Lithuanian drive for independence.[33]

By mid-June, apparats in Moscow had stopped sharing important party documents with the LCP, and Brazauskas called a special party congress to consider separation from the CPSU. Brazauskas had concluded that the Lithuanian Communists could not retain power unless they became independent of Moscow. The recent elections to the Congress of People's Deputies clearly demonstrated that fact.

Additional evidence that Gorbachev had blundered in encouraging the Balts to express themselves materialized with the "Baltic Way" demonstration of August 23, 1989. On that day an estimated two million people formed a human chain running from the Gedimino Hills in Vilnius, through Riga, to the Tompea tower in Tallinn. TV viewers worldwide had the opportunity to witness this amazing display of Baltic solidarity and opposition to Soviet rule. The event further emboldened the Balts in their determination to bolt from the USSR. And many other non-Russian viewers watched with keen interest, for now there was a growing number of them who began to ask why their nations should not be allowed greater independence from the Russian-dominated Center.

Gorbachev and the neo-Stalinists were appalled by this open rebuke of Soviet authority and shocked when the Balts requested the United Nations to condemn the Molotov-Ribbentrop Pact. Here was further evidence that "reactionary forces" were in control of the popular front movements in Estonia, Latvia, and Lithuania.

But the separatists were not the only ones that came under attack. In an August 25 statement, *Pravda* accused the LCP of "avoiding the political struggle and showing signs of confusion and appeasement." The next day Moscow television warned ominously, "The existence of the Baltic peoples is in serious danger. . . ."[34]

In September a plenum of the CPSU central committee was called to address the nationalities question, and Brazauskas argued in favor of providing

Lithuania with sovereign authority. In this way the republic could dramatically improve its economic situation. But his words fell on deaf ears.

On November 16, Brazauskas and the loyalists in the LCP were called to Moscow to meet with the Politburo. The meeting lasted for eight hours. "What is there to discuss with them, with Brazauskas?" declared Yegor Ligachev, the hard-line opponent of perestroika. "They have already accepted their Supreme Council's resolution on the superiority of Lithuania's laws to the laws of the Soviet Union. Juridically they have already separated from us."[35] In the past, any republic leader who angered the Politburo would have been dismissed, but Brazauskas survived the interrogation. Instead, Vadim Medvedev, who had earlier replaced Yakovlev as the official responsible for nationalities issues, was sent to Vilnius to set Brazauskas and his colleagus straight. "We favor broad independence for the Lithuanian Communist Party," he said, but "we cannot fail to express our negative attitude toward the desire to separate from the CPSU."[36] Brazauskas responded by arguing in favor of the LCP becoming independent of the CPSU and Lithuania joining "a new union of free republics."[37]

The old Bolsheviks rightly viewed the crisis in Lithuania as a direct threat to the sanctity of the Union and were prepared to play hardball. They lobbied the Poles and Russians in Lithuania (both communities were angered by the Sajudis-driven law to make Lithuanian the official language) to oppose the independence movement, encouraged Belorussian comrades to reiterate old claims on Vilnius, and warned that Klaipeda might be taken from the Lithuanians.

It was in the face of such warning that LCP gathered at the Opera and Ballet Theater in Vilnius on December 20, 1989. In his opening address to the Extraordinary Congress of the Communist Party of Lithuania, Brazauskas asked the Lithuanian people to forgive the party for its past actions. He said that "the Communist Party of Lithuania is politically guilty of having, as an integral part of the Stalinist totalitarian system, executed its will."[38] This was a gesture to the deportees and "forest brothers," and later he called for reconciliation with the Lithuanian émigrés. But that was just a start; he would take a much more provocative action— which would shock citizens throughout the Soviet empire—when he called for a vote on separating from the CPSU.

After a heated debate, 855 delegates favored severing ties with the CPSU while 160 voted against that resolution. At this time, Article 6 of the Soviet constitution, which provided the legal basis for the CPSU's supreme power, was being discussed in all fifteen republics. The Lithuanians demonstrated by their actions, not mere rhetoric, that they favored a multiparty system. Later that evening, Juozas Jermalavicius, an unreconstructed Bolshevik, invited those who opposed the independence option to meet in Vilnius at the Communist Party center. The 135 delegates who answered his invitation then voted to remain within the CPSU. Later this loyalist faction would be called the "night party."[39]

Many Lithuanians believed that Brazauskas was under orders from Gorbachev when he led the LCP out of the CPSU, that this was just the latest tactic in Moscow's strategy to have Brazauskas cooperate with Sajudis in the hope of coopting militants who proposed immediate independence. It is not unlikely that Gorbachev had concluded that the "outer empire" in Eastern Europe would have remained intact had men like Brazauskas ruled there. In allowing him to bolt from the CPSU, Gorbachev was providing the Lithuanian leader with the means to retain power with popular support. This, at least, was the argument which some skeptical Lithuanians made. Of course, even if there was a plot, it was not clear how much maneuvering room Gorbachev would grant the Lithuanian Communist reformers.

One thing was clear to Brazauskas: if the LCP did not distance itself from Moscow, its prospects for the Lithuanian Supreme Soviet elections, scheduled for February 1990, were poor. Unlike the 1989 elections for the USSR Congress of People's Deputies, in which the Lithuanians had little real political power, this election would determine who controlled the Lithuanian government. Should Sajudis form a new government, it would have the legal pretext to bolt from the union. Many diaspora leaders believed that Brazauskas left the CPSU to preclude this action. But once firmly in control of the newly elected Lithuanian government, Brazauskas would return to his Soviet masters with his tail between his legs. Moreover, by breaking away from the CPSU, the Communist reformers could "transfer Brazauskas's personal popularity to the party as a whole."[40]

Immediately after separating from Moscow, Brazauskas and the reform Communists took heart in displays of popular support for them. On December 26, a large crowd gathered at Gedimino Square in a sign of approval for Brazauskas and the independent Communist Party he led. *Tiesa,* the party's official newspaper, editorialized, "This was probably the first time that the people of Lithuania expressed such sincere solidarity with the Communists, the independent Communist Party of Lithuania."[41]

Brazauskas told me that he never colluded with Gorbachev to block Lithuania's drive toward independence. On the contrary, by leaving the CPSU, he and his colleagues had expedited the demise of the USSR; their exodus encouraged reform Communists in other parts of the Soviet empire to follow their example. Brazauskas claims Gorbachev was shocked by the Lithuanians' departure from the CPSU. "After we broke with Moscow, Gorbachev said, 'Algi, what have you done to me!' I responded it was not me, it was most of the Communist leaders in Lithuania. This was a democratic decision."[42]

After polls indicated a surprising sharp rise in the independent Communist Party's popularity, some Sajudis leaders feared that they had been tricked. But others concluded it was the party that had been co-opted by Sajudis since many of the most effective leaders in Sajudis were former Communists. As events indicated, this last interpretation was most accurate.

There is no dispute that on the eve of the 1990 elections, many Lithuanians were convinced that Gorbachev had crafted a strategy to place Brazauskas in the top spot in the new Lithuanian Supreme Soviet. Polls indicated that he was the most popular figure in the country, even though he was the head of the party that had served the hated "Center," Moscow. For example, in February 1990, a poll conducted for Gallup indicated that 89 percent of a Lithuanian sample gave a favorable rating to Brazauskas, while Landsbergis received a 67 percent rating. And even after the declaration of independence in April, the poll revealed that the rating was Brazauskas 93 percent and Landsbergis 76 percent.[43] A high school teacher during my first trip to Lithuania in February 1990 said, "Brazauskas is not like the rest of them. He listens to people . . . he even treats his critics with respect. Besides, he knows how to work with Moscow, and through his step-by-step approach, he can bring about independence. Eventually."[44] Brazauskas also impressed many Lithuanians because he had convinced them that he was a true Lithuanian patriot. "I recall one meeting," the libertarian Degutis told me, "when Brazauskas walked in a gathering with two of his aides and they told him they had to leave because the old 'nationalist flag' was being displayed. That would have been enough for his predecessors to turn and leave. But Brazauskas responded, 'You go, I'm staying.'"[45]

Later, when I met him and had time to watch him closely, it became clear to me why Brazauskas was such an effective politician. Tall, ruggedly handsome, this red-faced man with the linebacker's build would have had little difficulty securing votes from Lithuanian-Americans in Chicago's Marquette Park. I could envisage him knocking back a number of Buds in a neighborhood bar, cheering "da Bears" with gusto. According to Daryll Johnson, the U.S. ambassador to Lithuania from September 1991 to May 1994, "Brazauskas is a recognizable American type of politician. He is a pragmatist, not an ideologue. He is an Lithuanian Dick Daley."[46]

Brazauskas appealed to ordinary people because he, unlike so many of the academics who led Sajudis, easily moved among them and actually seemed to enjoy their company. Landsbergis, by contrast, was stiff and formal and was someone with whom only academics would feel comfortable. One foreign observer of Landsbergis noted: "His habitual tone of voice is nasal and low, and often halting—perhaps an affectation intended to give the impression of hesitancy, modesty and moderation. He has a tendency toward academic jokes and sarcastic remarks, after which he titters gently to himself."[47]

Few observers of the Lithuanian political landscape at the time would deny that Brazauskas was inherently a more appealing person than Landsbergis. But the musicologist would soon demonstrate that he was a man whose appearance on the stage of history was appropriate to the momentous events that awaited Lithuania. Indeed, he more than any single individual would help shape those events as Sajudis prepared for the fateful 1990 elections.

President Vytautas Landsbergis stands before the newly elected parliament on March 11, 1990, just after it had declared Lithuania's independence restored.

Unless noted otherwise, all photographs come from *The Gift of Vilnius: A Photographic Document in Defense of Freedom,* published in 1991 by the Public Affairs Council of the Lithuanian American Community, Chicago, Illinois.

A pro-independence rally in Vilnius's Vignis Park, where on April 7, 1990, in response to Gorbachev's demand that Lithuania renounce its restoration of independence, Landsbergis cited the battle cry of Duke Gediminas: "Iron will melt to wax and water will turn to stone before we will retreat."

On January 11, 1991, the first blood was spilled when pro-Soviet demonstrators clashed with supporters of the Lithuanian parliament. This view through a broken plate glass window shows members of the freedom movement pushing Communist loyalists out of the inner courtyard of the parliament building.

Soviet troops prepare to counter the surging independence movement. The crowd on January 11 at the Press House (the Lithuanian media center) is in good spirits; Bloody Sunday is still two days away.

Soldiers of the Soviet Motorized Rifle Regiment face a singing, flag-waving crowd at the Press House.

Independence Square on the morning of Saturday, January 12, after Landsbergis asked the Lithuanian people to gather there to save their independent government. On the left is the parliament building; to the right is the Mazvydas National Library.

Lithuanians also gathered at the Vilnius television and radio studios and the broadcast tower to protect them from advancing Soviet forces. Here Soviet troops surround the studios after seizing the building early on the morning of January 13. Shots were fired, but no one was seriously injured.

A young soldier of the Soviet Motorized Rifle Regiment confronts the crowd in front of the studios.

Soviet troops in control of the Vilnius broadcast facilities.

At the same time as the assault on the studios, Soviet troops attacked the crowd at the broadcast tower. A tank confronts the Lithuanian tricolor.

A Soviet tank crushes a young woman to death, as men try to push the tank off
her.

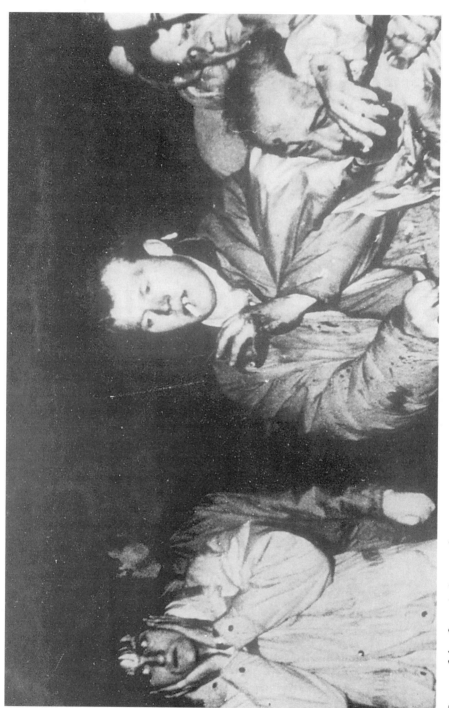

Some of the first victims at the tower.

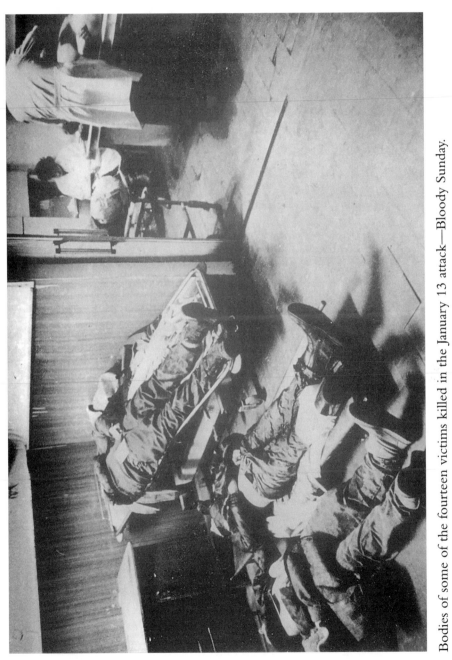

Bodies of some of the fourteen victims killed in the January 13 attack—Bloody Sunday.

Barricades placed around the parliament building during the demonstrations of January 1991. The sign at the top reads "Mr. Nixon save our independence!" *Author's photo*

5 FREE ELECTIONS

We stand here today and tell the world that we are strengthened by the spirit of Thomas Jefferson, of Abraham Lincoln, of Mahatma Gandhi, of Martin Luther King, of Nelson Mandela, and of all who have nobly carried the cause of liberty and human rights.

— *Arvydas Zygas, a young Lithuanian-American chemistry professor, on Independence Day, February 16, 1990*

It was February 16, 1990, and the crowd gathering in Parliament Square swelled as the hour for the draft-card burning approached. The protest had been organized by Sajudis, and its leaders reminded Western reporters covering the Independence Day events that Lithuania was an occupied country, forcefully annexed by Joseph Stalin in 1940, and there was no legal basis for its young men to serve in the Red Army. International law, under a 1949 Geneva ruling, proscribed subjugated peoples from serving under duress in the armed forces of an occupying power. "Our actions are legal," a young man waiting to destroy his draft card informed me as I watched with anticipation. Systematic mistreatment of recruits in the Red Army had shocked Western students of the Soviet military. It was a source of deeply felt resentment throughout the non-Russian republics, because there often was a real or perceived ethnic dimension to it: Russian officers and men brutalized recruits from the Baltics, the Caucasus, and Soviet Central Asia. In 1989, the Lithuanian filmmaker, Algimantas Zukas produced a documentary about the case of Arturas Soko-lauskas. After being subjected to a beating and gang rape, the young Lithuanian soldier shot and killed his eight attackers. He was tried and sentenced to a mental institution.[1] The case and film struck a responsive chord among Lithuanians, because many men who had served in the Red Army had been subjected to harsh treatment themselves.

A large throng of Western TV crews had gathered in the spacious square to witness the antidraft protest. It was the most recent example of the Lithuanian David defying the Russian Goliath. But the growing contingent of foreign journalists was in Vilnius to cover an even more significant event, the February 24, 1990 elections. They would be the first free elections in the history of the Soviet empire. Originally, I had planned to accompany the four U.S. members of Congress who also were serving as election monitors. They were Charles Cox (Rep., California), Richard Durbin (Dem., Illinois), John Miller (Rep., Washington), and Bill Sarpalius (Dem., Texas). I decided to leave earlier to witness Independence Day celebrations in Kaunas and Vilnius. If I had travelled with them I would have missed the elections, because the Soviet authorities refused the American legislators permission to enter Lithuania until after they were held.

The Independence Day activities would provide "background shots" for commentary on the election and its outcome. A large group of reporters who were staying at the Hotel Lietuva—a modern twenty story hotel built by the Finns early in the 1980s—had gathered in the foyer to cover the events at Parliament Square. The hotel was headquarters for the Mafiya, mostly men who were based in Vilnius or came from other parts of Lithuania or the Soviet Union to buy and sell merchandise in the underground economy. As in sister republics, Latvia and Estonia, living standards in Lithuania were higher than in nearby republics. Goods could be had in the Baltic republics that were scarce in Belorussia and Russia. The hotel, which had a nightclub on the top floor, also was a place where visiting foreign businessmen could find ladies of the night who would exchange soft bodies for hard currency.

The Lietuva was about a mile from parliament, across the Neris River, which separated old from new Vilnius. As late afternoon approached, journalists accompanied by cameramen and sound engineers hailed cabs or drove in rented vans to Independence Square. Until the late 1980s, officials in Moscow had not allowed Westerners easy access to Lithuania. The presence of so many of them in the city suggested to the residents that changes of significant, albeit ill-defined, dimensions were afoot.

Videotape depicting young men burning their draft cards would capture the attention of viewers back home—in Canada, the United States, Germany, France, England, Japan, and other countries that had sent TV crews to Lithuania. The Sajudis organizers knew that this affront to the mighty Red Army would serve as a hook and guarantee global coverage of their protest via satellite. The Americans and Canadians working with the popular front movement leading the fight for Lithuanian independence had helped craft an effective "media strategy." Perhaps because Gorbachev was so confident of his political skills and so sure that he could manipulate the Western press, there was no attempt to suppress it. Old Soviet hands marveled, nonetheless, that they were not impeded in their work by the authorities.

The TV crews pressed forward into a tight scrum to direct their cameras as a procession of young men began elbowing a path through the crowd to place their draft cards in a large brown box. When the last card was inserted, the impatient journalists waited for the expected flash of matches to incinerate the container. But they left disappointed when the organizers decided not to provoke Moscow, "the Center," and to ship the box instead to the "Russian capital" to protest Moscow's violation of the 1949 Geneva ruling. Such behavior, simultaneously bold but also solicitous of authority and legal norms, would exemplify Sajudis's actions in the ensuing confrontation with Gorbachev. Had the Lithuanians resorted to force as their counterparts did in the Caucasus, it would have been easier for Moscow to deal with them.

On a visit to Lithuania several weeks prior to Independence Day, Gorbachev had tried to dissuade the "radicals" in Sajudis from linking the election to the restoration of the Lithuanian state Stalin had crushed. Even this bold, intelligent, persuasive man must have made the trip with some trepidation. Gorbachev's policy of glasnost, encouraging the non-Russians in the empire to voice their concerns, had backfired. In 1989, Georgians in their capital of Tbilisi had protested Soviet rule, and Azerbaijanis had done the same in their capital, Baku, in 1990 after Gorbachev returned from Lithuania. Demonstrators in both cities were killed in cold blood by troops and police, presumably operating under the orders of opponents of perestroika in the Kremlin. Anyone who suggested that Gorbachev was connected with such brutality was pelted in the West by reminders that Gorbachev was the man who had peacefully dismantled communism in Eastern Europe. And who could challenge that truism?

In contrast to violent scenes of anti-Soviet (anti-Russian) protest in the Caucasus, the popular front movements in the Baltic republics were peaceful, but they represented a more serious threat to Gorbachev. Over the past several years, in all three Baltic republics, large numbers of demonstrators had taken to the streets in passive and orderly fashion to vent their displeasure with the Center. It would soon become apparent that Estonians, Latvians and Lithuanians had not become Sovietized even though many belonged to the Communist Party and most spoke Russian. Initially, Gorbachev had ignored the significance of this protest because he believed it had its roots in economic discontent and not old-fashioned nationalism. Everyone knew that Baltic living standards were among the highest in the USSR and believed they would be higher still were the Balts allowed greater economic freedom. Gorbachev had encouraged them to show Soviet citizens elsewhere (pinched by a paucity of goods and services) how the economy could be restructured to increase output and living standards for everyone in the USSR. In January 1990, the very month of his visit to Lithuania, Gorbachev had proclaimed the Baltic states henceforth would be free to control their own economic affairs.

In meetings he conducted while in Vilnius, Gorbachev said that as a result of economic reforms, living conditions would improve, but Lithuanians had to be patient. After listening respectfully to Gorbachev, his audience would eventually besiege the Soviet leader with the question "But Mikhail Sergeyevich, what about our independence?" Typically he would lose his composure and resort to harsh rhetoric and threats reminiscent of his predecessors. He just did not get it![2]

It had snowed occasionally throughout the day, and the demonstrators were bundled in warm garments to protect themselves from the evening chill. The following week, however, brought springlike temperatures, and I was puzzled to observe that Lithuanians of all ages remained wrapped tightly in their winter apparel. When I commented on this anomaly, a Lithuanian friend responded, "But it's winter." Such formal behavior was typical of the Lithuanians I encountered during my first visit to the country. They were deliberate, un-impulsive people, but on March 11 they would proclaim the restoration of Lithuanian independence and shock the world. This bold gesture would set into motion a series of events that would lead to the collapse of the Soviet empire seventeen months later.

I had arrived in Vilnius at 4:00 A.M., Independence Day morning, on a flight from Moscow that had been delayed by inclement weather. The heavy snow that had been falling in the Russian capital was not the problem, I was told, but the fog that had covered Vilnius. The airport there did not have adequate equipment to land planes safely under foggy conditions. This situation was typical of the Soviet Union. It possessed some of the world's most sophisticated weapons and was a pioneer in space travel, but its civilian infrastructure suffered because there were insufficient funds to meet the needs of both the military and civilian sectors.

The delegation of North Americans to which I belonged had been greeted at the Moscow airport the previous day by several young men associated with Sajudis. Their chief was Lionginas Vasiliauskas, a tall, thin young man in his late twenties who was addicted to American cigarettes, was the father of two children, and had "made sausages" before his association with Sajudis. Lionginas spoke excellent Russian. But even more important, he was street-smart, an

Artful Dodger who was the popular front's troubleshooter. If a confrontation with the Soviet bureaucracy was anticipated, Lionginas, I was told, was sent to straighten things out. Presumably such duties were deemed beneath the dignity of his superiors. I observed afterward that the older men, primarily academics and intellectuals, relied on him because they simply were not as skillful as he was at performing practical, day-to-day tasks.

Lionginas both charmed and outwitted the customs agents, who were giving some of our party a hard time. Ginte Damusis, for example, had brought many large boxes of equipment for Sajudis, including a fax machine. The Soviet customs officials were stunned by the enormous load that she was bringing into the country, for which they had to secure duties.

What followed demonstrated the difference between American and Soviet bureaucracy. In the United States there was comparatively little red tape, but the authorities religiously abided by the book. In the USSR there were vast amounts of red tape, but the authorities were cavalier about enforcing it. On this occasion, after a long argument about what customs fees were required, the official in charge suddenly threw up his hands and quickly settled the dispute. We all provided rubles to help pay the bill, which was modest in light of the favorable dollar-to-ruble exchange rate. There simply was insufficient information to go by the book, so the regulations were ultimately ignored. Lionginas smiled with satisfaction that he had beaten the system. If only the Lithuanians would have the same success with the Kremlin, I thought.[3]

We were driven by van over a deeply rutted road pockmarked with huge holes to Sheremetyevo One, where domestic flights departed. It was the original airport, which had been replaced by the newer Sheremetyevo Two. Upon our arrival at the administration building, we encountered a large delegation of Lithuanian legislators who were members of the USSR Congress of People's Deputies. Kazimiera Prunskiene, who would soon become the country's prime minister and would charm official Washington and the media in the spring, was among the delegation. We were invited to join them in the airport's VIP (nomenklatura) lounge, where we would wait in comfort for our flight to depart. Entering the dimly lit, dirty building, I spotted Robert Abernathy, the NBC TV Moscow correspondent, sitting with his crew among the overflowing crowd of passengers in a decrepit waiting room amid the debris of wine, beer, cognac, and vodka bottles.

We mounted the stairs and entered a spacious, hall-like waiting room containing an enormous bust of Lenin, a television, several large potted plants, two tables with chess sets, and numerous couches and plush chairs. In the VIP lounge's small but clean snack bar, we consumed much coffee and tea, and a little Jack Daniel's that I had provided, and countless salami, cheese, and ham sandwiches.

I paced the massive room to fight exhaustion long enough to record my impressions on a small tape recorder. At one point, while reclining on an overstuffed sofa, I observed an incident that reminded me of a movie I once saw depicting a post–Civil War scene in the American South. It was during the early period of Reconstruction when newly freed slaves served in state legislatures throughout Dixie. During a recess in the proceedings the delegates gathered in a large foyer, whites and blacks standing apart in two well-defined groups. The whites looked with scorn and contempt upon their black counterparts, who rebuffed their detractors by ignoring them as they spoke in hushed tones and comported themselves with dignity.

The Russians in the lounge were behaving much like the lawmakers from the Old Confederacy that February evening, only the Lithuanian deputies were not cowed. After all, they had been elected in March 1989—just five months after Sajudis had its founding congress—and Sajudis-backed candidates won thirty-nine out of forty-two seats to the all-union Soviet parliament. The Lithuanian Communist Party still controlled the Lithuanian government. But as Hedrick Smith points out, "the Communist Party had been thoroughly rejected and discredited" months before "the dramatic unraveling of Communist power in Eastern Europe that took place in the fall of 1989." Given the whirlwind of monumental events that have swept across what was once Communist Europe, many people today forget Smith's observation. "The unofficial opposition—Sajudis—had overwhelmed the Soviet Communist Party in Lithuania as convincingly as Solidarity, the Polish labor movement, would defeat the Polish Communist Party three months later."[4]

The Lithuanians in the VIP lounge took keen pleasure in talking and laughing loudly and strutting around the room as if they were in Lithuania on their own turf. It was as if their antics were calculated to outrage their Russian colleagues. Antanas Buracas, a tall economist with a scruffy gray beard who was a member of the USSR Supreme Soviet, at one point bolted in front of two Russians viewing a string quartet playing Bartok and switched channels in search of news programming. Clearly, the Lithuanians were unafraid of their "Russian elder brothers." This rebuff was consistent with reports from other republics about growing displays of animosity toward Russians and disrespect for Soviet authority. Gorbachev seethed when such attacks on Soviet power (not initiated by himself) surfaced, but he had facilitated them. Similarly, he had to take responsibility for TV coverage of the scenes of fighting in Azerbaijan that were openly beamed to Soviet viewers that night.

I detected something else of political significance at Sheremetyevo, although I did not realize its import until I returned to the United States. The Lithuanian deputies were gracious to their North American guests, and their solicitude appeared to be genuine. But the eagerness with which Americans were befriended by the Lithuanian dignitaries was evidence of a politically important fact: the Communist apparatchiks realized that the party's days were numbered, that the regime was terminally ill. All but the most obtuse comrades realized that Gorbachev's courting of the West was a prudent course of action, was in fact imperative. The USSR's future depended upon close and harmonious relations with Americans in particular. They after all were the leaders of the Western alliance, which was destined to dominate the world once the Soviet empire slipped below the waves of history.

In subsequent trips to the USSR I observed that among the best and brightest it was conceded that in the near future there would be a single superpower, the United States of America. Given America's status in the world, anyone associated with that great power was to be courted no matter how humble his or her position. The Lithuanians we were eating, drinking, and laughing with in the VIP lounge had been successful in Soviet Lithuania because they had a keen appreciation for and understanding of power. The USSR's future was unclear, but there was one thing about which they were certain: an American contact was a prized asset and could be useful when an invitation to the United States was desired. Of course, there was an even more immediate incentive for befriending Americans. The Lithuanian people were uncertain about the motives of former Communists associated with Sajudis. Were they merely jumping ship to save their own skins, or were they really patriots? Being seen in the presence of Americans helped impart legitimacy to the Communists, who were being closely scrutinized by skeptical voters.

After a 2:00 A.M. announcement that the plane would not leave before daybreak, I located a sofa large enough to stretch out on and catch some sleep. I was now in my second day without any, and in spite of my excitement I was weary, my head pounded, and my body ached. No sooner had I begun to relax than we were informed the plane would take off immediately and we had to rush to board it. The bus carrying us to the plane was packed with bodies that had not bathed for days, and the air was musty with wet clothing and sour with well-aged perspiration. Welcome to the USSR!

Upon our arrival at the airport in Vilnius we were eager to find a bed and sleep. But that pleasant thought was shattered when the luggage machine coughed, sputtered, and died. The attendant tried to revive the engine, working over it with intensity but little skill; his banging it indiscriminately with a large mallet was unavailing. The incident, nonetheless, was an appropriate metaphor for Soviet efforts to salvage a broken economy. Several times the motor sputtered to life, producing a cloud of dark smoke and filling the air with the acrid odor of burned metal, only to expire again.

While we were waiting, I accepted an invitation from Antanas Buracas to stay in his apartment during my visit to Vilnius. Like many of the deputies, he was a leader in Sajudis and could educate me about the political situation in Lithuania. Furthermore, he spoke enough English to carry on a conversation, so I eagerly accepted his invitation. Told finally that the machine was unsalvageable, we retrieved our own luggage. But when Buracas carried my bags to his car—he insisted on it—I discovered one was missing.

This resulted in further delay as we searched the empty Aeroflot building for the night manager. We located him in a small closet where he was bent shirtless washing himself with brackish water. He ignored Buracas and calmly patted himself dry with a dirty hand towel. "This is a guest from America and it is a great embarrassment to me that we have misplaced his luggage," Buracas said, and pressed the man further until he responded with loud obscenities and said he hadn't the foggiest idea where my luggage might be. We followed him into his office, and he continued to shout at us over his shoulder until the Lithuanian deputy produced his card. That didn't seem to make much of an impact, but when Buracas resorted to shouting back at him with the confidence of a man who believed he had more clout than his antagonist, the Aeroflot manager disappeared. Buracas told me in disgust, "He's drunk," and then added, "Why have a Russian running Aeroflot in Lithuania in the first place? He can't even speak the language."

The manager returned with several baggage handlers and dressed them down before us. They scurried from the room and returned in a few minutes with my errant bag.

I had accepted Buracas's gracious invitation only for a single night. I had declined further hospitality because I wanted to be free to explore the city and speak with its residents. During the 1960s, I had worked on the Office of Economic Opportunity (OEO) poverty program and evaluated OEO community action programs throughout the United States. Frequently, the directors of these programs asked me to stay at their homes. I refused because after accepting their hospitality, I would feel uncomfortable if I had to return to Washington with a report critical of their project.

Buracas lived in a large Soviet-style apartment building, reminiscent of low-income housing built in the United States in the 1950s. It was poorly constructed both inside and out, but by Lithuanian standards it was a prize. In addition to a tiny kitchen, Buracas had a living room and two bedrooms, and his apartment overlooked a clump of trees, which he pointed out to me with pride. I offered his gracious wife a gift of coffee and tea in appreciation for her hospitality and noticed that the kitchen was filled with box upon box of soap powder and other commodities scarce in the USSR. A dignitary, Antanas traveled widely within the Soviet Union and abroad, and like his peers he was given a long shopping list by his spouse of products in scant supply at home.

After a three-hour nap, Buracas drove me and Romas Vastukas, a Canadian anthropologist at the University of Trent and a leader in the Lithuanian-Canadian community, to Sajudis headquarters, located across the street from the Vilnius cathedral. Below the office was a café once favored by the city's intellectuals, Literatu Svetaine ("Literary Café"). The door to the café was perpetually locked, guarded by a doorman who allowed only a select few to enter. But Americans were rarely refused entrance to any establishment in Lithuania. After I discovered I could get coffee, pastries, and decent Moldavian champagne there for pennies, I frequented it often. I especially fancied the whipped creamed puddings they made. The cream was richer, presumably because the butterfat content in the raw product was higher than in the United States. During my visits to the café, I observed future Lithuanian capitalists make deals and celebrate their successes with young women who would have been labeled bimbos in my old neighborhood in Newark, New Jersey.

Buracas whipped his small car at high speeds through the streets of Vilnius and stopped abruptly at the curb outside Sajudis headquarters. A bus that would take us and Sajudis activists to Kaunas, an hour and twenty minutes away, was parked waiting for our arrival. It looked new and was comfortable, but it belched awful fumes from a mangled exhaust system. It would transport us to Kaunas to witness the Independence Day celebration there. The second-largest of Lithuania's cities, Kaunas had been the country's capital during its independence period, 1918–1940, and in contrast to the more cosmopolitan Vilnius, about 90 percent of Kaunas's population was ethnic Lithuanian.

We parked the bus and walked to the demonstration site in the center of Kaunas. We arrived minutes before the ceremony was to begin, and as "celebrities from abroad," we were escorted through a massive crowd of people to a spot in front of the microphones near a group of Catholic clerics, who sat quietly and attentively throughout the proceedings. I recognized the newly appointed Cardinal Vincentas Sladkevicius from pictures I had first seen years before in *The Chronicle of the Catholic Church in Lithuania*. The bishop appeared to be in his late sixties, a small man with a countenance I found mysterious and compelling. Since I am a lapsed Catholic, my response had nothing to do with spiritual rapture, only secular curiosity. I later met him and was surprised that someone who obviously had little opportunity to use the language spoke English rather well. He was charming, articulate, and intelligent. I noticed during the ceremony that his cheeks became beet-red as the sun occasionally appeared to temper the February-morning chill.

During the several hours in Kaunas, I witnessed an amazing spectacle. After the cardinal gave his blessing, speaker after speaker boldly attacked the country's unlawful occupation by Soviet authorities. Sajudis leaders and guests from abroad spoke eloquently in celebration of Lithuanian independence. A Latvian guest delivered his address in halting English, made even more difficult to follow because he chewed gum throughout his speech. He said that while most people there understood Russian, that language would never again be used by Latvians to communicate best wishes to their Lithuanian friends. Surveying members of the procession who bore flags and the Lithuanian coat of arms, I noted several wore prewar military uniforms of the independent Lithuanian army. Other bystanders displayed photos of partisans who had bravely resisted the Red Army after World War II until the Lithuanian "forest brotherhood" was crushed in 1953. I wondered where the guardians of these precious photos had kept them hidden. My vantage point prevented me from walking through the throng to determine the approximate number of people in and around the site and their mood. But the crowd appeared large and the demonstrators exuberant. As I listened to the speakers I recalled that this park, Freedom Park, had been the site of Romas Kalanta's suicide. It had not been in vain.

Although I had slept only six hours in three days, I was wide awake and alert. Still I had difficulty processing the flood of thoughts and images flashing through my brain. I was overwhelmed by the sensation that the thousands congregating in the park had obtained a single, collective consciousness that was both powerful and organic. This truly was a significant display of political protest, yet there was no sign of interference on the part of the authorities, nor would I encounter any during my two-week visit to the country.

Immediately after the proceedings ended, we were bused to a restaurant outside the city. It was a large, modern structure, not unattractive, and it was located near a lake. I surmised it might be pleasant to dine there in the summer but noted that the water was gray and looked polluted. A pretty good guess, since communism's legacy to mankind for decades will be some of the world's most polluted waterways and poisoned earth. On the bus ride to Kaunas we passed a large power plant that was belching dark and ominous-looking smoke from its chimney.

The lunchtime conversation was hampered not only by language difficulties. Even the Lithuanians I conversed with in English were shy and reluctant to speak openly with their foreign visitors. I realized later they were numbed by the dramatic changes that appeared to be sweeping across their land. The word "appeared" is appropriate, because most could not believe that at long last Lithuania was achieving true independence. Yet our very presence suggested that something monumental was afoot. Many knew that the more radical Sajudis leaders were going to use the elections for Lithuania's Supreme Soviet as a springboard for true independence. The exact timetable was uncertain, but undoubtedly radicals like Vytautas Landsbergis were intent upon a date that many prudent people believed was dangerously early.

At one point, a crowd gathered around a TV set to watch the American senator Don Riegle (Dem., Michigan) extend a few words of support for the Lithuanians in their upcoming election. He ended his statement with a raised fist salute. No doubt the senator had been asked to make the gesture by his aide, Cindy Jurciukonis Harris. Cindy had been one of the Hill staffers who always was glad to lend a helping hand to the Lithuanians lobbying Congress. The Lithuanian bid for independence had prompted her, like many other Americans with some Lithuanian blood coursing through their veins, to acknowledge her heritage with pride.

After lunch we boarded the bus and drove to Vilnius, where there would be a massive Independence Day celebration at Gedimino Square. But before joining the crowd there, we had stopped outside of parliament to witness the draft card burnings.

When the cameras directed at the draft protesters stopped whirling, a line of marchers appeared with Lithuanian flags and large posters protesting Soviet occupation of Lithuania. "Red Army Go Home!" "Center Out!" "Free Lithuania!" Most of the protesters were in their late teens and early twenties, but as the column moved down Gedimino Street toward the old part of town to the square, it attracted supporters of all ages and included entire families. The young children bundled head to toe in heavy pants, parkas, and woolen hats marched as if they were on a school outing. Their round young faces with chubby red cheeks beamed happily from the cocoons of clothing in which their parents had encased them.

I was struck in particular by one family of four. Husband and wife were in their early thirties, both were tall, the woman pretty, the man handsome. Their boy was about six, their girl eight, both blonds with oversized boots and brightly colored ski jackets similar to those their parents wore. They could have been a young American family at a ski lodge in the States enjoying a weekend of fun. The presence of entire families in demonstrations that had only months before prompted a violent reaction from the police was not in keeping with the cautious and prudent Lithuanian character. I later mentioned this to a Lithuanian friend, and he said there were many parents who took their children to such demonstrations. "There may be some risk. Sure! But they want their children to witness the rebirth of a free Lithuania."

The marchers were single-minded in their protest but orderly and good natured. Few showed signs of hostility or taunted bystanders who stood silently in lines at shops and restaurants located along the main thoroughfare. Most of these were Russians and Poles, who together constitute 40 percent of Vilnius's population, or Lithuanians who felt it dangerous to participate in the demonstration. Weeks later, television viewers in the United States would witness similar resolute but controlled behavior in the person of Vytautas Landsbergis, the first "president" of the newly reconstituted Lithuanian state.

The marchers' excitement mounted as we approached the square. It was early evening and dark, and the poor illumination characteristic of Soviet cities cast a dismal gray pall over the demonstrators, even though the stores and shops on both sides of the street were open for business.

I am a political scientist, a third-generation Lithuanian-American on my father's side of the family, who neither speaks nor reads Lithuanian. I am a well-traveled middle-aged man who finds it difficult to get excited about much. I was enthralled! Scenes of crowds descending on the Winter Palace in St. Petersburg in 1917, precipitating the first Russian Revolution, flashed through my mind. The crowd had produced a surge of human energy that was palpable. Everyone in it sensed that they were witnessing a historical event of monumental dimensions.

At one point, Romas and I had dashed through several side streets to intersect the front of the procession. The warmth the short trot produced felt good. Having accomplished our objective, we observed the marchers moving slowly down the street. It was as if I were watching a film in a movie theater, a film through tinted lenses to convey the sense of time past. But this was not make-believe, a Hollywood invention depicting a historical moment, but the present, an event unfolding in real time before me.

The square was filled with people, about 25,000 according to estimates, and many of them had their eyes fixed on the walls of the cathedral, which were illuminated by a colored spectrum of lights. It had been used as a warehouse for years and only recently had been returned to the faithful. Now it served as a backdrop to a small, flimsy wooden platform where speakers were perched to address the throng.

As I approached the platform I thought about the 1963 March on Washington, where I had heard Dr. King deliver his famous "I Have a Dream" speech. On several occasions the American civil rights movement was mentioned. When asked about the prospects of their achieving independence, some Lithuanians would respond, "We shall overcome!" As I made my way through the crowd, I was startled to hear familiar words from the sound system. The voice was obviously that of an American seeking to attract the attention of the Western media by speaking the international language—English.

"Justice. The people of Lithuania seek no confrontation with the ruling powers of Moscow, but ask the great Russian nation to be fully truthful to the errors of history." The speaker was Arydas Zygas, a young American chemistry professor who taught at the University of Vilnius.

"I speak to you today as a member of an ancient culture, and I also speak to you today as a citizen of the United States of America, the land of freedom and justice. We ask the world to be just in its appraisal of the aspirations of the people of Lithuania." Then repeatedly using the phrase "Tell the people of the world" to punctuate his points, Zygas said, "Tell the world that Lithuania has awaken from the nightmare of fear and persecution . . . that we have long been forced to live under oppression." And "We have been forced to bury our history, to desecrate our churches and to lie to our children." The crowd had grown silent, and he continued: "The genocide of the Lithuanian people did not end with the end of World War II. The genocide did not end with the death of Stalin. . . . Tell the people of the world that what you witness today in Lithuania is not nationalism. This is a movement for human rights, which have been violated for half a century and whose restoration we now seek."

Zygas spoke eloquently and with special feeling when he said that the human rights Lithuanians seek "are rights that are granted by the Constitution of the United States" and the Soviet constitution as well. "We stand here today and tell the world that we are strengthened by the spirit of Thomas Jefferson, of Abraham Lincoln, of Mahatma Gandhi, of Martin Luther King, of Nelson Mandela, and of all who have nobly carried the cause of liberty and human rights."[5] I thought of these words later when I read Soviet press accounts that characterized the Sajudis leaders as "dangerous reactionaries."

When the last speeches were given and the demonstration ended, I noticed many flags being carried by young people clearly not Lithuanians. With dark complexions and speaking languages other than Lithuanian, they were from outside the republic. Later I learned they were Georgians, Armenians, and people from Soviet Central Asia who supported the Lithuanian independence movement and watched its progress with keen interest. They too hoped to bolt from the Soviet empire, and to no small degree their timetable hinged upon the Lithuanian movement's success or failure in confronting Moscow.

The time had come for us to meet our candidates and travel with them to their districts. I was waiting in the Sajudis main meeting room when Egle Taurinskaite called to me, and as I approached she said, "Dick, the people driving you to Ukmerge are here!" Egle had majored in English at Vilnius University, and she was serving as a translator for one of the Canadian parliamentarians monitoring the election. She was a friend of Lionginas Vasiliauskas and had worked closely with Landsbergis and Mecys Laurinkus, another Sajudis activist. She was politically astute and well informed, and on subsequent trips to Lithuania she was often the first person I spoke with about the situation there. Had she been a man, there is no question that she would have been given a post in the first independent post–World War II Lithuanian government. Instead she would work as Laurinkus's assistant when he was elected to the parliament. Some of the founders of Sajudis were women, and women would serve in the "Landsbergis" government—the economist Kazimiera Prunskiene being the most notable example—but Lithuanian women often conceded power and influence to men, even men with less intelligence and political sophistication than they themselves possessed.

"Hello, my name is Saulius Skindulas. I'm your translator." The speaker was a man in his late thirties, about six feet tall, handsome, with blond hair and an engaging smile. He was a high school English teacher in Ukmerge, a provincial city about seventy kilometers northwest of Vilnius. I had been asked to monitor the voting in that area. He continued, "This is Mr. Kestutis Grinius."

His companion was several inches taller than Saulius, and his most notable feature was a thick black mustache and matching dark suit, which hung loosely over his gaunt frame. His bearing was somber, almost funereal. He was a high school principal, the chairman of Ukmerge's branch of Sajudis and formerly a leader in the Communist Party there. I resisted the impulse of being a captive of first impressions, but I did not like him. Unlike Saulius, he lacked warmth, and he was tense and apprehensive. This was not a man, I concluded, who acted upon impulse but who carefully calculated his every move.

In our van ride to Ukmerge, he told me that he was surveying the list of foreign monitors, which Sajudis had circulated to its branches throughout the country, when my Lithuanian name had caught his attention. I winced when Saulius translated the word "monitor," because I was puzzled about what my role would be in that capacity. In our briefings with Landsbergis over the course of several days and discussions with other Sajudis officials, little was said about how we were to conduct ourselves. I kept looking for cues from my colleagues, but if they were confident about their roles they were keeping it a secret. Finally, I had assumed that we were expected to detect gross attempts to rig the election or to sabotage it and that the local Sajudis representatives would help us identify such activity. And after it became apparent to me that the Sajudis staff had placed great weight upon our merely being in the country during this fateful period in their history, I stopped worrying about my duties. Like the other monitors, who realized that the Lithuanian elections would have an important bearing on the future of the USSR, I was eager to help in any fashion I could. Henceforth, I devoted my energies to gleaning as much information about the election and the general situation in Lithuania as I was able to during my stay there.

Kestutis said that he had turned against the Communist system for two major reasons. The first was that it was corrupt. Among other things, the party in Ukmerge worked closely with the criminal elements, the local Mafiya. Together they had controlled both the politics and the economics of the area. Western scholars, journalists, and others, who had begun to travel throughout the vastness of the Soviet Union as a result of Gorbachev's liberalization were discovering the same thing everywhere. Western students of the USSR had long commented upon the Mafiya, but it was only now becoming apparent just how closely linked the party apparatchiks were with these people. Often they were one and the same person.

Kestutis said, through Saulius, that the party "was like a giant octopus. Its tentacles were affixed to all profitable enterprises. By controlling access to consumer goods, it awarded its political friends and punished its political enemies." As the defects of the command economy drove domestic output down, the Mafiya's importance to the survival of the economy expanded. For many people, who previously had apologized for the system, the realization that its survival rested on society's criminals was the last straw. No honorable person could any longer support it.

But an even worse crime in Grinius's eyes was that the schools were denying students an opportunity to learn about their culture and to celebrate their language. Moscow claimed that it was encouraging the national cultures of the non-Russians, but in fact it was attempting to destroy Lithuanian national life. It was in resisting Russification and the Soviet culture, which thrived on deceit, lies, and deception, that he had finally turned against the system. Nonetheless, he feared his past party affiliation would lose him votes in the upcoming election.

Later, when I met his wife and his two lovely children, I scolded myself for my initial unflattering assessment of Kestutis. I reflected that it was easy for

Westerners to visit the Soviet Union and pass judgments on people whose country had been occupied by a foreign power and who had to provide for their families under oppressive and demeaning conditions. Many ambitious Americans if confronted with a similar set of circumstances would have joined the Communist Party and mouthed the prevailing dogma.

The countryside reminded me of the landscape one might find in many mid-Atlantic states—coastal Maryland, Delaware, or parts of Virginia: primarily flat with trees outlining large agricultural tracts, meadows, and grazing fields. It was only when the road ran close to rural housing, or one saw people working in the fields, that it was apparent that this was not the United States. A lot more draft animals were in evidence than on American farms, and occasionally I could see people along the road milking cows, which were tethered to wooden pegs in the ground. In one instance, I noted a women balancing a pail full of milk on the handlebar of her bicycle.

In another trip to Lithuania I met a Dutchman who was in the agribusiness, and he told me that the rate of growth in agriculture was higher in Lithuania than in any other republic. Since hand milking, often conducted in the field, was not a novel sight in Lithuania, one could only imagine how backward the conditions were in the hinterland of Russia. However, on larger collective farms, tractors and other modern farm implements were in evidence, and I was puzzled by the sight of fields that were kelly green in the dead of winter. Later I surmised that this greenness was produced by the profligate use of fertilizers and other chemicals that were polluting the country's land and water.

But when I entered the city of Ukmerge it was as if I had been sucked up into the vortex of a time machine and had been carried back to my young manhood. The older, pre-Soviet part of the city reminded me of the small German town of Hoechst, where I had been stationed with the U.S. Army in the mid-1950s. The buildings were run-down and dirty and had been neglected for a long time. That night in a stroll before dinner, I noticed the streets and stores were poorly lit and the air smoky, and I felt enveloped by an ominous grayness. As in postwar German towns, few residents owned private cars and there were lots of pedestrians walking the streets. Most of them were poorly dressed or wore clothes that were in fashion in the West decades ago. Still, many of the women were very attractive and ingenious in conveying a sense of style. Also, as I noticed in Vilnius, many Lithuanians of both sexes were tall. This national characteristic explained why for years four of the five starters on the Soviet Olympic basketball team were Lithuanians or other Balts. In my case (several inches short of six feet tall) there obviously had been a genetic malfunction.

As we entered the town and parked the van near the town square, I saw that a large crowd had gathered near a patriotic column of recent construction. I was stunned when I realized that the women adorned in traditional Lithuanian folk costumes, along with a young priest and several local political dignitaries, were waiting to greet me. I had dressed casually for the trip—a blue blazer, but with jeans—not dress pants, and I needed a haircut. I must have been a curious sight. "Look at that American! Congressman! So informal—not like our politicians." Perhaps that's what the younger people said, but I surmised the older ones were not pleased by my appearance. Coat and tie were always in evidence among the academics I had met in Vilnius.

I was not accustomed to being the subject of such attention and was ill at ease, but I soon got used to it. I was given the traditional Lithuanian gift reserved for an "honored guest," a large loaf of fresh-baked dark bread, and a massive bouquet of freshly cut flowers. Although it was February, I encountered fresh flowers frequently during my visit to Lithuania. They had been grown in one of the many hothouses that I had observed in my travels there. Two years later I would dine with a leading member of the Vilnius Mafiya who owned many such operations in the country.

After lunch I gave a brief informal talk about the U.S. Congress followed by a polite Q&A session. Several candidates from the Ukmerge region had attended the gathering. Later, in the mayor's office at city hall, I spoke with a member of the rump Communist Party, the Soviet Lithuanian Party, and his Sajudis opponent about the election. What struck me most about the unrepentant Soviet candidate was that he was unable to provide any explanation of why he did not join most of his comrades (about 80 percent) who broke with the CPSU. Unlike some of the Soviet loyalists I had read about, he did not display a strong ideological attachment to Marxism. I concluded, after trying to penetrate his defenses, that he remained loyal to the Soviet party because he deemed it in his interest to do so. Like many of his comrades, and ordinary Lithuanians, he just could not accept the possibility that Soviet rule would someday end in Lithuania. Perhaps he knew something we did not know, that the elections would be rigged and the old guard would return to power. Or that Brazauskas would prove to be a wolf in sheep's clothing and use his popular appeal to wrest control of the election from Sajudis even if its slate did well in the elections. Or that the USSR would use troops to crush the movement. At least, this is what many people had been surmising.

I had a strong hunch also that the unrepentant Soviet candidate had agreed to meet with me because he was as curious about me as I was about him. And I had the impression, sustained by other encounters with such men, that even the hard-liners had a grudging admiration for Americans. The next day some-one told me I had hurt his feelings when I indicated that in the West his inability to identify issues which would attract votes to his candidacy would hurt him at the polls. Later, it became clear to me that even some hard-liners wanted to be liked by Westerners, because like children they had lost their way and were looking for someone who would direct them to a safe harbor.

Like Kafka's bug in the story "Metamorphosis," they had developed in the Soviet system unique antennae which worked only in the bizarre society that had evolved in the USSR since 1917. Being compelled to leave that environment, they found themselves disarmed and vulnerable. This psychological condition explained why the apparatchiks in Eastern Europe did not resort to force to maintain their regimes after Gorbachev refused to support them.

Captives of Brezhnevite logic, the old Bolsheviks became disoriented as they entered a world where the truisms of the Cold War no longer prevailed. But they were not alone in their confusion, for the Bush administration also suffered from Brezhnevite thinking and failed to exploit the confusion and crisis of confidence that prevailed in Moscow. Had Washington been fully aware of the collapse in morale among the Soviet old guard and the openness of the reformers to any Western initiative, it might have implemented a continent-wide plan that would provide the Russians a nonaggression pact and generous economic and technological aid in exchange for Moscow's allowing some of the former satellite countries and the Baltic states to become members of an expanded NATO.

After a brief walk through the center of Ukmerge, I was taken to a state restaurant, which had been rented that night for a private banquet honoring "our esteemed friend from America." The bill was paid by a group of "deportees," who lived in the city and its environs—that is, men and women who had been deported by Stalin to northern Russia and Siberia during the first phase of Soviet occupation and in the aftermath of World War II. Deportees numbering in the tens of thousands would die in the frigid wastes of Russia and Siberia, but after Khrushchev became general secretary of the CPSU, most of the survivors were allowed to return to Lithuania. About one hundred thousand did, but others, numbering twenty thousand, did not have the resources or were too frail to return, and they and their offspring remain in Russia today.

Among the diners were several men who had fought the Red Army in the Lithuanian resistance, which was not finally crushed until the early 1950s. One elderly gent told me that if Moscow did not allow the Lithuanians to hold free elections, he was prepared to return to the forest. I studied him closely. He was about seventy, no more than five feet six inches tall, but he was thin and fit, and his eyes were clear. I believed him! Stasys Lozoraitis, who would become Lithuania's ambassador to the United States in 1991, recalled: "There were two views of the armed resistance. Some people associated with the government in exile supported the resistance with the expectation in mind that World War III was about to begin." The Lithuanians then would soon be joined by the West as it fought to overwhelm Stalin's army of occupation. "A second view, favored by young diplomats like myself, was that it was a lost cause and the 'forest brothers' should return home and go about their lives." Lozoraitis said, however, that the people who fought in the resistance had not died in vain. "I am convinced that because of the Lithuanian resistance, many Russians for years afterward were afraid to migrate to Lithuania" and preferred Latvia and Estonia instead. "Without the forest brothers, we might have a much, much larger Russian population in Lithuania today." He would add that he had nothing against Russians, but clearly if they represented the proportion of the population that they did in Latvia, about 40 percent, Lithuania would have a much more serious ethnic problem than it had today.[6]

When I entered the banquet room, the table, as customary in Lithuania, was covered with what Americans would call a Swedish-style smorgasbord. There were fillets of herring in onions, pickles of all kinds, several varieties of smoked ham and other cold cuts, a salad of canned peas and mayonnaise, fresh cucumbers, carrots and cabbage—the staples of the Lithuanian diet in the winter—apples and pears, and several dishes brought in from the kitchen. The most celebrated of the latter was *cepelinas,* heavy potato dumplings filled with chopped meat, a Lithuanian national dish that was appropriate to a people who lived in a cold climate. Of course, there was fresh dark bread, which tasted much like the bread my mother occasionally purchased from a Lithuanian bakery in Elizabeth, New Jersey. During the meal we were serenaded by a local folk group, which sang many beautiful, haunting tunes, several of which I had heard before in the United States. Most were traditional, centuries old, but some depicted the dark years in the gulag. In eleven months, on "Bloody Sunday," they would be sung again as Lithuanians stood defenseless surrounding the Vilnius TV tower and station to protect them from Soviet troops. As a consequence, millions of people throughout the world would be captivated, as I was that evening, by the beauty of the songs, and they would give added resonance to the world's appreciation of Lithuanian courage that fateful Sunday.

The next day I visited several voting districts in the city, and it was clear that nothing was amiss. There were no reports of voter fraud or ballot tampering as the Lithuanians participated in the first free election in the history of the Soviet Union. As always, the Lithuanians were calm and reserved, even though they were players in a very important drama. Here was further evidence that Gorbachev was serious about democratizing the Soviet Union. But just how far would he go? Would he allow the Lithuanians to bolt from the USSR if Sajudis won the election? On the basis of my random sampling it was clear that Sajudis would sweep the election.

A young couple who lived on a collective farm told me that they had voted for Sajudis and had ignored "the advice" of their farm administrator, who suggested they stick with the Communists. An elderly woman, also a collective farm worker, said that in the past she always had been too afraid not to vote the way her administrator told her to, but this time she did not care what he thought—she had voted for Sajudis. What struck me even more than such declarations of independence was the mood of the people, which was upbeat and marked by good humor. Lots of people smiled.

There was one tense moment in our tour of the voting districts. As we walked from Kestutis's voting station to another one across town, we spotted two policemen in a patrol car speeding down the street, and the three of us stopped our conversation as it screeched to a halt at the curb where we were walking. One policeman jumped out but ignored us and ran down a lane off the street, not in pursuit of a lawbreaker but presumably because he was late for lunch. Saulius smiled in relief. "Not for us!"

The next year, however, Saulius had little to smile about when he became a target of Soviet law enforcement officials. He was serving as a translator for several Western journalists when he was beaten senseless. Presumably, Soviet authorities had decided he was an activist who had be to taught a lesson. Such attacks were part of a campaign of intimidation that had always worked in the past. Saulius suffered a concussion and was in the hospital for several weeks.

In the afternoon, we drove to a collective farm, where I would meet several men and women whom I would interview at length to determine what they thought about the election and the situation in the country. The building where I was conducting the interviews was a new one, rather tastefully constructed. It did not have the shoddy run-down look that typified Soviet construction throughout the USSR. After my first trip to Moscow I had concluded that whoever designed the Berlin Wall was the same person who designed most apartment buildings in the Soviet empire. But it was at this point that my worse fears were confirmed. Two high school colleagues of Saulius, also English teachers, joined us to help with the onerous translating duties. While alone with one of them I asked, "Why is it that you introduced me as a U.S. congressman?" On several occasions, I had heard words that led me to that conclusion, but I was only guessing; I was by no means certain I had understood. "Because Kestutis told me to," the women answered in embarrassment.

When I confronted him, he at first lied, claiming that he thought I was a congressmen, since my name was on the list of monitors. But I pointed out that the Canadian parliamentarians and the U.S. congressmen had appropriate titles pre-fixing their names. Then he conceded that he had lied about my identity because he thought that it would help him with the voters, that his being seen with a Lithuanian-American U.S. congressman would help resolve their doubts about his Communist past. He assumed, correctly, that being seen with an American college professor would not help him as much. He got an A for his political sophistication but an F for honesty.

Here was a man who had spoken eloquently about the promises of democracy and had derided Homo Sovieticus for two days now engaging in the most stupid lie. The local paper had taken several pictures of us and had run a story identifying me as a member of Congress, but someone who knew better was bound to see it and take him to task for lying about my true identify. But he reasoned, no doubt, that by then he would have benefited from the ruse, and besides, he knew something else of which I was ignorant: no one would really care that he had lied.

Outraged, my ego bruised, I rejected his offer to meet with the local Sajudis leadership in a farewell dinner. It was a hard call to make, since I had grown accustomed to being treated like a celebrity, showered with gifts, displays of deference, and laudatory speeches. That was not something to which American academics were accustomed. I had already prepared a speech for my family upon my return to Fairfax, Virginia, the essence of which was that they were most fortunate to be living with a person of such prominence and international renown.

Upon returning to Vilnius I went directly to Sajudis headquarters and, with barely concealed outrage, told my story to the first person I encountered, the office manager, Andrius Kubilius. I liked and respected Andrius because in contrast to his older colleagues, he was outgoing and quick to laugh, and he possessed a keen mind and self-confidence. He listened patiently and then . . . laughed. It was a big joke to him, and he did not understand why I was so upset. I realized then that even the people who had taken risks to fight the system remained wedded to Soviet culture, a culture in which people were taught that it was good form to lie and cheat to accomplish their goals. Perhaps in the face of Soviet autocracy it made sense for Lithuanians, Russians, and others to be deceitful, but what would happen after the Soviet system collapsed? How long would it take before Homo Sovieticus was cast on the ash heap of history . . . and along with him, his unsavory values and practices?

On election day, Saturday, February 24, my last full day in Lithuania, I returned to Vilnius to hear the results. Early the next morning I had to catch an Aeroflot flight to Moscow and then get a return Pan Am flight to the United States.

The election returns would not come in until about 8:00 P.M., so I slept for a couple of hours at my hotel and then took a cab to Sajudis headquarters to join in what I hoped would be a victory celebration. Everyone was in good spirits. The Canadian parliamentarians, who had spread throughout Lithuania with their own candidates, had returned, and they were joined by Sajudis's leaders and staff.

I will always remember my first visit to the five-story cement building, constructed between the world wars when "Wilno" was a predominantly Jewish and Polish city. Sajudis occupied most of the floors. The rooms on every landing were packed with desks, telephones, and typewriters, and in the small garret rooms on the top floor young people worked constantly at a computer and a fax machine that were a major link to the outside world. The building's ambiance and inhabitants reminded me of the 1960s, of the American poverty program, of idealistic young people who spoke with excitement and feeling about "changing the system," about "making a difference." Casual clothes, unkempt hair, air choked with tobacco smoke, incessant loud conversation, and outbursts of laughter—this was a 1990 Lithuanian analogue to the community action agencies I had visited in the late 1960s in Brooklyn's Bed-Stuy, Chicago's Mexican-American Pilsen, New York's Spanish-Harlem, and similar places in Appalachia and Alaska that were magnets to America's young and idealistic.

One morning in the main office, which seemed to be shared by all the Sajudis council, I was perching on an old couch soliciting information from someone about the current political situation. Landsbergis and Virgilijus Cepaitis, a council member, were conversing with Ginte Damusis and Gabija Petrauskas, while in the room's four corners several other conversations, face to face or over the phone, were in progress. Throughout the hour I was there, the conversation was nonstop but frequently interrupted when a young aide entered the room to speak with one of its inhabitants. In the foyer, there was always a crowd—staffers, reporters, well-wishers, and people from the street who were drawn into the building by the billboard on the wall outside, which that day carried the latest news and vivid pictures of the recent massacre in Baku. Buracas pointed to one that portrayed a car crushed flat, like a tin can, by a tank.

A week later, soon after the election returns began to arrive, it was clear that Sajudis had won in a landslide, and even though a runoff election would be held two weeks later, 80 percent of the delegation to the Lithuanian Supreme Soviet would be Sajudis supported deputies.

I was drinking champagne in the Literatu Svetaine with a Canadian parliamentarian and Algimantas Cekuolis, the old Communist apparatchik who had had a long career in the Soviet foreign service and in journalism but now was one of the most outspoken proponents of Lithuanian independence. Several weeks after returning home, I would see him on ABC's *This Week With David Brinkley,* a popular Sunday news show. In the midst of the interview the Soviet authorities would pull the plug on him by halting satellite transmission from Vilnius to Washington.

"I want to thank both of you for what you have done," he said. We responded that he was welcome but we really had not done very much. "Oh, but you have," he insisted. "When you arrived we were overjoyed, because we realized that there was going to be an election." We discovered that Sajudis had feared, up to the last day before the election, that Moscow might cancel it. After all, unlike the 1989 elections to pick Lithuanian delegates to serve their country in the Soviet parliament, this election would determine who ruled Lithuania. Moreover, if Sajudis gained control of the Lithuanian government it could use that platform as a springboard for independence.

"There is something else," he told us. "When Moscow allowed the Western delegation to witness the election, we knew that the tanks would not roll."[7]

The next day when I flew to Moscow I reflected on Cekuolis's comment and wondered if he was really serious about tanks rolling. Gorbachev was the person who had made all of this possible. Why would the tanks roll?

Of course, I was thinking of Gorby I, the Soviet leader who allowed communism in Eastern Europe to collapse and permitted the reunification of Germany within NATO. But Gorby II was waiting in the wings and would make his appearance soon.

6 INDEPENDENCE

Gorbachev was about to receive new powers as the Soviet president. This was a trap! We had to move before these things happened.

—Vytautas Landsbergis on why he led the fight to restore an independent Lithuania in March 1990

Gorbachev had made a great error in not understanding that the Lithuanians' commitment to independence was driven by a powerful, organic attachment to their language and culture and a fear that Soviet rule placed both at risk. He first gained a personal glimpse of this deep emotional commitment to Lithuanian nationalism when he became the first general-secretary of the CPSU to visit Lithuania.

"Independence? Let's have it! At the workplace, in cities, in the republic, but together." This is what Mikhail Gorbachev told Lithuanians who had gathered in Gedimino Square to hear the Soviet leader during his three-day visit in the second week in January 1990.[1]

It was estimated that 200,000 had gathered at the square adjacent to Sajudis headquarters. I recall seeing, via TV, several scenes of Gorbachev debating with Lithuanians during his trip to the republic. One stands out in particular. Gorbachev is arguing with a Lithuanian bystander over the hood of his limousine while a crowd of onlookers witness this amazing exchange. The general-secretary of the mighty CPSU is being confronted by an ordinary citizen who is asking him pointed questions about independence. Years later, Laima Pangonyte, a former filmmaker for Sajudis, showed me TV outtakes she had taken during Gorbachev's visit. At one point, he is leaving his limo with Brazauskas and turns toward Laima when she asks him a question about independence. Brazauskas, irritated, tries to wave her off, but Gorbachev responds to her question dispassionately, remarking that he plans to talk to Lithuania's leaders about this and other issues.[2]

In a meeting with factory workers, Gorbachev indicated that he understood why so many Lithuanians spoke about national self-determination. "It is
only natural that Lithuanians have the right to decide their fate—to be within
the Soviet Union or to leave the Soviet Union." And at a rally, in "a pleading
tone," Gorbachev noted: "We have embarked on this path, and I am the one
who chose it. My personal fate is linked to this choice. The two states must
live together."[3]

Lithuanian friends who had met Gorbachev in large and small groups during that visit reported that he was not always "conciliatory." At the outset,
when discussing perestroika and the opportunities it would give Lithuanians
to experiment with new economic initiatives independent of apparats in
Moscow, Gorbachev was friendly, charming, winning his listeners with his
famous smile. But his mood darkened when he was pressed, "Mikhail
Sergeivich, what about independence?"

The famous Gorbachev smile would be replaced by an ominous scowl. "If
there's anyone here," he told one gathering, "who thinks that it's all so easy
that today or tomorrow you just have an election, get together and raise your
hands, and leave the Soviet Union, well, that is not politics. It doesn't even
remotely smell of politics. It's simply not serious."[4] And in a meeting with
party reformers and intellectuals in Vilnius he said: "Today I am your friend,
but if you choose to go another way, then I will do everything I can to show
that you are leading people to a dead end."[5]

Such angry words were undoubtedly fed by his knowledge that hard-line
critics like Yegor Ligachev had been more adroit in their assessment of Sajudis
than he had been. Developments in Lithuania had reached a very dangerous
stage indeed. Even the normally upbeat Aleksandr Yakovlev spoke on Soviet
TV about the Lithuanians' provoking a "domino" effect that could lead to the
USSR's disintegration.[6] Also, Gorbachev knew that separatists in the Ukrainian SSR and the Caucasus were observing with profound interest the Lithuanians' bold declaration and his response to it. KGB agents in Lithuania noted
that people from other republics—like the ones I spotted on Independence
Day—were traveling to Vilnius and consulting with the Sajudis activists seeking their advice on the proper strategy and tactics to adopt in dealing with
the Red Bear. Buracas told me that Sajudis was talking to reformers in the
Caucasus and Central Asia in the expectation that they might help if Gorbachev punished Lithuania economically.

From the perspective of the Old Bolsheviks in Moscow, collaboration
among "separatists" was cause for grave concern. So was Brazauskas's break
with the CPSU, since party elites outside of Russia were courting the masses

with nationalistic appeals at a time when Marxism–Leninism had lost its legitimacy. (In Russia, of course, Yeltsin was manipulating Russian nationalism in his confrontation with the Old Bolsheviks.) In some cases these newly converted nationalists were acting upon principle, while in others they were motivated by political opportunism. Whatever their motives, even apparatchiks who were mere opportunists emboldened the authentic nationalists and advanced their cause at Moscow's expense. Consequently, if Landsbergis did not rescind the declaration of independence, other radicals elsewhere in the empire would follow his example. He had to be stopped!

It was during my first trip to Lithuania that I truly understood the power and pervasiveness of Lithuanian nationalism. Like the other monitors, I was puzzled by the casual attitude the Sajudis leadership displayed on election eve, especially in the face of efforts to sabotage the campaigns of Sajudis candidates by restricting access to paper, printing shops, and, most important of all, the media. At least this was what we were told during our visit to Kaunas days before the election when we met with Sajudis leaders there. I remember, in particular, Aleksandras Abisala, because he had a dark beard counterpointed by icy blue eyes. A scientist who was born in Russia, where his family had been exiled, Abisala was a bright, charming, and clearly self-confident man—his enemies called him arrogant—and would become prime minister in July 1992. Earlier in 1992, when he held a cabinet post without portfolio and headed the delegation of Lithuanians seeking to negotiate the removal of Russian troops from their country, I had lunch with him in a private room in the Draugyste Hotel, formerly a hangout for Lithuanian Communist *nomenklatura*. Like other former opponents of the Soviet system (belated, since he at one time was a Komsomol leader) he was keenly relishing the perks that the apparatchiks had enjoyed. The meal was first-rate and we had our own private waiter taking care of us. Even the wine was good.

As a result of the lunch and other conversations with him, it was clear to me that he listened carefully to what people said and had a good grasp of the climate in the West. Also, it was apparent that he had considerable intellect and character. Victor Nakas, after becoming political officer at the Lithuanian embassy in Washington, reported that once Abisala became prime minister, governmental affairs in Lithuania were conducted with greater discipline and order than had been the case.[7]

The "Kaunas radicals," on the eve of the February elections, had conveyed a much more extensive effort on the part of the Communist hard-liners to sabotage their campaigns than was to be the case. The fact is that the candidates who received support from Sajudis had every reason to be supremely confident about their chances.

The Canadian parliamentarians had expressed amazement that in conducting their monitoring duties, their candidates did very little campaigning. That was my experience as well. On the afternoon before the election in Ukmerge, I had met with Sajudis activists there, and they spent most of the time plying me with gifts and taking me from venue to venue to show me off. That night Kestutis Grinius did not leave the banquet given in my honor to mobilize his campaign workers. By law, campaigning was forbidden the day before the elections, but one would have assumed that he and his colleagues would take "informal" measures to coax their candidates on to victory.

But he remained with me, and after we left for his flat we drank and ate until early in the morning—all this the evening before the biggest event in his life. But what he, and other Sajudis candidates, realized was that the vast majority of the Lithuanian people were behind them. For most of them the issue was the right of Lithuania to exist as an independent nation; for others it was the right of Lithuanians, at a minimum, to have a voice in decisions that previously were made by Russians in Moscow. In short, the issue was nationalism, and it was the single most important factor in Sajudis's success at the polls. Indeed, 96 percent of the delegates at the popular front founding congress were ethnic Lithuanians.[8]

By serving as my guide, Grinius helped himself with the deportees, who were the most vocal opponents of the Soviet occupation. If Grinius had their blessing, other Lithuanians who might have doubts about his Communist past, might think of him as a true patriot on election day. His bid for a seat in the parliament was successful, and once in office he moved toward the right and adopted an aggressive nationalist posture.

I left Lithuania before the results of the runoff elections (necessary because of the requirement that a candidate had to receive a majority of the votes cast), conducted on March 4 and 10, were posted. Sajudis won a smashing electoral victory, while the Communists were soundly thrashed. Sajudis elected ninety-nine deputies, the pro-independence Communists received twenty-five, the pro-Moscow Communists got seven, and there were five deputies who ran as independents. Brazauskas ran against Landsbergis for chairmanship of the newly established Lithuanian Supreme Council, the single most powerful body in the new Republic of Lithuania. Landsbergis won by a vote of 91 to 38, with some deputies abstaining. Among the Sajudis deputies were twelve who belonged to the Lithuanian Communist Party including Kazimiera Prunskiene, who was chosen prime minister. Two other Communists Brazauskas and Ozolas, became deputy-prime ministers. Ozolas had won the honor because he had become a prominent leader in Sajudis, while Brazauskas was awarded the post because the pragmatists in Sajudis realized that he and his supporters had access to important centers of power in the country and remained well organized, with an extensive infrastructure throughout Lithuania.

On March 11, 1990, as the deputies and guests applauded, a curtain slowly descended and blanketed the Soviet hammer and sickle, which had covered the wall of the Lithuanian parliament's main auditorium. Led by Landsbergis, the vast majority of delegates had voted to restore Lithuanian independence in the belief that the administration of President George W. Bush would provide diplomatic recognition to the newly resurrected state. On this score they were badly misinformed.

Soon after my arrival, every Lithuanian I spoke to of any import expressed confidence that the United States would recognize their country upon the restoration of Lithuanian independence. It was over dinner with a freelance journalist who worked in Sajudis headquarters that I had decided to give a speech explaining why President Bush would not extend diplomatic recognition to Lithuania. We were dining at Stikliai, which is adjacent to what once was the Jewish ghetto in Vilnius. Since it was the best private restaurant in the city, it attracted most of the powerful people in Vilnius and foreign guests to Lithuania's capital. Even at this early date, one could get a glimpse of the country's future, because in addition to diners like Prunskiene and foreign businesspeople, one spotted the country's "new entrepreneurs," members of the local and visiting Mafiya and their lady friends. They made a special effort to display the U.S. dollars they possessed in abundance. Some of the people I had invited to dine with me at the restaurant expressed anger at such crude exhibitions of new wealth. I remember having lunch with an academic from Kaunas who said, "I fear that after independence the Mafiya will get even more powerful and run things!"

Upon approaching the entrance to the restaurant, on Zydu Street (Jew Street), I saw a Hasidic Jew, dressed in a long dark overcoat with black hat, studying a building across the narrow street. He appeared to be about my age, and it struck me that this man had probably lived here when he was a boy. I wanted to ask him if that were indeed the case, and if not, what he was doing there. Had his parents or other family members once lived there? Had they died in the Holocaust? Why had he returned?

On subsequent visits, I met Jews who once lived in Lithuania, including Joseph Kagan, who had resided in Vilnius at a young man but fortunately had escaped the fate of many of his coreligionists. He had settled in England, where he was eventually made a lord for his good works. Returning to the scene of the Lithuanian Holocaust was a painful experience, but like other

Jews I met who once lived there, Kagan wished the country and its inhabitants well.

Upon reflection, I decided not to approach the man whose eyes were firmly fixed on the third floor of the building on Jew Street in a country where a large Jewish community once thrived. Today, only twelve thousand Jews remain in Lithuania, and older members of the Jewish community fear many of the younger generation will emigrate to Israel or the West. (The actual number of Jews might be higher, since many Lithuanian Jews sought a Christian identity during the Soviet era to spare themselves the fate of most of their coreligionists.) I decided to leave this man with his memories, undisturbed by a curious American. Besides, how could I ever adequately explain to him that I attended a high school in Newark, New Jersey, Weequahic, where most of the students were Jewish and some of them had escaped the Holocaust, perhaps just as he had? Also there were men and women in my old neighborhood who had numbers tattooed on their arms, imprinted there by their Nazi jailers at Auschwitz, Treblinka, and other death camps.

Ever since, I have frequently thought about the horrors that tens of thousands of Jews suffered in a country where some of my forebears once lived, and pondered how one could ever make sense out of that horrible demonstration of evil. It was with similar thoughts in mind that two years later I would live in a flat in a seventeenth-century building which had an entrance on Jew Street. From my third-story window I could look down at a small grammar school that occupied part of the space where the Grand Synagogue of Vilnius once stood. It had been gravely damaged by the Nazis during the war and later was bulldozed by the KGB. The Lithuanian government has since made preparations to place a memorial on the spot to commemorate one of European Jewry's greatest houses of worship.

After I explained to my dinner companion that there was no chance that President Bush would respond positively to a Lithuanian bid for diplomatic recognition, she urged me to give a lecture. The topic could be the U.S. view of Gorbachev and perestroika. I had made a decision before leaving the United States that I would not give any advice to the Lithuanians, since I knew little about their situation, but if they asked me about the political situation in my own country I would do my best to answer. I had appeared on Lithuanian TV, but while I shared my convictions with the viewers that Lithuania would be free one day soon, I did not discuss U.S. diplomatic recognition.

Upon entering the Central Lecture Auditorium in Old Town Vilnius, close to Vilnius University, I was impressed by the large crowd that had already gathered. About three, maybe four hundred people had responded to circulars and spots in the local media, print and broadcast, announcing my lecture. I had welcomed the opportunity to share my views with the audience and was confident that they accurately reflected political developments in the United States. Anyone who was a close observer of the Washington scene might speak with the same confidence. But even though I had been encouraged by Sajudis staffers to give the speech, I remained worried that it might do more harm than good.

From the outset, I had assumed that the Sajudis council members I had been meeting with had a hidden agenda for proclaiming that President Bush would grant Lithuania diplomatic recognition immediately after a new government in Vilnius restored Lithuanian independence. I reasoned that they could not really believe this would be the case, but were somehow advancing their cause by taking that position. But once I realized that this was what the Sajudis leadership really believed, I bowed to several people who had urged me to share my views explaining why this was not likely—indeed, I deemed it out of the question.

Rather than choosing to sit next to my translator at a table in the center of the hall, I stood at a lectern where I could maintain eye contact with most of the audience. The men and women who had attended maintained a serious demeanor, but they acknowledged my presence with smiles and good humor and listened to my address attentively. To break the ice I started my talk by making the following observation.

> My first day in Vilnius, I accepted Antanas Buracas's offer to rest at his house after two days without sleep. The next morning as we walked toward his car, he insisted that he carry my bags. I shared that story with you because it symbolizes what this election really means for Lithuania. Henceforth, the deputies you elect must carry the people's bags for them.[9]

Most of the audience smiled at the metaphor and only a few laughed. Tough audience, I noted.

In the heart of my speech I had provided several reasons why President Bush would not extend diplomatic recognition to a newly resurrected, sovereign Lithuanian government:

> Most Americans cannot locate Lithuania on the map, and many of them confuse the Baltics with the Balkans. Most informed Americans support Lithuania's bid for independence and wish the Lithuanian people well. But they cannot forget Hungary. They cannot forget that after our secretary of state, John Foster Dulles, encouraged the peoples of Eastern Europe to resist Soviet imperialism, the U.S. remained silent

when the Hungarians pleaded with Washington to send them arms to fight the invading armies of the Warsaw Pact. Many Americans believe it would be immoral for them to encourage you to declare your independence and face a similar attack.

At that point, someone from the audience asked: "Will America provide help if we declare independence and Moscow sends troops to crush us?"

I hesitated, hoping that the hesitation would make it apparent to the audience what the answer was. I finally said, "Probably not." What I meant to say, but did not have the heart to say, was "Certainly not." I held to this view because of the third reason why the Bush administration would not recognize Lithuania:

"The most powerful argument that President Bush will receive from his advisers not to recognize Lithuania is that Mikhail Gorbachev would be toppled as a consequence."

As I expected, the audience responded to this point with outbursts of displeasure, although there was irony, not anger, in their voices. Most Lithuanians I had met refused to acknowledge that Gorbachev had taken measures advancing the cause of democracy and Lithuanian independence—whatever his original motives might have been. When someone from the audience took issue with the positive view Westerners displayed toward Gorbachev, I responded: "Look, if were not for Gorbachev there would be no election in Lithuania next week. And certainty his predecessors never would have allowed me into the country to express my views openly in this forum and on Lithuanian TV." Even though the questioner had to concede that point, he, like most Lithuanians, was reluctant to give Gorbachev credit for anything—even for the obvious role that he had played in the collapse of communism in Eastern Europe in 1989. I continued:

> For many months after entering office, President Bush, his vice-president, Dan Quayle, and most of his advisers believed Gorbachev was not to be taken seriously, that like all of his predecessors, he was not intent upon reforming the Soviet system. But after the events of 1989, and in light of the elections to be conducted in the USSR in 1990, they changed their minds. Indeed, President Bush is convinced that Gorbachev's political longevity is vital to U.S. interests and his demise would be a disaster for the United States.

Before proceeding further, I paraphrased a remark that Landsbergis had made to Western observers, although I did not identify him as the speaker. He had said, in effect, that the West should allow Lithuanians to make the decision

whether or not to restore Lithuanian independence because it was the Lithuanians who would have the most to lose—not the West.

I said to the audience:

> But the American people believe that they have a stake in Gorbachev's
> survival—that is, if he is prepared to end the Cold War we must help
> him remain in power. After all, Americans have made many awesome
> sacrifices since the end of World War II. Over 100,000 Americans have
> lost their lives in wars during the Cold War, and about 300,000 have been
> wounded in battle. And billions of dollars have been spent which could
> have been invested to provide housing to the homeless, decent incomes
> for the poor, and better medical care for everyone. Don't tell Americans
> that they do not have a stake in Gorbachev, because they believe they do!

After the lecture, I spoke with several members of the audience and gave a
lengthy interview to newspaper reporters, but no one from Sajudis asked me
about my remarks. However, the evening before I was scheduled to catch an
early-morning Aeroflot flight to Moscow, and then Pan Am to the States, I
encountered Aidas Polabinskus on the stairwell of the Sajudis building. A
young Lithuanian-American from Illinois who was studying at Vilnius University, Aidas had been operating the fax machine in the attic of Sajudis headquarters and on occasion helped translate material from Lithuanian to English.
He said "Dr. Krickus, someone from the council heard about your speech and
would like you to share those views with the entire council early next week."
I said that was impossible, since I had to catch a six-thirty flight the next
morning.

During the long flight home I pondered whether the Sajudis leaders would
accept my analysis, and if they did, whether or not if would have any bearing
on their decision. Now I know that it probably would not have made any difference to them.

In his briefing with the international monitors on the eve of the 1990 elections, Landsbergis had indicated that if Sajudis was successful at the polls and
formed a government, it would declare independence. But he was unclear
about what that declaration would precisely entail, the restoration of a fully
independent and sovereign state operating independently of the USSR, or an
entity enjoying greater independent action yet still tethered to the Soviet
Union. Furthermore, he seemed to be saying that the declaration of independence would not occur right away but over time, after Lithuania had moved
gradually away from Moscow's authority. At one point, for example, he said
that "Moscow may be allowed to maintain military bases in Lithuania."

Clearly, he implied, Sajudis had no intention of confronting Gorbachev but would rather seek an accommodation with the man whose powers would be expanded once he was "elected" president of the USSR in the March 1990 elections.

Why did Landsbergis change his mind and declare independence immediately after a new government was formed in Lithuania? Was the position he stated on the eve of the elections merely a ploy to lull Gorbachev into a false sense of security when he had planned all along to move quickly and decisively? Anatol Lieven has observed:

> In the elections of February 1990, Sajudis stood on a platform of complete independence, and won on it; but the general expectation was that independence would come in stages, beginning with a declaration de jure, the course that Latvia and Estonia in fact pursued. In practice, the independence process as it actually occurred was a response to objective factors, but also to the determination of the radical nationalist minority in Sajudis, who succeeded in galvanizing the more cautious majority.[10]

On February 3, 1990, speaking before a gathering of Sajudis faithful in the Sports Palace in Vilnius, Landsbergis indicated that there were two paths that could be taken to achieve independence. The first involved "an agreement on moving step by step, reestablishing equal state relations" with the Soviet Union "without causing an upheaval on either side, preparing and establishing economic, military, and transit agreements, and coordinating the final hand over of power to the legal Lithuanian government." This was the position that would be associated in the minds of most Lithuanians with Brazauskas. The second path would involve an immediate and full declaration of independence with the restoration of Lithuanian independence. But Landsbergis cautioned, "We would have to foresee the risk of chaos, yet without knowing the views of foreign countries or the extent of their support."[11]

On the eve of the March 11 declaration, Lieven had attended an allegedly closed meeting to hear the Sajudis deputies debate the merits of moving step by step or achieving independence in one giant leap. The Sajudis assembly had authorized them to declare independence without providing specific instruction about the timing and the nature of the action. Lieven reports that three factors had a bearing on the decision to move at once. First, during the campaign they all had pledged to support independence. Now that a motion had been made to move at once, it was unthinkable to do otherwise. Eduardas Vilkas, a deputy himself, had declared, "To have voted against an immediate declaration would have been seen as voting against the declaration itself, not against the date, and no-one wanted to be recorded as against the declaration."[12]

A second factor was that if they did not move at once, the Soviet Congress of People's Deputies would convene in Moscow in March and give Gorbachev new presidential powers and approve of a plan that would made secession more difficult.

The third, and according to Lieven the most decisive, factor was that the Kaunas faction promised to support Landsbergis as chairman of the Supreme Council and Prunskiene as prime minister, if they opted for an immediate restoration of Lithuanian independence.

On the eve of the March 11 restoration of Lithuanian independence, Romas Sakadolskis, the head of the Lithuanian desk at the Voice of America, was in Landsbergis's kitchen late in the afternoon when the phone rang. It was Lozoraitis, who told Landsbergis that "things looked good in Washington"— that is, the American government would presumably look favorably upon recognizing Lithuania.

Lozoraitis believed Washington was prepared to extend diplomatic recognition to Lithuania. "I had informed Landsbergis that President Bush would recognize Lithuania," he told me in an interview in the Washington legation on 16th Street. "On the tenth of March, Mr. Landsbergis asked me about the declaration of independence. I was amazed that it was not already made. If we made the declaration, there would be no turning back, and it would foreclose any countermoves that Brazauskas or Gorbachev could have made."[13]

At the State Department, there was a group of people who were sympathetic to Lithuania—such as Paul Goble, Nicholas Burns, and James Swihart—and Lozoraitis concluded that their position was indicative of what Bush was thinking. (Perhaps he believed this because he had not spent much time in Washington and did not have a sophisticated grasp of the political dynamics of the Bush White House.) Lozoraitis said he was told by Department of State officials that they had anticipated Lithuania would declare its independence in the fall of 1989. Lower-echelon officials had prepared a statement of U.S. recognition, and they had informed Lozoraitis that they were pleasantly surprised that after it was sent up to the "seventh floor," where Secretary James Baker had his office, it returned without revision.

Also there was another influential Republican who reputedly favored extending recognition to Lithuania—Ronald Reagan, Bush's predecessor. Lozoraitis had been told that the former president had been urging George Bush to do so. "Therefore," he said, "I was convinced that the U.S. was prepared to accept Lithuanian independence and was encouraging it. Only later

did I find out what Bush had in mind . . . he was so enamored with Gorbachev that he thought Landsbergis's decision was a destabilizing one. Even if
Bush were opposed, I approved the move because it was important that we
show the communists that there was no going back, that it was the right thing
to do."

After pausing, he remarked: "You know my grandfather in Lithuania would
take me on his boat, and once he said that it was not possible to see around
the bend of the river but we had to go forward nonetheless. That is the way
history is. You cannot always predict the future. But you must go ahead if
what you are doing is right."

But the Sajudis leadership should not have been surprised that the Bush
administration would not extend recognition. The U.S. ambassador to the
USSR, Jack Matlock, met in March 1989 with Sajudis leaders who had been
elected to the Soviet Union's Congress of People's Deputies. He arranged the
meeting in his residence, Spaso House, "because I wanted to make sure that the
Soviet authorities could see that we were meeting openly!" Landsbergis was
out of Moscow and could not attend, but among the delegation were Ozolas,
Genzelis (the head of the Communist Party at Vilnius University), and
Virgiljius Cepaitis (the writer who would become a powerful leader in Sajudis).
They were open with Matlock and informed him that they hoped "to achieve
complete independence by mid-1990." They would move deliberately and by
stages. "They would remove the legal basis of their inclusion in the Soviet
Union by declaring the secret protocol to the 1939 Nazi-Soviet pact null and
void and reversing the Act of Accession, which had been forced at gunpoint out
of a rump Lithuanian parliament in 1940."

Matlock marveled at the fact that these mature, responsible men really
believed that they could break free of the Soviet state within a year. "Only
three or four years back, a prison camp or insane asylum would have awaited
anyone who called openly for secession. Forty years ago, it would have been a
bullet at the base of the skull."[14]

When asked what the U.S. response would be were the Lithuanians to
declare their independence, Matlock said that recognition was out of the question and warned it "might encourage Soviet hard-liners to use force," and "if
things go wrong and the Soviet use force, there is no way we can protect
you." The delegation responded that if Gorbachev used force, that was the end
of perestroika, and consequently they did not think he would resort to
violence.

As a result of the meeting, Matlock concluded: "These are acts of a psychologically free people, and from that day in 1989 I never doubted they would

prevail, not in some far-off generation of the next century, but before the end of this one."[15]

On 7 March 1990, the Soviet foreign minister Eduard Shevardnadze, asked Matlock to meet with him at the ministry. Shevardnadze warned that if the Lithuanians declared their independence the Soviet Union could be struck by civil war. "Without specifying precisely how a civil war might start, he pointed out that there were many defense plants and troops stationed in Lithuania, implying that the Soviet military might attempt to seize power there without Gorbachev's approval—or perhaps that they would even attempt to remove Gorbachev." Shevardnadze indicated, however, that if the Lithuanians waited until after Gorbachev secured the powers of the Soviet presidency, "Gorbachev could deal with the situation without undue risk."[16]

Shevardnadze then said that he knew that Matlock had a scheduled meeting with the Sajudis leaders that morning. He urged the American ambassador to postpone it until the Lithuanians had settled the issue of independence, so it did not look as if the United States were involved should the Lithuanians proclaim independence after they formed their new government. Matlock said he could not cancel the meeting which was scheduled for 11:00 A.M., in half an hour, but observed that the United States was not encouraging the Lithuanians to declare their independence and that even though the United States did not recognize Soviet annexation it would not extend diplomatic recognition to Lithuania.

In the meeting, Landsbergis said that a declaration was likely and asked how the United States would respond. Matlock said the United States extended diplomatic recognition to a country only "when it is in effective control of its territory. A declaration of independence alone would not give them that control, and therefore they should not expect recognition."[17]

When I asked Landsbergis why he decided to make the declaration restoring Lithuania's sovereignty, he responded. "Gorbachev was about to receive new powers as the Soviet president, and he was planning to impose a new law of secession. We were not a Soviet republic. This was a trap! We had to move before these things happened."[18] It was for this reason that one might surmise that Landsbergis would have made the bold move and bolted from the USSR even if he accepted Matlock's prediction of non-recognition. He was convinced that the time was ripe and he was not deterred from the action by anyone.

When the Lithuanians issued their historic proclamation, Gorbachev was preoccupied with developments in Moscow, where perestroika was at risk. As opposition from the party reactionaries became more pointed, he needed to find new sources of power to promote his reforms. Initially, Gorbachev had assumed he could embark upon fundamental reforms without challenging the monopoly status of the CPSU as stipulated under Article 6 of the Soviet constitution. He was a party man and dismissed any talk about the need to create a multiparty system in the USSR. By the winter of 1989–90, however, it was clear that he had to expedite the expulsion of people he deemed "unimaginative" apparatchiks, who were "mindlessly" opposed to reform, and replace them with new blood. But the party hacks demonstrated greater staying power than he had anticipated. He also wanted to transfer power from the party to the government, which he would lead as president once he was selected by the USSR Congress of People's Deputies in March 1990.

The Lithuanians' challenge to the imperial Center, therefore, could not have come at a less propitious time. The Lithuanians were placing Gorbachev's campaign to strengthen his position in the Kremlin hierarchy and the future of perestroika at risk.

Moreover, Gorbachev had no intention of allowing the Lithuanians to leave the union, ever. He instead began taking actions in Lithuania to force Landsbergis to rescind the declaration of independence.

March 18: Soviet military planes and helicopters begin unscheduled military maneuvers over Lithuania.

March 19: The Soviet government orders its ministries to step up protection of vital installations in Lithuania.

March 21: Gorbachev issues an executive order directing Lithuanian citizens to surrender all weapons and instructs the KGB to tighten border checks, including restrictions on foreign visitors.

March 23: Soviets order two U.S. diplomats out of Lithuania. Moscow also begins to limit travel and access to Lithuania for foreign diplomats and the press.

March 25: Soviet soldiers seize two Communist Party schools and the Vilnius Communist Party headquarters.

March 27: Soviet paratroops occupy two buildings of the independent Lithuanian Communist Party and hand them over to Moscow loyalists. Soviet soldiers also seize and brutally beat a dozen draft resisters harbored in a Vilnius psychiatric hospital.

March 30: Soviet forces occupy the state prosecutor's office in Vilnius and install a Moscow loyalist. Troops also seize the main printing plant where the republic's main independence newspapers are printed.[19]

Meanwhile, from Moscow, Gorbachev launched a "constitutional" offense against the government in Vilnius. On March 15, Gorbachev declared the Lithuanian action illegal and the Congress of People's Deputies began consideration of a new secession law. There was a provision for secession in the Soviet constitution, but precise details specifying how the process worked were not defined. The new law proposed that if the Lithuanians were to bolt from the Union, they would first have to meet three requirements.

1. Two-thirds of the voters had to approve of Lithuanian independence through a referendum.
2. This would be followed by a five-year waiting period to settle many outstanding questions. For example how would Lithuania compensate the USSR for improvements that had been made in the country since 1940, and how would individuals who wished to leave Lithuania be compensated for their property? Also, how would the rights of minority peoples—Russians and Poles—be safeguarded?
3. Assuming all of the issues associated with the second step were adequately resolved, the Soviet parliament had the final say in whether or not Lithuania would be allowed to leave the union.

Landsbergis's response was that Lithuania had been forcefully incorporated in the USSR and therefore was not subject to Soviet law. The Soviet constitution had no legitimacy in Lithuania and so neither of the first two conditions was relevant. Landsbergis and his colleagues had conceded that the reparations issue was legitimate, but the Lithuanians were the ones who had the right to demand reparations. A system of payments to compensate Lithuania for the Soviet occupation had to be negotiated. And payments to families whose loved ones had been murdered by Soviet authorities or had died when forced to live in the gulag had to be arranged. And what about those deportees who had returned from forced exile? They too had to be compensated for the horrors they had endured, not to mention the work they had provided as slave laborers. One of the Sajudis speakers, who had briefed the international monitors before the 1990 election, calculated that the Soviet Union owed Lithuania many billions in U.S. dollars.

The Lithuanian people perceived Soviet displays of military prowess as a real threat, not merely a symbolic gesture, but they remained resolute. So did Landsbergis, who had refrained from criticizing Gorbachev for more than two weeks. Then on March 27, after Soviet troops occupied the headquarters of the Lithuanian Communist Party and two dozen Lithuanian "deserters" from the Red Army were subdued at a psychiatric hospital, he sent a telegram to Gorbachev. Landsbergis said the arrests "are clear indications that Lithuania remains a country on whose territory an occupying power can commit acts of violence and remain unpunished."

But the frustrated Lithuanian leader also leveled charges at the West. In comments to reporters, Landsbergis said, "All we can do is raise the question to the democracies of the West: Are they willing once again to sell out Lithuania?" Only "bold declarations" of support for Lithuanian independence would protect Lithuania from aggression, he added. If the West played the role of bystander, the world would experience another Munich.[20]

In a formal statement issued to the Lithuanian people and parliament several weeks after the March 11 declaration, Gorbachev proclaimed: "The actions being taken in Lithuania have no legal foundation. They are being taken at a time when we have begun to resolve vital issues of the Soviet federation on a really democratic basis." Insofar as Gorbachev was prepared to give the republics a greater voice in matters previously dominated by Moscow, this last statement was accurate. But then, turning to the issue of Lithuania's status under the Soviet constitution, Gorbachev observed: "Did the Lithuanian citizens not support the USSR constitution, by which Lithuania abided for years honestly and strictly as a fully fledged republic?" This was simply false; Lithuania had been forced into a union with the USSR. And so Gorbachev's concluding remark was baseless as well: "I propose that the Lithuanian Supreme Soviet immediately annul the illegal acts it has adopted."[21]

Gorbachev's legal ploy was meant to cloud the merits of the Lithuanian cause and to provide the West with a pretext not to support Landsbergis. Gorbachev knew that George Bush was anxious to resolve the confrontation between Moscow and Vilnius, and he believed other Western leaders would pressure Landsbergis to reach a compromise that satisfied Moscow.

But after he failed to force Landsbergis to repeal the declaration in March, he resorted to his ace in the hole—an economic embargo in April. On the 17th of that month, Landsbergis received a telegram from Gorbachev with the warning that if Vilnius did not repeal the declaration, an economic blockade would begin. At the outset, Moscow would halt the flow of oil to Lithuania. As a result of that move, the oil refinery at Mazheikai halted operations on April 23. It was the only refinery in the country, and one-fourth of its output was distributed throughout Lithuania. Later Moscow would stop sending other raw materials to Lithuania in the expectation that Landsbergis would ultimately bow to economic pressures.

To the surprise of his friends and the delight of the Lithuanian people, however, the diminutive, mild-mannered professor refused to kowtow to Moscow, and he displayed great courage, resolve and determination in standing up to Gorbachev. The Lithuanians were not alone in their struggle, for at this point allies in Russia offered them help to break the embargo.

Liberal mayors and democratic-minded officials in Moscow, Leningrad, Omsk, Smolensky, Saratov, Arkhangelsk, Pskov, Tyumen, and Minsk, and even supporters in Uzbekistan, together with factory and state enterprise managers, provided the Lithuanians with oil they desperately needed to heat their buildings and fuel their industry. Smith reports, "The Lithuanian government claimed that through barter deals with parts of the Soviet Union, and not counting old Soviet contracts, it had imported 892 million rubles' (nearly $1.5 billion) worth of goods during the embargo and had shipped back an equal volume."[22]

The abortive economic blockade not only failed to produce the result that Gorbachev expected it would—the repeal of the March declaration—it helped mobilize the Lithuanian people around Landsbergis. On April 7, an estimated 200,000 resolute patriots massed in Vingis Park in a show of support for him and the parliament. Repeating a battle cry of Duke Gediminas, Lithuania's fourteenth century national hero, Landsbergis said, "Iron will melt to wax and water will turn to stone before we will retreat."[23]

Later that month, Landsbergis characterized a letter from German chancellor Helmut Kohl and French president François Mitterrand as "important and positive." The two leaders had asked him to consider a temporary "delay" in implementing the March 11 declaration. In late May, Gorbachev said that if the Lithuanians denounced the March declaration, they could become independent within two years. Landsbergis countered that he would suspend implementation of the declaration for one hundred days—but not the declaration itself—in exchange for negotiations and the lifting of economic sanctions. "Gorbachev wanted me to use the word 'moratorium,' so that he could tell the upcoming party congress that the Lithuanians had capitulated." Landsbergis's position was that talks could begin only after the blockade was lifted.[24] Prunskiene favored Gorbachev's deal, but the right in the Lithuanian parliament was opposed. Landsbergis and Prunskiene traveled to Moscow and conferred with Gorbachev on June 26–27. On June 29, Landsbergis said he would accept a moratorium, but it would begin only after both sides agreed upon terms to negotiate a settlement to the crisis. The Lithuanian parliament, by a vote of 61 to 35, accepted the moratorium, and Gorbachev immediately announced the lifting of the economic blockade.[25] The two sides, however, would never agree upon the ground rules that would allow formal negotiations to begin.

By choosing to define the "compromise" to fit their own interpretations of the informal agreement, Vilnius and Moscow had reduced the tension. Gorbachev had no intention of accepting the Lithuanians' demands for independence, but Prime Minister Ryzhkov was appointed chair of the Soviet negotiation team. An American scholar contends Landsbergis moved slowly in appointing a delegation because he hoped "to disassociate himself from the stigma of having supported the moratorium."[26] Prunskiene, by contrast, was being attacked by the Lithuanian right for being too anxious to negotiate with Moscow.

The two Lithuanian leaders also were at odds over the composition of the delegation: Landsbergis said it should be appointed by the Supreme Council, and Prunskiene the government. Landsbergis won, and his deputy chairman, Bronius Kuzmickas, was selected to lead the commission that would draw up principles for negotiations while the parliament would choose the team to negotiate with Ryzhkov. On August 21, Landsbergis was selected as chairman of the Lithuanian delegation. Representatives from Estonia and Latvia and the émigré community were invited to join the delegation.

Alfred Eric Senn, the dean of Lithuanian studies in the United States, claims that Landsbergis at this time believed political developments in Russia were moving in Lithuania's favor. On May 29, Boris Yeltsin was selected as chairman of the Supreme Soviet of the Russian Republic, and he demonstrated immediately that he planned to use that post to challenge Gorbachev. The Russian parliament would soon contend that Russian law took precedence over Soviet law. Senn writes, "In Moscow on June 1, in a spectacular display of solidarity between rebellious republics, Yeltsin had talked with Landsbergis for an hour, agreeing in principle on cooperation between their governments."[27] Some Lithuanians believed that the struggle between the two Russian titans would ultimately lead to the Soviet Union's demise. Even if that colossal event did not occur, the Gorbachev-Yeltsin competition could work in Lithuania's behalf.

By the summer's end and under mounting pressure from the neo-Stalinists, Gorbachev made two historic decisions. The first was that the liberals no longer were a political asset and his political survival rested on his reaching a new accommodation with the hard-liners. The correctness of this decision would become even clearer as Gorbachev confronted powerful opponents to perestroika in the fall.

On November 11, 1990, he met with 1,110 military officers who also held legislative seats at all levels of government, running from local councils to the Congress of People's Deputies. They told him that the military was in disarray and was being derided by the people, that draft dodging had become pandemic, that military installations were being attacked, and that the Red Army's ability to defend the nation was on a steady path downward. The country, they concluded, was on the edge of a great precipice, and if Gorbachev did not reverse his course, disaster was inevitable.

On November 16, the Politburo held a special meeting, and party reactionaries confronted Gorbachev with similar warnings and urged him to restore law and order and take strong measures to halt the spread of nationalism. The next day, Gorbachev announced that he had acquired new emergency powers, that he had disbanded the presidential council, and that he had formed a new security council composed of the KGB, the ministry of interior, and the ministry of defense. Democrats greeted this news with grave forbidding, for it was liberals like Aleksandr Yakovlev, who served on the presidential council, who were being removed. The reactionaries controlled all three "power ministries" after the liberal head of interior, Vadim Bakatin, was replaced by an old Stalinist, Boris Pugo, late in 1990.[28]

Gorbachev's second fateful decision was that the Lithuanian cancer, which was a lethal threat to the Soviet Union, had to be excised at any price. That summer, he appointed Mykolas Burokevicius, the Lithuanian Bolshevik, to the Soviet Politburo, along with other loyalists in the non-Russian republics, to stem the tide of separatism. Burokevicius's appointment was an attempt to give him political legitimacy and indicated that Gorbachev was preparing to move against Landsbergis.

In this connection, Oleg Shenin—a supporter of the ultra-conservative Soyuz ("Union") faction in the Congress of People's Deputies—was appointed as the CPSU's secretary for organizational questions. In August he was sent to Lithuania and was shocked by growing evidence that the Lithuanian situation was getting out of control. Senn notes that "once back in Moscow he called for action by Soviet authorities, warning that the Lithuanian government was aiming at 'total dismantling of Soviet power and the renewal of the totalitarian dictatorship of the bourgeoisie in Lithuania.'"[29]

Henceforth, Moscow would work closely with Burokevicius and Vladislav Shev—the Soviet loyalist in the Lithuanian Communist Party, and member of parliament, who founded the "Committee of Citizens of the Lithuanian SSR," in March—and ignore both Landsbergis and Brazauskas in the process.[30] Presumably, Gorbachev really believed that the Soviet loyalists in Lithuania had significant popular support behind them. Or perhaps he really did care whether they had such support or not. For example, Gorbachev had indicated in a meeting with Prunskiene as early as July that negotiating with Lithuania was no longer a major priority for him. Things had changed.

But having decided to remove Landsbergis with whatever measures were necessary, Gorbachev still had to accomplish this objective without harming relations with the West, whose financial assistance was necessary to revitalize the Soviet economy. His reliance on Western help would become even more urgent after he received reports indicating that the 1990 grain harvest had been a disaster and the provision of food from abroad was absolutely imperative. In May, Gorbachev would meet with Bush in Washington and plead for American assistance.

To placate the democracies, Gorbachev had to provide justifications for his move against the Lithuanians that the West could accept as consistent with "democratic values." Toward this end, spindoctors in Moscow and Russian leaders in Lithuania intensified charges that the "Lithuanian nationalists" were placing the human rights of non-Lithuanians at risk.

The Russian population in Lithuania had followed the rise of Sajudis with misgivings, even though some ethnic Russians, like Nikolai Medvedev, were Sajudis activists and would be elected to high office in the February–March 1990 elections. Representing approximately 9 percent of the population, the Russians did not have the numbers to influence developments in Vilnius as they customarily did in Tallinn and Riga. But through the Communist Party and Soviet ministries they enjoyed what the Lithuanians deemed privileged status in the country. To countervail the power of Sajudis, the Russians on November 4, 1988, had announced the formation of their own "Socialist Movement for Perestroika in Lithuania," Edinstvo ("Unity") The so-called international fronts that were established throughout the Baltics in opposition to the popular front movements (which were accused of narrow nationalism) henceforth became known as "interfronts." The organization, which included Polish Communist loyalists, openly declared itself as Soviet, and its organizers said that they had found it necessary to organize because of the Lithuanian Communist Party's ineptness in handling Sajudis.[31]

On February 4, 1989, Edinstvo had held a rally of eighty thousand people in Vilnius to protest demands by Sajudis that Lithuanian replace Russian as the republic's official language. If the law, which had been passed on November 19, 1988, was not rescinded, Edinstvo threatened, among other things, to conduct strikes of protest.[32] When Edinstvo conducted such rallies, people were brought in from outside Lithuania to fill the ranks of protesters. On one occasion, Sajudis activists noted the presence of many cars in Vilnius with

Belorussian license plates. Of course, even Russians residing in Lithuania, who were neither attached to security agencies nor party activists, were fearful about their status in a free Lithuania. "Suddenly the Russians felt like strangers, aliens in what they saw as their own country" observes Hedrick Smith.[33]

Although the Poles in Lithuania as a group were not as privileged (the intellectuals and middle class had fled or were expelled by Stalin's anti-Polish policies), they too felt vulnerable. Some Polish leaders, like Czeslav Okinczyc, belonged to Sajudis and were elected deputies in the 1990 elections, but in largely rural Salcininkai and parts of the Vilnius region the locals looked to Polish Soviet apparats to protect them from Lithuanian nationalists. And even Okinczyc criticized Sajudis for not displaying greater sensitivity toward the Polish community in Lithuania.[34] Under these circumstances, many Polish peasants believed the apparatchiks, who warned that the Lithuanians would embark upon an anti-Polish campaign after they gained power.

In August 1990, I had spoken with several Polish leaders in Warsaw. Among them was Henryk Wujek, a close confidant of Bronislaw Geremek, and Senator Tadeusz Klopotowski, the first Polish official to speak before the Lithuanian parliament after it issued its March 11 declaration. Klopotowski, who had lived and worked in Washington for several years, headed a commission in the Polish senate responsible for the status of Poles living in the diaspora. Although the newly independent Polish government deemed it imprudent to anger Moscow by extending diplomatic recognition to Vilnius, Solidarity leaders like Adam Michnik, Bronislaw Geremek, and Jacek Kuron had traveled to the Lithuanian capital in a bold display of support for the new government there. Authorities in Warsaw believed that Landsbergis and his closest supporters would treat the Poles in Lithuania fairly.

Public declarations to the contrary, officials in both capitals continued to view their counterparts with suspicion. Warsaw, for its part, had expressed anger that the Lithuanians persisted in the claim that the Poles living in Lithuania were really Polonized Lithuanians. This "misreading of history," authorities in Warsaw believed, was a pretext to ignore the legitimate concerns that Poles in Lithuania had about the future of their schools, language, and economic prospects. Many Lithuanians displayed appalling ignorance about the Polish community in their country. For example, a women who was the administrator in charge of Polish schools in Vilnius led me on a tour of one of them, but she did not know that Poles outnumbered Lithuanians in the city before World War II. Perhaps she knew the truth but preferred to ignore it; if so, here was evidence, as the Poles claimed, that the Lithuanians did not want to treat their grievances seriously. What Polish leaders feared most was that Landsbergis, under mounting pressure from Moscow, might exploit anti-"foreign" feelings among ordinary Lithuanians to rally them around their embattled government.

The Lithuanians, in turn, noted that the Polish apparatchiks who held local political positions in the Vilnius area and the largely agricultural Salcininkai region in eastern Lithuania had remained loyal to Moscow. Indeed, in addition to opposing Sajudis and the independence declaration, they had threatened to secede from Lithuania and join some adjacent Soviet entity, perhaps Soviet Belorussia. The myths and half-truths that the Lithuanians held about their Polish fellow citizens aside, they had reason to fear that the neo-Stalinist apparatchiks were bent on subverting Lithuanian independence. And while they welcomed bids of support from Warsaw, the Lithuanians remained wary of their larger neighbor. They could not forget that Poland was ten times the size of their own country and had imposed Polish culture upon Lithuania over the centuries.

Polish and Lithuanian authorities had discussed their mutual concerns immediately after the March declaration, but the Poles believed further discussions were necessary. Wujek and Klopotowski had asked me to organize a meeting between them and the Lithuanian deputy prime minister, Romualdas Ozolas. In a visit to Vilnius in the fall of 1990, I informed Ozolas of the Poles' request, and he said I should arrange the meeting. But he urged me to revise its scheduled date, which I had previously set for early in 1991, and to conduct it before Christmas of 1990. Because of financial difficulties, the meeting never occurred, but later I presumed that Ozolas wanted to meet with the Poles in mid-December to prevent Moscow from exploiting any real or imagined dispute between the government in Lithuania and the country's Polish minority before the U.S.-led attack against Saddam Hussein's forces began.

From the Western vantage point, the very fact that Gorbachev was debating with the Lithuanians and not sending in security forces to coerce them into silence was a positive sign. And, at the time, one could be hopeful. Not many weeks before Gorbachev became the first Soviet general-secretary to travel to Lithuania, the Berlin Wall was destroyed. That event symbolized the ending of the Cold War for millions of people throughout the world, and Western observers knew that without Gorbachev's compliance this historic event never would have taken place.

The Wall's construction and brave attempts to cross it created scenes that would remain forever in the memory of millions of people on both sides. How could anyone forget still and TV pictures depicting Germans risking death by dashing across minefields or picking their way through barbed wire while dodging bullets in the hope of crossing into West Berlin? Or the sight of people jumping from buildings in East Berlin to freedom in the western half of the city? Or most of all, the sight of people who were shot dead in their mad but abortive dash for freedom? Such vivid, heart-wrenching scenes had demonstrated to the entire world that communism was an evil system that could not prevail.

At the same time, such scenes must have devastated the morale of those of the Communist elite who had not altogether surrendered their humanity. Only those who had lost the capacity to think and feel like civilized human beings could have been unaffected. It was in this sense that the wall's demolition had practical consequences. As it crumbled, so did the resolve of many Soviet apparats to preserve the pathological society that the Bolsheviks had established in 1917. As Timothy Garton Ash, one of the most prolific and perceptive chroniclers of communism in Eastern Europe, has written, the "ruling elite's loss of belief in its right to rule" explained why the Communist leaders gave up in most countries without a fight.[35]

Finally, who could forget Christmas Day 1989, when Leonard Bernstein conducted an orchestra and chorus of musicians from both sides of the old Iron Curtain in East Berlin's Schauspielhaus? They played Beethoven's masterpiece the Ninth Symphony to an enthralled crowd of thousands. *"Freiheit!"*

While applying pressure on the Lithuanians, Gorbachev had good reason to believe that the Western media and publics would accept—albeit reluctantly—his spin on his confrontation with Landsbergis. Soviet propagandists inferred that it was Landsbergis, whom Gorbachev personally detested ("that piano player," he called him), who was being unreasonable. There were many Westerners, not unfriendly to the Lithuanian cause, who were prepared to accept this distortion of the situation. They knew Gorbachev and they liked what they knew about him; they had no idea who Landsbergis was and were unsure about his motives.

Gorbachev, after all, had earned enormous goodwill and popularity in the West. His charm campaign had started with Prime Minister Margaret Thatcher. The Iron Lady of Great Britain had been the first Western leader to meet him in 1984, a year before Konstantin Chernenko, his predecessor, died. In a TV statement she had issued the much quoted remark "I like Mr. Gorbachev. We can do business together." After he gained power and began to travel widely in the West, this positive assessment was endorsed by adoring crowds and admiring leaders alike. Gorbachev's intelligence, wit, and broad, inviting smile had captivated foreigners, and his attractive, stylishly dressed, articulate wife, Raisa, was a real asset to him. Pundits in many Western capitals reported that

"Gorby" was enjoying greater popularity with Western voters than their own chief executives were.

Gorbachev's PR successes abroad helped him at home. Even after it was reported that he himself was more popular in the West than in the USSR, Gorbachev skillfully used his popularity abroad to enhance his domestic political position. It helped him with those who believed the West could do no wrong, with people who supported him but remained skeptical about his commitment to pluralism, and with those hard-liners who marveled at his public relations skills and who, although they would not admit it publicly, paid great attention to what the West said about their society and its leaders.

Gorbachev's exalted international reputation and his uncanny ability to manipulate Western mass media had protected him from criticism from that quarter. For example, he knew that the Red Army did not enjoy a reputation for subtlety, but he used troops and other security forces known for their brutality against the Georgians in Tiblisi on April 9, 1989, causing twenty nationalist demonstrators to be killed, some with infantry entrenching shovels. While he was in Lithuania, ethnic fighting had erupted between Azeris and Armenians in Azerbaijan's capital, Baku, and a week later, Soviet forces entered the city to end the killing. Hedrick Smith reported:

> The films I saw of that operation, which took place overnight on January 19–20, showed a brutal, overpowering assault: tanks and armored personnel carriers spraying apartment buildings with gunfire, tracers fired back from Azerbaijani snipers on rooftops, civilian buses riddled with machine-gun fire, rows of passengers slumped against the windows, forever motionless. Some top leaders of the Azerbaijani Popular Front were arrested. More than one hundred Azerbaijanis were killed, and a million people turned out two days later to mourn them and denounce Gorbachev.[36]

Smith characterized the incident as "Gorbachev's crackdown," but among Western observers it was generally assumed that neo-Stalinist opponents of perestroika were responsible for the brutal killings. That was not an altogether surprising conclusion, since Gorbachev had been responsible for the destruction of communism in Eastern Europe while he orchestrated truly pluralistic reforms in the USSR. Such good and evil acts coming from the same man were deemed psychologically incompatible, and there was no evidence to suggest that he had ordered the brutal actions in Georgia and Azerbaijan. At least it had not come to the attention of the Western media. But the world would soon learn that there were two Gorbachevs: Gorby, the good Gorbachev, who allowed communism to expire in the "outer empire," and the other one, who would use the mailed fist to preserve Leninism in the "inner empire."

7 AMERICA'S RESPONSE

In a closed-door meeting with four congressmen, who visited Lithuania Feb. 24–25, Mr. Bush and his senior aides said keeping the Soviet leader in power was a higher priority than the Lithuanian independence drive, although they hoped the choice wouldn't surface, according to the lawmakers.
—the Washington Times, *March 29, 1990*

At the Malta summit of December 2–3, 1989, Gorbachev asked Bush not to exploit Moscow's problems with the Baltic countries. Bush had no intention of doing so but warned the Soviet leader that the Baltic states would be mentioned in the press conference at the end of the summit. Gorbachev replied that he would be ready for any questions that might be asked about the Baltics. Echoing what Shevardnadze had been saying to Baker for months, he told Bush that "the Kremlin was 'determined' to avoid repression if at all possible." In keeping with what other Soviet officials had been telling their American counterparts, to use force "would be the end of perestroika."[1]

Bush reminded Gorbachev that the United States had never recognized the Soviet Union's annexation of the three states. "Nor," according to Beschloss and Talbott, "had it relinquished its desire for Baltic independence." Bush said that the use of violence in the Baltics "'would create a firestorm' of anti-Soviet feeling in the United States."[2] In this connection, the president and his aides were undoubtedly thinking about attacks upon the administration by conservative columnists and members of Congress who supported the Lithuanians in their struggle with Gorbachev. But the Americans were grateful to Gorbachev, for he had terminated Communist rule in the satellite states, had adopted pluralistic reforms in the USSR, and was ending the global Cold War competition.

Therefore, in the weeks before the Malta summit, President Bush and his secretary of state, James Baker, were worried that the Balts and Moscow were on a collision course. The president's national security adviser, Brent Scowcroft, and Bush himself had concluded that Gorbachev was sincere—"he was perestroika"—and that if the Balts pushed him too far, civil war could break out in the Soviet Union. Scowcroft said in private, "It is not necessarily in the interest of the United States to encourage the breakup of the Soviet Union."[3]

This was the thinking in Washington when the Lithuanians made their March 11, 1990, declaration. That same day, the White House released a press statement reiterating that Washington had never recognized "the forcible incorporation of the independent states of Estonia, Latvia and Lithuania." It stated, furthermore:

> The new Parliament has declared its intention to restore Lithuanian independence. The United States would urge the Soviet government to respect the will of the citizens of Lithuania as expressed through their freely elected representatives and expects the government of Lithuania to consider the rights of its minority population. . . . We call upon the Soviet government to address its concerns and interests through imme- diate constructive negotiations with the government of Lithuania. We hope that all parties will continue to avoid any initiation or encourage- ment of violence.[4]

At first reading one might deem this statement even-handed, until one con- siders the implied suggestion that the Lithuanians respect the rights of minor- ities and refrain from violence—as if Moscow and Vilnius were morally equivalent and of equal size. Also, given its favorable tone, one might assume that Landsbergis had reason to conclude that U.S. diplomatic recognition would be forthcoming. But in subsequent press conferences and statements, Bush indicated that the United States could not recognize the Lithuanian gov- ernment, since it was not in control of its territory. Bush could take comfort in the cover provided him by editorials in major American newspapers such as the *Washington Post* and the *New York Times,* which had adopted his position.

Still, he could not rest easy, for on March 28, under pressure from Capitol Hill, Bush was forced to take his case to Congress. Overall, the reception was favorable but mixed. The Speaker of the House, Thomas S. Foley, and the House Republican whip, Newt Gingrich, both supported the president's posi- tion on Lithuania. Foley said, "I don't criticize the president at this moment in recognizing that circumstances are very delicate, very serious, and I think he should be given the benefit of the doubt as he deals with this." Gingrich responded, "We had a very spirited exchange and he won. We don't gain any- thing by forcing a confrontation." But some Republican aides, who chose not to be identified, noted that not all Republicans on the Hill were happy with Bush's position. One said, "For the arch–cold warriors this is vindication of all

their suspicions and there are those who have viewed things a little less cyni-
cally and are concerned that they may have been naive."

One Republican senator who was prepared to make his displeasure with
Bush public was North Carolina's Jesse Helms. He had his aide, Ann Smith,
telephone the government in Vilnius and state that the Congress would "turn
out the lights" on détente if the Lithuanians did not prevail.[5]

The next day, March 29, the *Washington Times* reported, "In a closed-door
meeting with four congressmen"—the men I had originally planned to visit
Lithuania with—"Mr. Bush and his senior aides said keeping the Soviet
leader in power was a higher priority than the Lithuanian independence drive,
although they hoped the choice wouldn't surface according to the lawmakers."[6]
This conclusion was not unique to the Bush administration, for it was held by
leaders in Western Europe as well. The Europeans were concerned lest the crisis over Lithuania negate the American-Soviet summit scheduled for Washington in late May and disrupt East-West talks over German reunification and
arms control. Some Europeans chastised the Lithuanians for pressing too forcefully. A source inside NATO said: "There's a sense that people in Lithuania
went a little too far and a little too fast and that if everyone would just pull up
a bit, it might give things a chance to work."[7]

Fortunately for the Lithuanians, there were influential columnists in the
American press who were unrelenting in criticizing Bush for not providing
more overt and steadfast support to the Lithuanian independence movement.
Among the most vocal were syndicated columnists Roland Evans and Robert
Novak. The fire from such influential opinion-molders on the right fed fears
in the White House that Republican conservatives would oppose Bush's 1992
bid for the party's nomination and during the election provide him only lukewarm support. This meant that Bush could not altogether ignore harsh measures that Gorbachev might adopt to resolve his problem in Vilnius. Because
Gorbachev, in turn, was aware of this, he could not crush the Lithuanian
rebellion with one swift and brutal stroke as Soviet troops had done in Tbilisi
in 1989 and Baku in 1990.

During my first visit to Lithuania, I was in the crowded Sajudis office and
noticed Roland Evans enter the reception room. He was just another reporter
to the Lithuanians, but I knew that he was a staunch supporter of Lithuanian
independence and it behooved Sajudis officials to spend time with him and
help him in any way they could while he was in the country. The column he
wrote with Robert Novak (known in Washington as the Prince of Darkness
for his hard-right political views) was carried by more newspapers than any
other political column in the United States. Also, it was read by the people

whose support the White House was most concerned about losing in Bush's reelection bid.

Politically, I was left of Evans and the other columnists who had been offering such effective support for Lithuania. I had always identified myself as a *Dissent/New Leader* liberal, that is, like the editors and writers of both small New York–based journals (to which I had contributed), I had adopted what might be appropriately called a "social democratic" stance on domestic issues while I was a hard-line opponent of Soviet Marxism on international issues. It pained me that many liberal writers like those who appeared in *The Nation* (to which I also had once contributed) avoided the issue of recognition for Lithuania and by their silence endorsed the Bush administration's policy of nonrecognition.

Evans wanted to travel outside of Vilnius and had asked me if I could help him get a car. He, of course, would pay for all expenses. I urged Andrius Kubilius, who ran the Sajudis office, to provide him with transportation and a translator, and he did so free of charge. It was a good deal for the Lithuanians, because the Evans and Novak column fought for Lithuanian independence right up until the day the United States finally recognized the small democracy in the fall of 1991.

Two other influential conservative syndicated columnists, the *New York Times's* William Safire and Abe Rosenthal, also would champion the Lithuanians cause even before the March 11, 1990 declaration of independence. Perhaps because of their conservative tendencies, they were less likely to become victims of Soviet disinformation campaigns such as the one Moscow was conducting against Landsbergis and his supporters in an attempt to brand them ultra-extremists who wanted to restore the fascist regime that existed before World War II.

During the Cold War, there were those associated with the old American left who saw the "Communist menace" with clarity. The most balanced assessment of the "Soviet threat" available to American readers had appeared in the pages of *Dissent*. But only a small percentage of even well-informed Americans were familiar with the prestigious quarterly, long edited by Irving Howe and his social democratic colleagues. In its pages one found cogent articles depicting the Soviet Union as an oppressive empire but one in advance stages of decay and hardly capable of leading a global Communist movement even if the aged men in the Kremlin were so inclined. Of course, there were liberal organizations like the AFL-CIO that openly endorsed the Lithuanian March 11 declaration and provided help to Sajudis.

Still, in the spring of 1990, it was primarily the conservatives in the American press who provided vigorous, open, and steadfast support for the Lithuanian independence drive.

In spite of fears of losing conservative support, the Bush administration was reluctant to press Gorbachev on the Baltic question. For example, after the Soviets announced their economic embargo, U.S. officials on April 23 said that President Bush would take countermeasures—e.g., suspend one or more sets of trade and commercial negotiations with Moscow. But the next day, after consulting with key members of Congress and allied leaders, the president changed his mind. He told a gathering of agricultural writers: "I am concerned that we not do anything that would cause the Soviet Union to take action that would set back the cause of freedom around the world."[8] Of course, that is precisely what Gorbachev was doing in Lithuania.

Nonetheless, the administration could not ignore the Gorbachev-Landsbergis confrontation, and in a trip to Moscow in May, James Baker discussed the issue of Lithuania with Gorbachev and Shevardnadze. "When Baker suggested that a distinction could be made between the legal status of the three Baltic states and that of the other republics, Shevardnadze objected that people in the Caucasus felt just as strongly as the Balts did about their forcible incorporation into the Soviet Union and so did many in Central Asia." The next day, Baker met with the Lithuanian prime minister, Mrs. Prunskiene, who was accompanied by two Landsbergis deputies, Bronius Kuzmickas and Ceslovas Stankevicius. "Until then I had been unaware of the tension that had developed between Prunskiene and Landsbergis," Jack Matlock noted. "[B]ut the composition of her party suggested that Landsbergis had sent two of his deputies to keep an eye on her."[9] Prunskiene informed Baker that the Lithuanians were reluctant to suspend their action on independence lest Moscow deem it as evidence that the Lithuanians had accepted "Soviet jurisdiction. Baker assured her that, whatever the Lithuanians decided to do in this regard, the United States would hold firmly to its nonrecognition policy."[10]

Meanwhile, notwithstanding Bush's failure to display his displeasure with Gorbachev by taking concrete countermeasures, the Soviet leader realized that the scheduled May 30 summit in Washington could be canceled if he did not end the economic embargo. The summit proceeded as scheduled, but only after Gorbachev agreed to lift the embargo. His confrontation with Vilnius was not cost-free, for it denied him the opportunity to address the U.S. Congress. Since he was convinced that he could work his magic upon the Congress and the millions of Americans watching the event on TV, this was a setback. Later he would learn something most disconcerting to him—that TV was one of the greatest assets Landsbergis possessed in his struggle with Gorbachev.

In late February 1990, upon my return from Moscow, I was asked by CNN to appear live on its afternoon news show, which emanated from Washington. The studio was only twenty minutes from my home in Fairfax, Virginia. My proximity to downtown Washington would be an asset over the next two years as I attempted to promote Lithuania's independence drive via appearances on TV and radio and through newspaper interviews and my own op-ed pieces. I remember once telling Victor Nakas, with whom I had conducted daily telephone conversations and strategy sessions during this critical period, that Gorbachev up to now had very skillfully manipulated the Western mass media but was going to find out that it can be a two-edged sword. Victor, who would become a very effective advocate of Lithuanian independence in his TV appearances, agreed. He was knowledgeable about developments in the Soviet Union, and his liberal-minded views helped refute the line that Moscow was perpetrating, that the Lithuanians were far-right philistines and analogues to the most primitive Lithuanian politicians of the interwar period. There were some people who fit that description among the émigré leadership, but fortunately none had materialized up to that point in Lithuania itself.

American political scientists, even as late as 1990, were marveling at TV's power to shape public attitudes on world affairs and to influence the actions of decision-makers. Initially they dwelt on TV and U.S. politics, in particular on the impact TV had upon American political campaigns and domestic circumstances in particular. Richard Nixon's "Checkers speech," the Kennedy-Nixon debates of 1960, and Nixon's skillful use of TV in his successful bid for the presidency in 1968 as depicted in Joe McGinnis's book *The Selling of the President* were customarily discussed in political science courses.[11]

Later, after Vietnam, the "first television war," political pundits acknowledged the power of TV to influence world affairs. Examples included the taking of American hostages by terrorists in Tehran during the Carter administration, which hurt Jimmy Carter's chances for reelection, and the killing of 241 marines in Lebanon during the Reagan administration, which, under the urging of his political advisers, caused Reagan to withdraw American troops from the Middle East even though he wanted to keep them there. Such developments, underscoring the close connection between U.S. foreign policy and a president's electoral prospects, had been firmly imprinted in the minds of President Bush's political advisers. After all, the Republicans, a minority party, had adroitly manipulated TV for years to defeat their Democratic opponents in races for the White House. Bush's people had been brilliant in portraying Michael Dukakis in the 1988 presidential campaign as a polluter, as soft on defense, and as a patsy on crime.[12]

It was clear that the Bush administration was attempting to distance itself from Landsbergis because it feared vital U.S. foreign policy objectives, such as German reunification, would be placed at risk. This was a legitimate concern, and it made sense to work with Gorbachev to end the Cold War and reduce risks to U.S. national security. But the Lithuanians were not going to back down, and by refusing to negotiate with Landsbergis, Gorbachev was only running the risk of placing himself in a situation in which he would feel obliged to use force against the government in Vilnius. If he did, Soviet–U.S. relations would be placed in peril. Indeed, the 1990 Washington summit could be aborted if a violent confrontation occurred. That is what I said in my interview with Paula Zahn on CBS's *This Morning* show several weeks before it was to begin. A crackdown against the Lithuanians would provoke a backlash in Washington; it would be very difficult for Bush to conduct talks with Gorbachev while Gorbachev's security forces were oppressing Lithuanians.

Prior to the February elections and the March declaration of independence, few Americans knew or cared about Lithuania. But the national mass media had projected the Lithuanian cause before U.S. audiences and had won Landsbergis and his people support from the best informed segment of the American population. Most important, opinion molders throughout the United States were supporting the Lithuanians even if they had accepted Bush's rationale for not recognizing the government in Vilnius at that time. In their newspapers, and on "local" radio and TV, they provided coverage of the confrontation between Vilnius and Moscow that worked in the Lithuanians' favor. From Moscow's perspective it would have been better if Lithuania had been ignored altogether. Furthermore, Americans love underdogs, and clearly Lithuania was David to the USSR's Goliath even though the person playing Goliath had high approval ratings among the audience. It must have annoyed Gorbachev that on this issue, the Western media, with their capacity to reach millions of people and make international events "newsworthy", were not working in a manner consistent with his needs.

Although the White House was not unmindful of the support the Lithuanians had enjoyed among the American people and influential opinion-molders, the president and his advisers felt they could not confront Gorbachev on this issue. President Bush was pressing Gorbachev to allow the German people to decide the crucial question, whether or not a reunified Germany should have membership in NATO. The American position was that a reunified Germany in NATO would be less dangerous to European stability and to the Soviet Union than one that was outside the alliance and left in limbo. Over time, the Germans, fearing they were isolated, might become paranoid and ultimately decide to develop their own military deterrent (perhaps including nuclear weapons) to safeguard their security.

The Bush administration had concluded that it could not allow the Lithuanians' bid for independence to prevent the United States from achieving vital international interests. Furthermore, Bush's advisers feared that U.S. recognition would precipitate Gorbachev's political demise. In reference to the Lithuanian crisis, Yegor Ligachev—the hard-liner who initially had given perestroika lukewarm support and later turned against it—said: "We must resolve this by political means. Tanks will not help in this matter." But Soviet military leaders were talking tough. The chairman of the U.S. Joint Chiefs of Staff, Admiral William Crowe, was told by Soviet defense minister, Dimitri Yazov, that his colleagues were prepared to "crush" Lithuania. "If one republic secedes, Gorbachev is through. And if he has to use force to prevent one from leaving, he's out too."[13] The White House's bottom line was that Gorbachev's political survival took priority over Lithuanian independence.

My view was that the Bush administration could not be induced to recognize Lithuania under these circumstances. But as the Kremlin disinformation experts perused the Western press and read about American endorsements of support for recognition, they would realize that it would be a grave error for them to use force against the Lithuanians. Also, it was in their interest to reach some kind of accommodation with Landsbergis, because a showdown with him lost them support in the West. One might also make an additional argument, that the Lithuanians were providing a peaceful solution to the non-Russians' legitimate demands for a greater voice in political, economic, and cultural decisions shaping their lives, from which Moscow had excluded them in the past. Indeed, if Gorbachev had permitted them a voice in decisions Moscow always had monopolized, this concession might have prevented them from bolting from the USSR in the first place.

At any rate, President Bush had accepted a questionable proposition: that if he refrained from taking any action, the problem would be peacefully resolved. But there was no going back and no risk-free position to take. Under these circumstances the Bush administration had no option but to do the right thing. It was against this backdrop that I wrote the following op-ed piece on March 23, 1990:

> The Bush White House remains mute in the face of pleas from Vilnius that the U.S. recognize Lithuania's newly reconstituted government. Such silence is puzzling. Washington claims the 1940 forceful incorporation of Lithuania into the USSR is unlawful, yet it refused to

extend diplomatic recognition to the government of President Vytautas Landsbergis.

President Bush argues his position is justified. He claims U.S. recognition of Lithuania could possibly undermine Mikhail Gorbachev at a time when the new Soviet president faces serious economic problems, mounting popular discontent and violent ethnic strife at home. Bush contends it is in the vital interests of the United States to spare Gorbachev from a setback that his neo-Stalinist opponents could exploit to topple him.

The chief U.S. State Department spokesperson, Margaret D. Tutwiler, said after Lithuania's declaration of independence in March, it has been the practice of the United States "to establish formal relations with the lawful government of any state once that government is in effective control of its territory and capable of entering into, and fulfilling, international obligations." Since that time, President Bush has urged both sides to refrain from threats and to negotiate their differences.

Supporters of the administration's viewpoint argue that even if Lithuanians were capable of controlling their country politically and achieving economic viability, the United States could not force Gorbachev to recognize the Landsbergis government. They say, this factor probably best explains not only Washington's failure to recognize Lithuania, but why no other government has extended diplomatic recognition. [Iceland would be the first government to do so.]

Others in the Bush administration say 'not to worry.' Gorbachev's modus operandi has been to bluster and rage in the face of opposition, but he has always in the past sought reconciliation. They say he will do the same with the Lithuanians. There is no need for Washington to press, and to risk his good will.

In truth, however, these justifications strike a growing number of Americans as disingenuous, cynical, and flawed. The following reasons outline why:

—Gorbachev has wrested considerable concessions from the West. He has done this by skillfully manipulating the notion that while law and morality are on the Lithuanians' side, politics dictate he deny them their freedom. Otherwise, he says, hard-liners in the Kremlin will depose him. American Kremlinologists agree Gorbachev's internal problems are mounting, but they argue simultaneously that he has consolidated his power. Gorbachev is a political genius. His opponents are demoralized and in disarray. As George Kennan told Congress in January, they are afraid of toppling him because, even if they could, they are terrified by the chaos that would accompany his demise.

—President Landsbergis is a resolute, single-minded proponent of his nation's independence, but he is also a pragmatist. He expects negotiations with Moscow to be detailed and protracted, before the recent declaration of independence can become a reality. He knows that Lithuania will continue to have close intimate economic relations with the USSR. It is in both sides' interests that this continue. He knows his country initially will experience economic difficulties, but he also believes in Lithuania's capacity to achieve a level of economic prosperity at least equal to the present.

—Landsbergis favors negotiations with Gorbachev and is willing to make concessions. As an example, he has said the Red Army must leave Lithuania, but concedes Moscow should be allowed to maintain naval bases on the Baltic in such strategic areas as Klaipeda. On the other hand, it is Gorbachev who has been making threats and refusing to talk with Lithuanian authorities. Lithuania has the capacity to "control its territory" and fulfill "its international obligations" . . . if Moscow does not place barriers in its path.

—The multitude of problems threatening the Soviet Union cannot be resolved without Western assistance and good relations with the U.S. If resolute, President Bush could induce Gorbachev to halt his bullying tactics (such as current military exercises in Lithuania) and intimidating rhetoric, which could easily lead to violent outbreaks that neither Gorbachev nor Landsbergis wants. Gorbachev is a political visionary. He knows the Soviet empire is an anachronism, and cannot long survive as presently constituted. The Lithuanians have provided him with a peaceful solution to that problem.

—Soviet threats to use force to take away the personal firearms of Lithuanians (which Moscow knows would never be used against the awesome Red Army) and the arrest of young Lithuanians who have deserted the armed forces could lead to bloodshed. Once violence occurs, it would be very difficult to control its destructive course. Gorbachev could not possibly desire another Baku, and certainly President Bush does not either.

The United States can wait no longer, nor act like a bystander, in a drama that could turn into great tragedy for the Lithuanian people, and possibly destroy the constructive course of East-West relations. By recognizing Lithuania, currently the only democratically elected government in the USSR, President Bush could help avoid impending disaster.[14]

As the first republic to risk the wrath of Moscow by declaring its independence, Lithuania captured the attention of the entire world. Favorable international public opinion would prove to be an asset to Landsbergis and his people as they approached a fateful showdown with Gorbachev and those hard-liners in Moscow who had decided to crush Lithuanian independence. I first realized that Gorbachev was prepared to use force to settle the vexing Lithuanian problem when I traveled to Vilnius and Moscow in October 1990.

I stood at the desk to the Lithuanian embassy hotel in Moscow weary from the early-morning flight from Vilnius. It was October 30, 1990, and I had welcomed the opportunity to register and catch a few hours of sleep before meeting with my contacts. I had not slept much the previous evening, having enjoyed a late-night meal at Stikliai with Egle Taurinskaite on my last day in Vilnius. As always, she had provided me with an overview of the political scene in Lithuania. Over the summer and in face of mounting pressure from Moscow, the Lithuanian people had rallied around Landsbergis and the government. Gorbachev was mistaken if he believed troop movements, threatening rhetoric, and an economic blockade would crush the Lithuanians' morale. Also, it was clear to officials in Vilnius that Gorbachev had no intention of reaching an accommodation with them. Soviet authorities were participating in "negotiations" with the Lithuanians to please the West and mislead the Americans into believing that Gorbachev was pursuing them in good faith while Landsbergis was being "unreasonable" in not rescinding the Lithuanian declaration of independence.

After a phone call to Lionginas in Moscow, Egle had arranged a room for me at the Lithuanian legation hotel there free of charge. During the Soviet era, each of the non-Russian republics had an embassy in Moscow with a hotel and quarters for the staff attached. I was on a tight budget and had accepted the offer with gratitude. But even if I had had the funds to stay in one of the city's first-class hotels, such as the Metropole, I would have chosen the legation hotel. It was strategically located in downtown Moscow not too far from the Kremlin and other interesting venues, such as the Russian White House, and it was filled with fascinating characters.

During the day, the small restaurant that adjoined the hotel's foyer served the personnel who were assigned to the compound's staff. For twenty-five cents you could have breakfast there, and lunch and dinner for less than a dollar. Meat was scarce, or of poor quality, but delicious pancakes and eggs were usually on the menu, and sometimes there was smoked salmon. Unlike the smoked salmon in the States, it had white flesh, and the flavor was even more delicate than that of the pink meat to which we are accustomed. The dark black Russian bread and brown Lithuanian variety were provided in abundance and were always terrific. It was in the beverage department that the situation was especially critical. I never drank milk, and fresh juice was unavailable. But so was water. Instead, a concoction of raisins immersed in water was often provided. It was absolutely dreadful. There was an ample supply of mineral water, but it had the flavor of Stalin's sitz bath. It was salty and laced with chemical compounds, which were proudly listed on the label. And it was difficult to purchase quality beverages such as beer from East Germany or Czechoslovakia on the street in Moscow for rubles.

The people who took their meals at the embassy compound restaurant included drivers, cooks, janitors, and secretaries, not just the diplomats and their aides. They were housed in a dormitory adjacent to the hotel. Most were Lithuanians, many of whom had resided in Moscow for years, but some were Russians. Indeed, one of the "characters" at the embassy was a Russian, Natasha. Anyone who visited more than once knew her or had heard about her. Natasha was the secretary to the Lithuanian counselor in Moscow, while Lithuania was in the union, and she remained in that job after independence. At that time her boss was Egidijus Bickaukas. She spoke Lithuanian and English in addition to her native Russian. When I first met this small, effusive women it occurred to me that she was a Hollywood construction, not a real person. Her laugh and frequent exclamations of surprise and mock anger filled the large outer office she occupied with a surge of energy. She moved around with blinding speed, bounding from her desk to file cabinets in quick, frenetic movements.

After the evening meal, the restaurant became a café for the embassy staff where men and women of all ranks drank Lithuanian beer, vodka, and inexpensive wine from Georgia, Moldavia, or one of the other southern republics. The room took on a decidedly different character after nightfall. It was dark and smoke-filled, and the chatter of many tongues emanating from the tables and the small bar reminded me of Rick's Place in the movie *Casablanca*. At any moment I expected to see Sydney Greenstreet and Peter Lorre enter, take a table, and share dangerous secrets in hushed tones. In this single setting, one could appreciate the diversity of the vast, mad, wondrous, multiethnic Soviet empire, because people from other republic embassies as well as a motley collection of Westerners frequented the café.

In Vilnius I had discovered that ethnic activists from all parts of the USSR frequently visited Lithuania to learn how Sajudis had managed to get away with its challenge to Moscow. Since the March 11 declaration, nationalists throughout the Soviet Union were watching the struggle between Gorbachev and Landsbergis with keen interest. Would the Lithuanians succeed in their bold challenge, or would Moscow prevail? Like the Soviet leader, they too anticipated that the prospects for their bolting from the union would be diminished or enhanced by the outcome of the struggle. Few believed that the Lithuanians would achieve real independence but each day that passed with Landsbergis still in office encouraged leaders elsewhere to think that maybe they should follow the path of the uppity Lithuanians.

Before leaving Vilnius, I had a phone conversation with Lionginas about scheduling appointments for me in Moscow. In addition to obtaining an interview with Landsbergis, I had hoped to learn about the status of negotiations between the Lithuanians and the Soviet prime minister, Nikolai Ryzhkov, as both sides attempted to resolve the dispute over the March restoration of Lithuanian independence. Even though he had to know they were phony, President Bush was using the negotiations to screen himself from critics who attacked him for not extending diplomatic recognition to Lithuania.

The criticism was pervasive and hard to deflect, because it existed within Bush's cabinet. Marlin Fitzwater, Bush's press secretary, reports that on one occasion Jack Kemp, the former NFL football star who was the secretary of housing and urban development, expressed his displeasure with the administration's failure to recognize Landsbergis's government. In a White House gathering, he told Secretary of State James Baker that he was wrong on Lithuania.

> Secretary Baker, recognizing the kind of personal confrontation better avoided, started to leave by the front door. Kemp kept talking. Baker stopped as he held the door wide open, could contain himself no longer, then turned to shout across the Oval Office, "Fuck you, Kemp!" For a second, time stood still. Everyone froze: the president behind his desk, Scowcroft next to the president, Gates near the windows, and I near the rear door. Then Kemp reacted.
>
> The Oval Office suite of furniture, two couches with end tables, a coffee table, and two wing-back chairs, was between Kemp and Baker. Baker started down the hallway, past my office, and toward the West Lobby. Kemp reacted like a quarterback who had just been victimized by unnecessary roughness. He started running through the furniture, sidestepping the couch, dodging the end table, and breaking into the clear near the door. He chased Baker down the hallway, catching him just outside my office door. They were nose to nose when General Scowcroft caught up to remind the secretary of housing and urban development that the president was ready to leave.[15]

Bush's advisers must have realized that Moscow had no interest in reaching a settlement with which both sides could live. So should have Secretary of State James Baker, who remained in close contact with his counterpart, Eduard

Shevardnadze. Gorbachev had demanded that Landsbergis renounce the declaration of independence pure and simple. There was no other outcome that was
acceptable to him. But as long as the talks were "in progress," Bush could cite
them as a rationale for standing aside as the parties worked out their differences. This ploy also could be used by Baker in his press conferences and
appearances before congressional committees.

"Mr. Krickus, how are you?" I turned from the receptionist and saw Lionginas. I had detected his presence before I actually turned toward him, for when
he approached me I smelled the cigarette smoke and essence of vodka that
surrounded his person. In the young man's defense, he had the capacity to
consume lots of alcohol without effect. Moreover, it was difficult to attend any
function in Moscow and not accept a drink to celebrate a victory, mourn a
defeat, or toast some event. Lionginas, tall, thin, and about thirty, was at first
unrecognizable to me because he was decked out in a dark suit, white shirt,
and tie and not the old ski jacket and jeans he had favored during my stay in
Lithuania early that year. I recalled how helpful he had been to all of the
international monitors and how he had conducted his tasks efficiently and
with good humor.

After the March events, Lionginas was given a job as an assistant to Bickauskas, the Lithuanian spokesman in Moscow, who told me that October that
the "Russians" were not negotiating in good faith and were uninterested in a
settlement, and that it was a farce to characterize the meetings as negotiations.[16]

Lionginas told me that the talks between Landsbergis and Ryzhkov had not
gone well. Ryzhkov had said that the Molotov-Ribbentrop Pact was illegal
and had nothing to do with Lithuania's annexation by the USSR. The Soviet
leader had said that Lithuania was part of the Soviet Union because of a
people's revolution in 1940. It was ominous news indeed that the Soviet prime
minister was rejecting Lithuania's right to restore its independence by asserting that the Lithuanian people had voluntarily joined the empire in 1940. It
indicated that Gorbachev was not interested in reaching an accommodation
with Landsbergis but would settle the crisis with the mailed fist. The question
was when.

Although I did not know it at the time, the answer to that question had
materialized in August when Saddam Hussein's forces invaded Kuwait. My
scheduled trip to Lithuania that summer had been canceled, since the Soviet
embassy in Washington was refusing to provide visas there during Moscow's
struggle with Vilnius. Therefore I had witnessed the invasion via CNN in my
hotel room in Warsaw, where I had gone to confer with several Lithuanian
contacts and to find out from them what was happening in their homeland.

The three Lithuanians I met with were all politically well placed. Alvydas

Medalinskas, one of the Sajudis initiators, was an articulate young economist who was well informed about developments in Vilnius. Bronius Genzelis, the head of the Communist Party at Vilnius University and a Sajudis leader, had become an outspoken advocate of Lithuanian independence. The third member of the group was Arvydas Matulionas, a sociologist, who once belonged to the Politburo of the Lithuanian Communist Party and was a close associate of Brazauskas. Later, I would get to know him well, and in visits to Lithuania I would always have a couple of beers with him to acquire the left-wing perspective on developments in the country.

Matulionas was Victor Nakas's cousin. While they had met, and spoke to each other without rancor, there was a wide ideological gap between them. As member of the LCP's Politburo, Matulionas had served the system that Nakas had fought from the distant shores of North America, making career and financial sacrifices to do so. In 1992, Matulionas would be accused of being a KGB agent. I recall meeting him afterward. His face was gray and drawn and he had lost a lot of weight. He denied the charges and said what troubled him most was that his mother was taking the accusations very hard. I was unable to judge whether there was merit to the accusations. Until I was presented with concrete evidence, I was inclined to assume they were untrue. Anyone who traveled abroad during the Soviet era had to report to the KGB upon returning to Lithuania. What's more, after independence, politicians on both the left and right were accused of being "secret agents" by their opponents, and since cries of wolf (more appropriately "Red wolf") were so pervasive, it was difficult to distinguish truth from fiction. What I do recall vividly was a trip I made in the summer of 1991 with Arvydas to the predominantly ethnic Russian city of Snieckus to survey the Ignalina power plant there. A sociology professor at Vilnius University, he had a team of students conducting surveys in the city to determine what the Russian population thought about becoming citizens of a Lithuanian state. I observed that the young people liked him and he related to them in an informal and congenial manner. That won him my approval.

The threesome had traveled to Warsaw by overnight train, a hot and uncomfortable journey. I thought it curious that they had bothered to make the trip to speak to an American academic, but like many other Lithuanians I met, they probably assumed I was a government agent, perhaps a CIA operative with an academic cover. After spending time with them I found their motives varied; Medalinskas was looking to snag an overseas scholarship and hoped I might help. The other two made the trip believing that I represented the U.S. government or assuming that I had influence with the diaspora, which reform

Communists were courting. Since they remained close to Brazauskas, they did not have the same opportunity to meet friendly Americans as Landsbergis's supporters did.

Our discussions were candid, and as a result of subsequent conversations I concluded that the information they were providing was accurate. Even when it was slanted I had the opportunity to make that determination, because I spoke to people whose politics ran left, center, and right—academics, journalists, government officials, and minority ethnic leaders, as well as Sajudis activists. Many Lithuanians from the diaspora made the mistake of ignoring Brazauskas and did not confer with his associates or people who supported his step-by-step approach to independence. Simultaneously, they accepted without qualification whatever was told them by people close to Landsbergis. The diverse body of Lithuanians I consulted ultimately realized that I was not involved in émigré political organizations and did not have a political agenda of my own. Also, it helped that I shared my articles with them and they could see there was no discrepancy between what I said in print and what I told them in private conversation.

After the United States had prevented the Iraqi despot from moving into Saudi Arabia through Desert Shield, President Bush announced that if Saddam did not remove his troops from Kuwait, America would remove them through Desert Storm. His pronouncement that the U.S.–led coalition would take the offensive early in 1991 caused a stir in both Moscow and Vilnius—in Moscow because Gorbachev saw an opportunity to crush the Lithuanians while the West was waging war in the Gulf, and in Vilnius because Landsbergis assumed Gorbachev was thinking in just such terms. Lithuanians reminded Westerners of an incident that had occurred a half century earlier that could be repeated in 1991. In 1940, while the world was preoccupied with Hitler's occupation of Paris, the Red Army that same day had entered Vilnius.

It was in face of the neo-Stalinists' reassertion of power in Moscow that Landsbergis was granted a meeting with President Bush on December 10, 1990. The Lithuanians desperately wanted to share their fears that Gorbachev was about to resolve his dispute with them through force. They believed that the American president had the influence to prevent the Soviets from resorting to force. But they left the meeting unsettled and anxious. Landsbergis recalls: "What I remember very well was that President Bush was surprised by my prediction of the future that we would be attacked." Bush responded that "such an action would be a loss for Gorbachev and his country" and that "he would not resort to force."[17]

Landsbergis told Bush that Gorbachev was "waging constitutional aggression" against Lithuania by asserting that it was legally bound by the Soviet constitution. But Lithuania was a sovereign country and Soviet law did not apply to it. Landsbergis asked President Bush to use his influence with Gorbachev and get a categorical commitment from him not to use force against Lithuania under any circumstances. All parties would benefit from such an outcome and the "zone of peace" in the world would grow accordingly.

Even though Landsbergis implied otherwise in a press conference at the Lithuanian legation on 16th Street afterward, Bush gave no indication that he took the Lithuanian president's warning about a Russian attack seriously. At the time, Landsbergis's grasp of English was not good, but Bush had insisted that he speak English rather than use Victor Nakas as an interpreter. Perhaps that was the reason the American president did not understand just how concerned Landsbergis was about an imminent attack.

Landsbergis never learned whether Bush made a categorical request to Gorbachev to refrain from using force against the government in Vilnius. One thing is clear: Bush was convinced he needed Gorbachev's goodwill on the eve of what Saddam Hussein had declared "the mother of all battles." If the American president pressed Gorbachev on Lithuania, he might run the risk of losing Moscow's support.

In the weeks after the meeting, Gorbachev, in an obvious effort to woo Western public opinion, attacked the Lithuanian government for violating the human rights of the Russian and Polish minorities in Lithuania. I interpreted this campaign as especially ominous, since Gorbachev knew that the charge was unfounded, that demonstrations in Lithuania by the so-called aggrieved minorities were organized by Soviet agents. And in contrast to events in the Caucasus and Central Asia, Russians were not being killed anywhere in the Baltics.

Clearly, many Russians who held important all-union posts in the Lithuanian Republic and Polish apparatchiks in areas like Salcininkai were bitter opponents of Landsbergis and Lithuanian independence. Other ordinary Russians and Poles, loyal to the Soviet state, expressed fears about their status in an independent Lithuania and voluntarily joined such demonstrations. But many others, while harboring fears, supported independence. And some Russians, like Nikolai Medvedev, and Poles, like Czeslaw Okinczyc, were Sajudis activists and had been elected deputies running under its banner. Even before the Communist regime collapsed in Warsaw, the leaders of Solidarity were encouraging the Poles in Lithuania to cooperate with Sajudis.[18]

One thing could be said with certainty: the human rights of ethnic minorities were not at risk in Lithuania and there was no need to be concerned about their physical safety. Gorbachev, by suggesting the contrary, was clearly establishing a pretext to take harsh measures against Landsbergis. He hoped to exploit Western ignorance about the Baltics and the disparaging views of Eastern Europe that had prevailed in the United States, many Americans assumed that Eastern Europeans simply could not live in peace with one another. Gorbachev also reasoned that, preoccupied with the coming clash with Hussein, neither the American president nor the American people would pay any attention to his settling of the Lithuanian question . . . once and for all.

8 BLOODY SUNDAY

Only fourteen killed and all that fuss!
— *Mikhail Gorbachev on Bloody Sunday*

By the fall of 1990, Gorbachev had turned his back on his reformist allies and moved toward the right. On October 13, he announced that the Shatalin Plan, designed by reform-minded economists to introduce a free-market economy, had been scrapped. Then in November, Gorbachev proposed a new union treaty that would maintain the Center's control over powers that the republics had coveted. Although most leaders in the republics rejected it, here was further proof that Gorbachev was bowing to pressure from the neo-Stalinists. And several days later, Marshal Dmitri T. Yazov, the Soviet defense minister, warned that the armed forces would defend military installations and soldiers threatened by ultranationalists in the "rebellious republics." Yazov said that Gorbachev had authorized him to make that statement.

The Lithuanians considered Gorbachev's courting of the reactionaries a direct threat to them, and their fears were reinforced on December 20, 1990. That day, Eduard Shevardnadze stunned the Congress of People's Deputies and the world with the announcement that he was resigning from office. "I cannot reconcile myself with what is happening in my country," he said. "The reformers have gone into hiding. A dictatorship is approaching—I tell you that with full responsibility. No one knows what this dictatorship will be like, what kind of dictator will come to power, and what order will be established."[1]

Two days later, emboldened by the resignation of the man they held responsible for the collapse of communism in Eastern Europe and the reunification of Germany within NATO, the hard-liners made bold public accusations they had previously stated in private. The KGB chairman, Vladimir A. Kryuchkov, warned, "There are attempts from abroad to exert overt and covert pressure on the Soviet Union and to impose doubtful ideas and plans to pull the country out of the difficult situation."[2] These words were especially ominous because the neo-Stalinists were now asserting that developments within the

USSR—including the Lithuanian rebellion—had emboldened foreign enemies and that the security of the Soviet Union itself was at risk.

On December 26, in a further attempt to mollify the old guard, Gorbachev appointed Gennady I. Yanayev, a heavy-drinking apparatchik, to fill the new Soviet post of vice-president. Appointments of other typical Soviet bureaucrats, such as Valentin Pavlov, who replaced Ryzhkov as prime minister, and Boris Pugo, who replaced the liberal Vadim Bakatin at the ministry of interior, signified that Gorbachev was desperate to placate the neo-Stalinists, believing they held his future in their hands.

Shevardnadze was right—the democrats in Russia were demoralized and in disarray, while the forces of reaction were confident and mobilizing to reverse the reform process. The fact that Kryuchkov and his colleagues in the party and military were openly vocalizing their contempt for perestroika and issuing warnings that the West was exploiting Gorbachev's reforms suggested that they felt quite confident about their position. It was against the backdrop of these developments that Landsbergis had sought a meeting with Bush in December 1990.

Meanwhile, the neo-Stalinists in Lithuania, who belonged to the loyalist Lithuanian Communist Party, were urging Gorbachev to crush the Lithuanian rebellion. The LCP's first secretary was Mykolas Burokevicius, a professor of Communist history who, according to Matulionas, "really believed in Marxism-Leninism, he never doubted the dogma." Burokevicius had met frequently with hard-liners in Moscow, who responded favorably to his recommendation. Another Moscow loyalist was the "night party's" second secretary, Vladislav Shev, a deputy in the Lithuanian Supreme Council who had demanded Landsbergis's resignation for his "anti-Soviet" activities.

On Monday, January 7, 1991, Burokevicius sent a memorandum to Gorbachev warning that the "separatist leadership of Lithuania" was preaching "secession of the republic from the Soviet Union and the establishment of the bourgeois system." He also mentioned "flagrant violation of political and human rights of the Soviet citizens in Lithuania." He said the rebellion was "being inspired by Western and émigré centers." He claimed that the lives of loyal Communists in Lithuania were at risk. He concluded: "It is absolutely clear that there can be no kind of political settlement of the constitutional conflict between the union and V. Landsbergis and his circle."

In light of these dangerous and subversive circumstances, ". . . the central committee of the Lithuanian Communist Party believes that at the present time there exists in the republic a really urgent need for presidential authority." The imposition of presidential rule would not spawn widespread opposition from the Lithuanian people. "Even by their supporters' assessment, the possible introduction in Lithuania of the president's rule would most likely cause no mass opposition."[3] Gorbachev would cite this document to justify the measures he would take later in the week.

That same day, Monday, January 7, Prunskiene flew to Moscow to discuss Soviet troop movements in Lithuania and to explore the resumption of negotiations, but Gorbachev would not discuss the issues. "Go back and take care of the situation and restore order so that I do not have to do it myself," he said upon her departure.[4]

Lithuania was in political crisis. Relations between Landsbergis and Prunskiene had been fractious for some time, but now they had reached a breaking point. A major area of disagreement between the two leaders involved relations with Moscow. Landsbergis resolved to remain firm and not make any concessions to Gorbachev regarding independence, while Prunskiene favored a more cautious approach. Some American commentators believed they saw evidence of bad blood between the two as early as her spring 1990 trip to Washington. The press inaccurately claimed that Prunskiene received a cool reception from President Bush during her "unofficial call" at the White House. Bush was not happy about her visit because it complicated relations with Moscow, but as was his custom, the president was gracious and friendly. Several times in their brief meeting, however, he reminded Prunskiene that the U.S. position of non-recognition was not "another Munich."

In a tour of Congress, Prunskiene had received a hearty welcome. She impressed both members of Congress and American reporters with her defense of Lithuanian independence. She had orchestrated her trip with Landsbergis, and they had remained in daily contact, discussing strategy throughout her American visit. But at home, the more radical elements in Sajudis were unhappy with her appointment to high office in the first place. Prunskiene had never been liked by the right in Lithuania, which had accused her of being too cozy with Moscow and with Gorbachev in particular, whom she reputedly had impressed. Opponents in the parliament also accused her of moving too slowly on economic reform, privatization in particular, and for being involved in corruption. Lieven claims that it was no secret that Landsbergis had approved of such attacks on his prime minister.[5]

In January 1991, the growing rancor between Prunskiene's government and the Sajudis faction in the parliament came to a head. Her government was labeled Communist by right-wing parliamentarians like Virgilijus Cepaitis, and Prunskiene herself was accused of being too accommodating toward Moscow. She, in turn, proclaimed that the parliament had no business interfering in her legitimate duties. She was outraged, then, when on December 30, 1990, the Supreme Council resolved that the price hikes she had ordered were not to be implemented. While economic logic was on her side—the government's budget deficit was soaring—political logic was on the side of her adversaries. Moscow would cite the public outcry against lifting price supports as further evidence that conditions were out of control in Lithuania and that Gorbachev had to resort to presidential rule to achieve order there.

On Tuesday, January 8, leaders in Edinstvo and the "night party" organized a demonstration to protest the proposed price hikes. An estimated five to seven thousand pro-Soviet demonstrators marched toward parliament, and some of the throng crashed through the main door of the building. After a brief struggle with the young guards in the building's foyer, they were forced back out into the square when the guards turned fire hoses on them. The demonstrators, some of whom Landsbergis claimed were Soviet soldiers in civilian garb, had demanded his resignation and the parliament's dissolution. By employing Russian "workers" throughout this fateful week, the Soviet authorities hoped to convey the fiction that the massacre that would occur on Sunday the 13th had started as a mass-based revolt against Landsbergis's "authoritarian rule."

In turn, Landsbergis and his supporters mobilized Lithuanian patriots who, through nonviolent tactics, would nullify efforts to crush their independence movement. Landsbergis would be criticized for risking the lives of these defenseless people, but they heeded his call for assistance and were prepared to risk their lives because they no longer could tolerate Soviet despotism. Besides, Landsbergis had no other weapon in his arsenal.

After meeting with a delegation of demonstrators, the Lithuanian Supreme Council immediately canceled the prime minister's price increase. This is what the council had decided to do in the first place; it was not caving in to Soviet pressure. Some conservatives saw Prunskiene's action as an overt attempt to provoke a crisis in Lithuania and thereby give Gorbachev the pretext he needed to intervene. Upon returning from a trip to Moscow, Prunskiene resigned, and later, after she went abroad and accused Landsbergis of acting like a fascist, her accusers cited her unseemly behavior as evidence that their charge was sound.

For Landsbergis, the January 8 incident was a dangerous provocation. Clearly it was designed by Moscow with the expectation that the parliament guards would resort to force against the demonstrators. The day before, additional Soviet troops arrived in Vilnius, and the clash at the parliament would provide them with the pretext to declare a state of national emergency. Gorbachev then would place Lithuania under his rule, "presidential rule," because the government in Vilnius had "lost control of the situation." On Monday, Landsbergis questioned "the strange coincidence between the threats of the Soviet military and such a sharp price rise."[6] The next evening he addressed the nation over radio and urged people to gather in Independence Square as a demonstration of support for their embattled government.

On Wednesday, January 9, Edinstvo conducted a late-afternoon protest demonstration at the Mazvydas library, which is located next to parliament. Armored personnel carriers (APCs) entered Independence Square in what was a show of support for the Edinstvo group. According to Landsbergis, "Young men were in the crowd from well-trained KGB units, and they tried to provoke Russian workers" to storm the parliament building in the expectation that the guards might lose their composure and fire upon them.[7] A much larger crowd of pro-government Lithuanians prevented them from achieving that objective. They heeded Landsbergis's plea to avoid violence, and they blunted the move on the parliament peacefully by dint of their sheer numbers. The Russian Orthodox Archbishop Khrisostom called for calm, and after the provocation failed, the pro-Soviet demonstrators left the square and the APCs roared away from the area without incident.

On Thursday, January 10, Dr. Albertas Simenas, a meek mathematician with no government experience, replaced Prunskiene. Opponents accused Landsbergis of violating constitutional procedures and complained that Simenas had no political experience. But Landsbergis, his nation's independence in imminent jeopardy, ignored his critics. If a new prime minister was not immediately appointed, Moscow would exploit the power vacuum to justify intervention. Indeed, in a gesture reminiscent of the 1940 Soviet occupation of Lithuania, Gorbachev had sent a telegram to the Lithuanian authorities and warned them not "to restore the bourgeois order."[8]

That same day, January 10, the Soviet authorities tightened the noose around Vilnius. According to Senn, the airport was declared closed by a strike of the Russian workers there. Members of the government staging their regular television discussion show chose not to go to the television studio but rather to originate their broadcast from the safety of the parliament building." That night, "an estimated 30 Soviet tanks and 1,000 paratroopers roamed through the city, passing by the Press House, where most of the central newspapers were published, and the television tower. As news of the troop movement spread, Lithuanians hurried to both sites, but no conflict occurred."[9]

But the next day, Friday the 11th, the first blood would be spilled. In a replay of earlier tactics, "Russian workers" operating under Edinstvo conducted demonstrations in strategic parts of the city. But once again, the threat to parliament was blunted by a large crowd of Lithuanians who prevented the Edinstvo demonstrators from moving upon it. Kazimeras Motieka, a lawyer and Sajudis leader, then urged some of the pro-government supporters to proceed to the Press House to protect it instead.[10]

Lithuanian TV (in film that was sent to the United States) documented what happened next. Large numbers of Lithuanians had gathered at the Press House, the high-rise building that was home for many of the country's newspapers and journals. A cross section of people, men and women, young and old, had congregated there as a show of solidarity. At times they greeted the heavily armed troops supported by tanks with patriotic songs. On other occasions they argued with the young men and their officers, demanding that they leave the area. Coffee was distributed to the people who had gathered there in a display of support for their country's independence. At one point the camera settled on a young woman who, with woolen gloves to her tear-stained face, observed the mayhem with alarm.

Shouts of protest erupted when the troops stormed the building, broke the glass doors, and entered and occupied it. Following the practice of peaceful resistance, one young man in the building doused a Soviet colonel with water, and the colonel raked the building with his Kalashnikov. The TV cameras then showed the young man being led from the building to an ambulance, blood streaming from his face, but he had only suffered a flesh wound. The colonel, moving from the crowd, then mounted his tank as he was pelted with demands to explain why he had fired upon the youngster. The TV cameramen also showed the remains of a truck that had been struck by a tank, and later showed the vehicle's injured driver. Given the fact that its cab was badly crushed, it was miraculous that he survived with only minor injuries.

No one was killed in the Press House incident, but the show of force was deemed the beginning of what everyone assumed would be a far more brutal display of muscle that weekend. The Soviet authorities also learned something from the incident: before they took decisive measures to crush the rebellion, the Lithuanians had to be denied access to their most powerful weapon—television. Lithuanian TV coverage of the incident had reached audiences outside the country. This time the Soviet authorities would secure control of the city's TV station and tower before launching the attack upon the parliament building.

Gorbachev did not appreciate the degree to which his policy of glasnost had empowered the Lithuanians and other opponents of the Soviet system. In allowing Soviet journalists to adopt standards of openness approaching—if not reaching—those practiced in the democracies, Gorbachev was taking a great risk. Preoccupied with his own problems, he, like other Kremlin leaders, did not observe the Western media on a consistent basis. The Soviet elite, who lived and worked in the closed, parochial world of the CPSU, had no means to measure just how powerful TV had become . . . anywhere.

They appreciated the potential of TV as a propaganda tool, and Gorbachev's opponents in the Kremlin had opposed glasnost for that reason. But they, along with Gorbachev, remained naive about its truly revolutionary potential. Nor did they realize that in democracies, leaders could not ignore public pressure generated by TV coverage of events. Gorbachev had adroitly manipulated the Western press, but even he did not realize the extent to which the U.S. press operated independently of official Washington. He did not understand either that once TV became fixed on a story and provided almost nightly coverage of it, public support for or against a particular issue could obtain proportions that even the American president could not ignore.

Moreover, given their ability to manage the flow of information in their own society, the Soviet elite failed to appreciate that once their people were exposed to objective reporting on a relatively consistent basis, the Kremlin could not resort to old practices of censorship and distortion when the news was "bad." Glasnost had helped peel away the tissue of lies and distortions that had been a hallmark of the Soviet media, and the public could not be induced to accept the reimposition of the old ways. Moreover, Soviet journalists, who had the opportunity to operate like their peers in democratic societies, henceforth could not be as easily intimidated as they had been in the past. Operating like a journalist in a free and open environment was intoxicating, and the young men and women who experienced this rush became addicted. Finally, gutsy journalists could exploit the fissures in the upper reaches of the party to provide objective reporting.

Television was a vital weapon for the Lithuanian rebels, and so were the Western media. If aroused, American journalists could put unrelenting pressure on Bush to use his influence with Gorbachev to spare the Lithuanians the fate of the Azeris in 1989 and the Georgians in 1990. Early in January 1991, Victor Nakas, who was in daily contact with Vilnius, had phoned me to say that troops were on the move throughout Lithuania and had begun to occupy buildings and installations as part of an obvious campaign against the Landsbergis government. Something truly ominous was in the offing, and I had decided to add my small voice to those people in the United States who were warning that a tragedy was about to take place in the Baltics. On January 10, Gorbachev had announced that "people are demanding" the Kremlin impose its rule over the breakaway government in Vilnius.[11]

On Friday, January 11, I wrote an op-ed piece for the *Christian Science Monitor,* hoping it might arouse influential syndicated columnists who had become articulate and powerful proponents of the Lithuanian cause. Perhaps they could force Bush to contact Gorbachev directly and urge him to scrap his plans to oppress the Lithuanians.

"What should the United States do about Lithuania?" The question was rekindled when President Bush met with Vytautas Landsbergis last month but takes on a new urgency as Moscow sends paratroopers to Lithuania and other republics to round up draft resisters. At this writing, Soviet troops and tanks have surrounded the main TV station in Vilnius—an action that could be a precursor to a coup. Such events put the February summit in Moscow at risk. Significant suppression of the Balts by Gorbachev will gravely damage U.S.–Soviet relations.

The White House revealed little about the Bush-Landsbergis talks but the meeting sent an important message to Gorbachev: "We need your support for American Persian Gulf policies and want your reforms to succeed, but don't take the hard measures some Soviet hard-liners have been advocating in your press."

Mr. Landsbergis was more forthcoming in a press conference at Lithuania's Washington legation. The soft-spoken Lithuanian said yes, Moscow had threatened to cut off food, energy, and raw materials if the Lithuanians did not sign a new economic agreement. "The specific demand made on us was that we remain in the central planning, finance, and taxation system and . . . give over to the Soviet authorities the hard currency that we earn." He added that the Soviets hoped that "General Winter" would force the Lithuanians to bow to Moscow's demands. "But we are convinced that we are going to fend off the attack and emerge victorious."

Landsbergis said that when he requested political protections against oppressive Soviet policies, Bush responded favorably. But on reconciliation between Moscow and Vilnius, Bush alluded to a solution favored by Gorbachev, a referendum. Lithuania has rejected a referendum for two reasons. First, with large Russian populations, neither Latvia nor Estonia could achieve the two-thirds yes vote needed to bolt from the USSR. Secondly, the very acceptance of a referendum suggests that the Baltic republics have been legally annexed by the USSR. Instead, the former musicologist suggested that the "four plus two" talks that led to German reunification be modified for the Baltic crisis. His formula included: four; the U.S., USSR, Britain, and France, plus three; the Baltic countries. Bush did not pick up on the idea, reasoning, no doubt, that Gorbachev would never tolerate this interference in domestic Soviet affairs.

But like the talks that led to German reunification, the "four plus three" talks are an international matter, part of World War II. As long as the Molotov-Ribbentrop Pact, justifying Stalin's subjugation of the Baltic countries, remains intact, the last act of the great drama remains to be played. And like Shakespeare's *Hamlet,* ghosts are critical to the plot. In this case, they are Adolph Hitler and Joseph Stalin, who signed Lithuania's death warrant in 1939.

Unfortunately, Gorbachev has not exorcised Stalin's ghost from the Kremlin's halls. In October discussions with Lithuanian authorities, Soviet Prime Minister Nikolai Ryzhkov said a "people's revolution," and not the infamous pact, was the justification for Lithuania's annexation.

For those who wish Gorbachev well on democratic reform, Ryzhkov's Stalinist apologia is cause for concern. Red Army tanks and not a free election forced the Lithuanians into the Soviet empire. As Zbigniew Brzezinski, former U.S. national security adviser, has observed, until Gorbachev acknowledges the Balts' right of national self-determination, the fate of democracy in the USSR is sealed.

Indeed, oppressive policies may provide a short-term solution for Gorbachev. The Balts' refusal to serve in the Red Army rests on a 1949 Geneva ruling that citizens of an occupied country are not required to serve in the army of the invading forces. Gorbachev's refusal to recognize international law will preclude peaceful long-term solutions to his economic, political, and nationalities problems. And a worsening situation in the USSR could foster instability throughout Europe and sabotage U.S.–Soviet relations. Against this backdrop, the "four plus three" formula makes sense. There is no justification for the Baltics' incorporation into the USSR, and while the Big Four powers may deem their restoration of independence an inconvenience, it is legally and morally justified and must be addressed, not ignored.

Desperate, Landsbergis had tried to reach Gorbachev on several occasions, but the Soviet leader had refused to come to the phone and speak with him. At one point, an aide said that Gorbachev was sleeping. Clearly, if Gorbachev had wanted to prevent bloodshed he would have taken Landsbergis's call. He had reason to believe that under mounting pressure, Landsbergis might make concessions. But Gorbachev had decided to resolve the Lithuanian question by destroying the popular front that had precipitated like-minded movements throughout the USSR. Besides, there was reason to believe that Landsbergis and his supporters could be vanquished without too much bloodshed, perhaps none at all. As Arvydas Matulionas would tell me later, "The Moscow loyalists in the Lithuanian Communist Party had convinced Gorbachev that with a show of force, the Lithuanian independence movement would disintegrate."[12] This is precisely what Burokevicius had stated in his January 7 memo to Gorbachev.

Senn reports that after the Friday attack on the Press House, the Lithuanian authorities concluded that the worst might be over as "there were no longer public demonstrations against the Lithuanian government."[13] Also, while an estimated five thousand people had surrounded the TV tower on Friday to protect it from being occupied by Soviet troops, the feared confrontation did not take place. Tanks approached the area but reversed their course and did not confront the Lithuanians who were safeguarding it.

But then Juozas Jermalavicius, the pro-Soviet Lithuanian Communist Party leader who was chief of ideology, announced that a Committee for the Salvation of Lithuania had been established. Later that Friday evening, *Vremya,* the Soviet news broadcast from Moscow, "depicted the Committee for the Salvation of Lithuania as protecting the rights of the citizenry; and it reported that workers at the Ignalina Atomic Energy plant had threatened to go out on strike on January 15 if the Lithuanian parliament did not dissolve itself."[14] Meanwhile, Soviet troops had halted all trains at the Vilnius station and refused to permit them to continue on their journey. Elsewhere troops were conducting searches for arms and occupying military installations that were being used by the Lithuanian home guard.

Late Saturday morning, January 12, radio listeners were shocked to hear President Bush's press secretary, Marlin Fitzwater, state that no force had been used in Lithuania. They deemed this ominous, for it reinforced fears that Bush, relying upon Gorbachev's support for the imminent attack in the Persian Gulf, would not use his influence with the Soviet leader to prevent Moscow from crushing the independence movement.

Early in the afternoon, Brazauskas issued a statement proclaiming his support for Lithuanian independence and denounced the Soviet army's actions as "inhuman, antihuman."[15] News that Yeltsin had chided Gorbachev for using force in the Baltics was also gratefully received by the Lithuanians. The faint hope that they might not be subjected to further violence was bolstered by reports that the USSR's federation council had announced it favored a political solution to the crisis in Lithuania and was sending a fact-finding team to Vilnius for that purpose.

Nonetheless, on Saturday evening, Landsbergis appealed to the Lithuanian people to gather at the parliament and the Vilnius TV tower to protect these vital Lithuanian institutions from Soviet forces that were advancing toward them. Senn writes, "At 11:00 P.M. that night, the National Salvation Committee announced that it was taking power. An hour later, paratroops with armored vehicles left the main military base in Vilnius and made their way to the TV station and tower."[16]

The wishes of Mykolas Burokevicius and other Old Bolsheviks in the "night party" had been satisfied, but the only person publicly associated with the committee was Juozas Jermalavicius, the pro-Moscow LCP's ideological chief. It was his voice that would be heard declaring a state of emergency that evening by the crowd that had gathered to protect the TV tower. Many young people attending Saturday-night parties would leave the festivities and go to the TV tower. Upon their arrival, they found patriots young and old surrounding it, prepared to give their lives for freedom. A pivotal question that preoccupied Landsbergis and supporters in the parliament was whether or not the crowds at the tower and in the square would stand fast and not run once they were fired upon. If they ran, as Burokevicius and Jermalavicius assumed they would, an independent Lithuania was doomed.

About 1:30 A.M. on Sunday, January 13, Soviet paratroopers and members of the KGB Alpha unit attacked the tower, with the expectation that the crowds would flee in the face of small-arms fire and body-crushing tanks. They were operating under the command of General Valentin Varennikov, the commander of the Soviet ground forces. After the Lithuanians lost their ability to send TV images to the world community depicting their plight, a similar move would be made against the parliament, where Landsbergis and the deputies had gathered to resist the onslaught. But the people who had heard Landsbergis's appeal and congregated at the TV tower in a demonstration of solidarity and support for Lithuanian independence stood ready to die for their country—and they did not run.

At the TV tower, the KGB Alpha unit—the shock force supported by paratroopers from Russia—struck the demonstrators with their rifle butts, fired into their midst with live ammunition, and badly burned several of them with blank shells from their tank cannons. TV footage showed one man atop a bus being struck by a bullet and slumping to his knees and then a moment later several men trying to hold back a tank that had crushed a young women under its treads. All the while a tall figure in a leather trench coat walked among the killers, obviously one of the commanders of the operation. From the bowels of a tank the recorded voice of Jermalavicius could be heard in spite of the roar of tank engines, small-arms fire, screams, and voices singing in defiance. The civilians responded to demands that they disperse with shouts of "Lithuania" and taunted their attackers with the word "fascists." They were clubbed and shot . . . but they did not run.

The Lithuanian defenders were unarmed and did not respond in a violent manner but stood their ground in a heroic display of civil disobedience. They had restricted themselves to nonviolent resistance for almost a week, and their refusal to strike back at their tormentors defied human nature, but this weapon of the defenseless ultimately proved to be the more powerful one.

Several months after Bloody Sunday, in May testimony in Washington before the Conference on Security and Cooperation in Europe, President Landsbergis would share with the audience and officials an eyewitness account of the incident that led to the crushing of a young woman (Loreta Asanaviciute) by a tank. Algirdas Sukys, a resident of Vilnius, reported:

> We held hands as we stood in front of a huge moving tank which crawled by quite close to us. Hardly had I managed to pull my leg away from its treads when on the left, almost beside me, I heard a scream. Turning, I saw a woman or girl lying on her back (in the shade of the tank it was hard to see her face distinctly, but I noticed she had a light-colored kerchief or a cap on her head, and was wearing a light-colored scarf and a dark or gray coat). Her legs were under the treads of the tank. Men tried to push the tank back, to pull the victim out, but they could not budge such a heavy object (it was a heavy tank, not an armored personnel carrier). I began to hit the top of the tank with my fists, screaming in Russian that there was a woman under the tank. Then, cursing furiously, a soldier jumped up to me, gave me a poke in the back, kicked me in the stomach and pushed me from the tank. The tank drove backwards, but before moving forward, it pulled back a bit and ran over the woman once more. Several men took the injured woman and carried her off. At the same time on the right side shots were heard. One soldier wearing a helmet shot at a man who fell down and who was also taken away from the tower into the darkness. A young, well-built man in a soldier's uniform with medals on his chest, standing among us, jumped in front of the tank and fell down, shouting. "What are you doing? You're shooting at your own people! I served together with you in the army. Even in Afghanistan we didn't act like this. Crush me, too!" A soldier ran up to him. I don't think he managed to kick the man lying on the ground because our men pulled him to where we were. He stood and cried. Big tears were rolling down his face. We joined our hands and began to chant, "Lithuania! Lithuania! Lithuania will be free!"[17]

Thirteen Lithuanians and one KGB officer were killed that night, and 608 people sought medical attention in hospitals to treat wounds caused by gunshots, blunt instruments, and burns from blank tank rounds. Later, Gorbachev exclaimed to Brazauskas, "Only fourteen killed and all that fuss!"[18]

Meanwhile, the Lithuanians who had gathered to protect the parliament were prepared to defend their free and independent government. "Some former Red Army officers were monitoring the communications between the tank commanders and their superiors when they heard the order 'advance on the parliament,'" said Rita Dapkus, a thirty-year-old women who had left her home in Chicago in the late 1980s to join the Lithuanian drive for independence. "President Landsbergis had announced that all women in the building should leave. He also said that all deputies who chose to could leave as well. Most stayed."[19]

Included among the brave occupants of the parliament were young staffers, some of whom would not leave the building for weeks. Unlike Landsbergis and some of the military defenders who would be praised and given medals afterward, they would not be publicly recognized for their courageous behavior. They quietly but resolutely performed their duties as they anticipated the attack. One was Loreta Musanya, who worked as an English interpreter/translator for the parliamentarians and Landsbergis. She was a product of a Lithuanian-Polish marriage and had been raised in a "Red" area of Vilnius where both young and old believed in communism. "I never heard anything about the 1950s resistance until I attended the university. People in my neighborhood never spoke against the Soviet system," she said. Later, as a result of her desire to learn about the outside world, she became a pen pal with an African student—a Marxist-Leninist—who was studying in Moscow. She would eventually meet and marry him and return to Zambia with him. They had a child, but the marriage failed and she returned to Lithuania.

After Sajudis's formation, she became enthralled with the idea of Lithuanian independence and eagerly accepted the offer of employment in parliament as an interpreter/translator after the March 1990 victory. She remained in the parliament throughout the weekend. "I can't explain it, but I was not afraid even when we all thought the tanks would come. What I remember most vividly is reports we heard that Jermalavicius was driving through the streets announcing that Soviet power had returned. I said no way!"[20]

Loreta's friend Ona Volungeviciute, who had worked with Sajudis from the outset, also remained at her post in the parliament throughout the weekend and for days later. Her office had an open phone line to Moscow, and at one point when the Voice of America announced that no one had been killed in Vilnius, staffers called the U.S. embassy and informed them otherwise. Soon VOA reported deaths had occurred, and the realization that the world was watching developments in Vilnius uplifted their spirits. During the weekend the parliament maintained an open line with Romas Sakadolskis in Washington. The staffers kept Romas informed of events on a constant basis. He also remained in contact with ham radio operators in the United States who relayed messages from their Lithuanian counterparts to Washington.

Ona also indicated that for the most part she was not afraid when she remained at her desk in the parliament in the early morning hours of January 13. She recalls most vividly several scenes that occurred after the attack on the TV tower. "I recall Landsbergis, accompanied by a priest, pledging young defenders to protect their homeland." She remembers several of them asking her to join them in a toast before they manned their defensive positions. "I also recall calling my mother and sister to tell them that I was all right."

But the moment she recalls with greatest dread was when Landsbergis announced that an attack was imminent and anyone in the building and the square who wished to leave could do so. At that point, she reached a decision. She had been watching a woman in the crowd surrounding the parliament. "I guess I noticed her because she was wearing a bright plaid scarf." Ona decided that if this woman left, she would too. "But the women remained in place and I decided to stay as well."[21]

The men and women who heeded Landsbergis's call to gather at Independence Square knew about the slaughter that had occurred early that morning at the TV tower, which was situated a couple of kilometers from the parliament. It was a tourist attraction visited by Lithuanians from all parts of the country. A revolving restaurant was perched on the top of the tower, as on the Space Needle in Seattle. As it slowly moved, diners had a panoramic view of the city and its environs.

Everyone knew that Landsbergis and the parliament were Moscow's primary target, so the Lithuanians who congregated at the heart of their nation's government arrived with the expectation that they would be subjected to a bloody attack. Yet many would stay for days to deter the assault, and by dint of raw courage and sheer determination they succeeded in preventing it. Frequently, entire families were involved in the "freedom vigil." For example, while Vytautas Baukas remained at home with his two children, his wife, Rasa, joined the defenders at the square, where old farm implements, blocks of concrete, and industrial equipment were placed to blunt the expected tank attack. After Rasa served her eight-hour shift, Vytautas would take her place at the square while she cared for the children.[22]

A ragtag defense force had made preparations for the deadly attack with no expectation of success. But tanks approaching the square would be subject to attacks from the high-rise apartments on Gedimino and other adjacent streets. Armed with Molotov cocktails, the Lithuanians hoped to destroy armored vehicles as they advanced toward parliament. But there was no question about the outcome. If an all-out attack were launched, the defenders were doomed.

Landsbergis and his advisers had decided to greet an assault with passive resistance. If the troops, though unprovoked, began to kill the building's inhabitants, the defenders would fight back: not to seek retribution but rather to send a message to the world that the Lithuanians in 1991 did not voluntarily surrender their independence as Ryzhkov claimed they did in 1940.

Landsbergis said that on the days leading up to Bloody Sunday, "some people in parliament suggested that I leave the country with my family." He refused to identify these persons and said they "were not necessarily working in behalf of Moscow." Of course, Gorbachev would have achieved a victory if the president had followed their advice.[23] With Landsbergis out of the picture, the Lithuanian drive for independence would have disintegrated. He had become the person with whom the Lithuanian people and most steadfast rebels had identified as the leader of their bold drive for independence. With his departure, a replacement would have been found, but organized popular support for continued resistance would have collapsed. There would have been resistance, to be sure, but without leadership it would have fizzled.

But this mild-mannered man, who had accepted Soviet subjugation of his country without protest most of his life, refused to surrender and urged his people to stand fast in the face of overwhelming odds. Lowry Wyman, a Harvard lawyer, reported, "I was amazed by Landsbergis's composure. His calm steadfastness had a positive tranquilizing effect upon the Lithuanian population. Landsbergis did not want his people to resort to violence and give the Soviets the pretext to slaughter them."[24] She was on the scene that weekend with her husband, Barnabas. Both had been providing legal expertise to the Lithuanian government as it crafted a new post-Soviet constitution.

Following the vigil on January 11, 1991, when crowds had gathered outside the high-rise building that housed many of Vilnius's newspapers and journals, the people surrounding the parliament sang patriotic and religious songs as acts of solidarity and defiance. "The singing was beautiful, haunting, and had a powerful emotional impact upon everyone at the square," Barnabas Wyman noted. Henceforth, Lithuanians would speak of their "singing revolution."

"After hearing the news that the tanks were advancing on the parliament, I thought, 'Rita, this is going to be the last day of your life,'" said Rita Dapkus, the parliament's press secretary, in an interview a year after Bloody Sunday. Her parents were part of the DP migration, she too had attended "Saturday school," and she also had belonged to the community of young Lithuanian-Americans who dreamed of returning to a free Lithuania.

Rita, who would eventually open the first American-style restaurant in Vilnius, concluded:

> I decided to remain in the building because I had committed myself to Lithuanian independence and I had to see events through, no matter what the consequences. But then the men monitoring the tanks heard a Russian commander announce that thousands of people had surrounded the parliament and a move against it would result in as many casualties. Soon someone gave them the order to turn around. The siege was over![25]

But at the time, no one was certain of that fact. Landsbergis and his associates believed that the Soviet authorities behind Bloody Sunday might decide to forget about casualties and foreign reaction and storm parliament. That fear diminished after Major General Vladimir N. Uskhochik, the commandant of Soviet troops in Vilnius, met with a delegation of Lithuanian leaders led by Motieka. Both sides agreed that if the crowd in Parliament Square left the area, the Soviet troops would return to their bases and not attack the parliament building.

It was to avoid this awful prospect that the Lithuanian-American community and its supporters in the United States mobilized to rally Congress and public opinion in an open show of support for the brave Lithuanians.

On Sunday morning, January 13, I received a call from CNN bookers in Washington asking me to come to their D.C. station, which is close to Union Station. They had received film from Lithuania depicting a massacre in Vilnius. Would I comment upon the footage? I said I would leave at once for the studio. In my drive to the station, I thought about the men and women I had come to know personally since the March 1990 declaration. What could I possibly say that would have an impact upon their fate?

While waiting to comment upon the film at the studio, I saw President Bush walking from his helicopter to the White House. His press aides said that the Bushes had returned to Washington because the first lady, Barbara Bush, had injured her ankle, but it was obvious the president had returned to deal with the criticism he knew would be aimed in his direction. What would he say about the massacre in Vilnius? What would the American response be?

When the film rolled, CNN viewers saw Soviet troops firing live rounds into the crowd and tanks rolling over demonstrators, who had vainly sought to stop them with their bodies. Like everyone else who was watching, I was appalled by the brutality of the armed thugs but also inspired by the demonstrators, who, although defenseless, refused to run as people around them were being killed and maimed. The assault and Landsbergis's call for Lithuanian patriots to fill the streets in displays of support for their country's survival had drawn people of all ages to the scene. Virginija Kuklyte, a tenth-grader who witnessed the massacre, later revealed what a schoolmate had exclaimed as the attack began: "It is a good thing that I went to confession yesterday!"[26]

When asked by the CNN interviewer what my reaction was to the brutal footage, I said that it was curious that we were said to be fighting to save democracy in Kuwait, which in fact was run by a feudal despot, when a real democracy was at risk in the Baltics.

In the weeks following Bloody Sunday, replays of the slaughter on CNN and the networks reached millions of viewers around the world. The most gruesome frames were excluded from American television, such as the dying Loreta Asanaviciute, but the viewers could see the handiwork of Gorbachev's executioners firsthand. As a result, a growing number of Americans rallied to the Lithuanian cause and urged their representatives in Congress to support the embattled government in Vilnius.

In anticipation of a public outcry, the State Department had formed the Baltic Workshop Group on January 12. It received "countless calls from people throughout the country," proclaiming their support for the Lithuanians and demanding that the U.S. government help them. Paul Goble was part of the group and recalls: "The response was staggering and overwhelmingly favorable, and from ordinary Americans, not only those of Baltic heritage. I remember a call from a man in Richmond, Virginia, who said that he was a Republican and if President Bush did not stand up for the Balts, he would never vote Republican again."[27]

Members of Congress also received declarations of support for the Lithuanians. Through television, the legislators and their constituents shared a compelling collective experience. A vast audience of Americans witnessed the horrible scenes from Vilnius, and members of both parties in the Senate and House would express outrage against those in Moscow responsible for the horrors in Lithuania.

The images, which reached foreign audiences, told a story of amazing courage and incredible acts of heroism. While soldiers were firing into their midst, the demonstrators answered their tormentors in song, a traditional instrument of Lithuanian protest. One can surmise that millions of TV viewers who witnessed this scene from around the world were both awestruck and inspired by this gripping display of bravery. During the Bloody Sunday weekend, great courage was displayed in other parts of the city. For example, the TV station in Vilnius (located separately from the TV tower), which also housed radio studios, was stormed by Soviet troops. As they forced their way through the building indiscriminately firing their weapons, some of the broadcasters locked themselves in their radio booths and described the attack to their listening audience. They surrendered their soundproof cubicles only when ordered at gunpoint to do so or lose their lives. Afterward, the journalists published a pamphlet with pictures and text depicting the assault. They expressed outrage that the attackers needlessly trashed the building even after it was surrendered to them. Several said the troops' barbaric behavior just made them more determined to fight on whatever the consequences.[28]

As TV and radio reports of resistance reached audiences throughout Lithuania, people from all parts of the country traveled—by car, bus, and train—to their nation's capital in a bold display of support for their independent government. Without the presence of TV cameras that provided vivid, real-time shots of their countrymen courageously resisting Soviet oppression, the will to resist probably would have eroded. At the same time, it was almost certain that the authorities in Moscow would have launched a final lethal assault on parliament if they had not feared that a global TV audience would witness the slaughter.

Another deterrent was the presence of many Western journalists who were in Vilnius. Why Soviet authorities mounted the January 13 coup while they remained there was perplexing. Some Lithuanians believe the reason was that Gorbachev accepted the argument of the loyalists in the "night party" that Landsbergis would surrender his position by a mere show of force. Another view was that the Lithuanian Communists Burokevicius and Jermalavicius convinced themselves that they indeed were operating in a legal fashion and had no reason to apologize to the international community for their actions. A third view was that the Soviet authorities moved, in spite of an unfavorable international response, because they reasoned that the international press, preoccupied with the Gulf War, would pay only brief attention to the coup in Vilnius. But after the massacre was flashed before the world via TV, they lost their nerve.

The most plausible explanation was that Gorbachev and other members of the Kremlin hierarchy were badly divided among themselves. Victims of confusion, they were emotionally stricken by knowledge that the situation had gotten out of hand, and they had no simple cost-free solution to the problem. Consequently, they lurched from one position to another, knowing they had to act but without confidence that any action would work. In the final analysis, and out of desperation, they hoped Burokevicius and Jermalavicius's scenario would materialize.

Outside of Lithuania, there were two people especially upset about television's coverage of Bloody Sunday—Mikhail Gorbachev and George Bush.

Both men had been skillful practitioners of television politics and were acutely aware of the medium's power. Gorbachev, unlike his predecessors, was comfortable before Western TV cameras and was confident that he had the upperhand in the struggle between the TV producers and himself. It was via TV that the image of Gorby I had become deeply imprinted in the minds of Brits, Germans, and Americans who had urged their leaders to work with him. But as long as the struggle between Moscow and Vilnius was the subject of Western TV, Gorbachev's image was badly tarnished. In the minds of Americans, the contest was "unfair" and conjured up the image of a schoolyard bully beating up the frail little kid who spent all of his free hours practicing the piano. Over the next several weeks as the full impact of Bloody Sunday penetrated the consciousness of Western viewers, the outlines of a new image, Gorby II, began to take form.

Gorbachev contended that the local garrison commander in Lithuania had ordered the use of force, according to Hedrick Smith, but that commander, Major General Vladimir N. Uskhochik, "had told reporters that he derived his authority from Gorbachev and served only the president."[29]

Gorbachev realized that Bush could manipulate such malignant coverage to force concessions upon him. But worse yet, the TV coverage jeopardized what Gorbachev had deemed his ace in the hole as he sought to restructure Soviet society: massive infusions of Western loans and technological transfers. Once again the Lithuanians were preventing him from achieving that objective. For example, the European Economic Community withdrew its pledge to provide the USSR with a $1 billion food-aid package.[30] Gorbachev also received a rebuff from the Americans. Before the confrontation with Landsbergis, he had anticipated the opportunity to address a joint gathering of the U.S. Congress, at which he would ask for American aid. He was sure that he could charm the legislators and their constituents. The TV appearances he had made in the West had always worked in his behalf. But after Bloody Sunday, the White House balked. Bush's advisers feared supporters of Lithuania would make a great outcry of protest. The event would be a disaster when members of Congress and the public noted the irony that Gorbachev was asking American help to build an open society when he was closing the door on democracy in Lithuania.[31]

Gorbachev was naive to think that Western support would be massive in the first place and even more naive to believe that if provided it would revitalize an economic system that was unredeemable. The final irony is that Gorbachev had resorted to force in Vilnius to remove Landsbergis and his supporters from the TV screen so the image of Gorby I could be reaffirmed.

Instead, coverage of Bloody Sunday brought into full and sharp focus the image of Gorby II, the bad Gorby.

In Washington, George Bush was appalled as he watched the video depictions of Bloody Sunday. During the summer 1988 campaign against Michael Dukakis, he had overcome a massive deficit in the polls to defeat his opponent through the skillful manipulation of TV. After he took office, the Bush White House was occupied by media spindoctors who understood that by controlling TV coverage of its activities, the administration could look confidently toward a second term in office four years hence.

When Saddam Hussein invaded Kuwait in August 1990, Bush and his advisers concluded that the crisis in the Persian Gulf gave them an opportunity to ensure his reelection. But they feared the "Baltic crisis" could prevent them from securing Gorbachev's support for the American-led coalition which in the winter of 1990–1991 was poised to destroy Iraq's forces. Beschloss and Talbott write that before Bloody Sunday, ". . . Scowcroft, confided to Bush and Baker that he could all too easily imagine the Baltic crisis 'ripping the Soviets out of the coalition.'"[32] When the news reached the White House early Sunday, Bush feared that this awful scenario might materialize.

His fears were not altogether unfounded. It was unlike the 1940 Soviet occupation of Lithuania, for television in 1991 carried the brutal display of force in Vilnius to viewers worldwide hours after the slaughter occurred. And since the March 1990 restoration of independence, millions of Americans knew something about Lithuania and even could locate it on a map. Indeed, most thoughtful Americans knew who Vytautas Landsbergis was, and via TV many had seen Kazimiera Prunskiene impress members of Congress in her spring 1990 trip to Washington. Millions of Americans who had deemed Gorbachev a hero were perplexed as they followed his campaign to crush the Lithuanian independence movement after March 1990. They also watched in disbelief and admiration as the mild-mannered musicologist, who was the subject of unstinting pressure, refused to cry uncle. As the drama was highlighted by new acts in the confrontation between David and Goliath, TV and radio talk shows, syndicated columns, political cartoons, and op-ed pieces provided support for Landsbergis and his brave people.

At this point we can only speculate about the White House's reaction to such news coverage. Clearly, it dismayed Bush and his advisers that influential syndicated columnists like Evans and Novak, William Safire, and Abe Rosenthal continued to write articles attacking the administration for its refusal to support the Lithuanians in their struggle with Moscow. In one column, Safire proclaimed it was Landsbergis, not Gorbachev, who should have been awarded the Nobel Peace Prize. Throughout the United States, in newspapers large and small, editorials and op-ed pieces were published in defense of the gutsy Lithuanians. Schoolchildren, under the encouragement of their teachers, drew maps and collected articles of the Baltic countries that were struggling to wrest themselves free of the Red Bear.

Even without a well-financed, sophisticated lobbying operation, a small number of activists in the diaspora strove to alert the American people to the horrible slaughter that had occurred in Vilnius January 13. They distributed information to members of Congress, journalists, and academics and lobbied them in the hope that their expressions of outrage would encourage the Bush administration to warn Gorbachev against further violence.

Asta Banionis, the public affairs director of the Lithuanian-American Community, had been expecting the worst for several months prior to Bloody Sunday. She told me, "First, Ozolas late in 1990 had warned publicly of a military attack before Christmas. Then early the following January his son was murdered under mysterious circumstances. Some commentators believed that the Soviets were attempting to intimidate him."[33] Perhaps Moscow hoped that if a wedge was driven between Ozolas and Landsbergis, divisions in the independence movement's top leadership would eventually undermine the will of the Lithuanian activists.

When news of Gorbachev's threats against Vilnius and reports of troop movements and the occupation of several buildings in the Lithuanian capital reached her office in Arlington, Virginia, Asta contacted Lithuanian-American activists in the Baltimore-Washington metropolitan area to conduct demonstrations protesting Moscow's decision to settle the Lithuanian issue by brute force.

The Lithuanians were providing a peaceful solution to the Soviet Union's mishandling of the nationalities question. This was something no one in the Bush White House seemed to realize, at least not people with influence and authority. Paul Goble, who had been reassigned from Radio Free Europe/Radio Liberty in Munich to the State Department to serve as the expert on Soviet nationalities, had recognized this fact for some time. Goble and several other pro-Baltic State Department officials were among those who had helped shape the March 11, 1990, administration draft statement that had so encouraged Lozoraitis. It was Goble's sad duty to contact Asta about her request to meet White House staffers and discuss a U.S. response to Bloody Sunday.

Lithuanian activists in Washington had hoped to convince the president that if he took concrete measures—economic and diplomatic—to punish Moscow, Gorbachev would refrain from resorting to further bloodshed. Goble said that the meeting would take place in Room 100 of the New Executive Office Building next to the White House. "Room 100!" Asta responded in rage. "Paul, do you know what that room is? It is the fucking mailroom! The fucking mailroom! We won't meet there!"[34]

Asta and several other Lithuanians associated with her organization met with Sichan Siv, the Cambodian who had been appointed by President Bush as the director of the White House Office of Public Affairs. Arvydas Bardzukas was among the delegation. Like many men and women who were contributing their time and energy to the Lithuanian-American organizations during these fateful days, he was a political neophyte. An architect, he had become a part-time lobbyist after developments in Lithuania compelled him to take active measures in assisting his old homeland. Without large numbers of voters such as the Poles could deliver, or campaign financing, which the American Jewish and Greek communities could provide, the Lithuanians had to rely upon the merits of their cause along with perseverance and hard work.

Asta said, "Mr. Siv was a nice man, but to send him to meet the delegation was an affront to the people in Lithuania, who feared another Soviet attack." He played no part in the policy process and was sent as a mere palliative. The Baltic-Americans continued to press for a meeting with the president.

On January 22, representatives from the three Baltic-American organizations met with the director of the National Security Council, Brent Scowcroft, and the president himself, but they did not leave that meeting satisfied. Asta represented the Lithuanian-American Community. The threesome had been urging Scowcroft to accept their recommendations that the U.S. government take concrete measures against Moscow and demonstrate American displeasure with Bloody Sunday and the attack on Riga—which had occurred the Saturday prior to their meeting—with more than mere rhetoric. After ten minutes, the group heard President Bush's voice as he entered the room exclaiming: "I heard that my favorite Baltic leaders were here and I thought I would look in on them." He said he could stay for only a few minutes, but it was forty minutes later when he left, an indication that he was worried about how the public and Congress would assess his administration's handling of Bloody Sunday.

The group had recommended several concrete measures to punish Gorbachev for the killings in Vilnius and Riga: an economic embargo, a moratorium on visas for Soviet officials scheduled to visit the United States, and most important of all, cancelation of the scheduled Moscow summit. Only strong displays of displeasure would deter officials in Moscow who might be contemplating further violent actions against the Balts.

"We don't have influence over the Soviets," Scowcroft responded. There was nothing, the NSC director said, that the United States could do but issue verbal warnings. Mary Ann Rikken of the Estonian-American National Council spoke for the group when she retorted, "Mr. President, that's appeasement! That's appeasement!"

At this point Bush cut her off and said, "Don't use that word!" Asta Banionis noted that while there was not an edge of anger in President Bush's voice, his body language changed. To emphasize his displeasure, Bush leaned toward his accuser and said, "I think this is unfair, Ms. Rikken."[35] The delegation knew that the words "appeasement" and "Munich" would arouse Bush, since the rightwing of his own party had doubts about his steadfastness on foreign policy matters. Some would even have liked to deny him the GOP's presidential renomination in 1992 for being "a wimp on the Soviets" and "a patsy for Gorbachev."

Bush and his advisers believed a quick victory in the Persian Gulf would nullify any such campaign, but Gorbachev's support for Desert Storm was vital to a successful outcome. To pummel Gorbachev publicly for Bloody Sunday could place Moscow's support for the Gulf War at risk. Such unpleasant thoughts explained why the president had spent so much time with the Baltic-American delegation. They did not represent a large voting bloc, but they could help ignite opposition to Bush's reelection by feeding his enemy red meat labeled "appeasement."

Michael Beschloss and Strobe Talbott have provided an insiders account of the White House's mood after the president returned from his helicopter on January 13 to his residence.

On Sunday morning, in the Situation Room at the White House, Robert Gates used a secure video link to speak with officials at State, Defense, and the CIA. Condoleezza Rice [an NSC expert on USSR] said, "Boy, what a coincidence! Just when we're all tied up with the Gulf, Gorbachev sends in the tanks!" She recalled that in 1956, Nikita Khrushchev had cracked down on Hungary at a moment when he presumed the West was absorbed in the Suez crisis.

Gates replied that "whether it's deliberate or not," the Soviets "must understand we're not too distracted" by the Gulf crisis to react. David Gompert—who had become the principal European affairs expert on the NSC staff since Robert Blackwill's return to Harvard the previous fall—said, "This is a classic challenge to us as a superpower. We've got to prove to the world that we can walk and chew gum at the same time, that we can deal with two crises at once."

Bush returned to the South Grounds by helicopter from Camp David. Inside the White House, Fitzwater and Rice were waiting for him. Bush asked about the situation in Vilnius: "How bad is it?"

"Awful," said Rice. "They ran over a thirteen-year-old girl with a tank."

Hoping that Gorbachev was not directly responsible, Bush asked, "Do we know who ordered the attack?"

"No," she said, "but the buildup has been there for some time. There's no reason to believe that the military was acting on its own."

At one point, "Bush put his hand on Scowcroft's shoulder and thanked him for urging him to mention the Baltics during his telephone conversation with Gorbachev the previous Friday. 'It's a good thing we didn't let that subject slide,' he said."[36]

To break the silence after Bush told the Estonian-American representative that her charge was unfair, Asta interjected, "Mr. President, if you don't care about the Lithuanians, think about the Russian democrats." She was referring to the Russians who had demonstrated in Moscow protesting Gorbachev's attempt to crush the Lithuanian independence movement. Many Russian leaders, including Boris Yeltsin, believed that the hard-liners were prepared to use force against the Russian democrats just as they assaulted the Lithuanians in Vilnius. Bush ignored her remarks and did not respond, but John Sununu, the former governor from New Hampshire, who had excellent credentials with the Republican right and served as White House chief of staff, later warned Bush that the administration had to "put teeth" in complaints to Gorbachev. Conservative Republicans in Congress were outraged by the killings in Vilnius.[37]

The Lithuanian-American Community conducted demonstrations in Washington, but it did not have the personnel, organization, or financial resources to produce a massive turnout. Four thousand people joined a demonstration in the nation's capital after Bloody Sunday. Not discouraged, the activists lobbied on Capitol Hill and provided newsletters and other material to its branches throughout the United States. By keeping Lithuania in the news—specifically in the minds of TV producers, columnists, and print editors—they maintained pressure on the U.S. government and on the disinformation experts in Moscow, who closely followed the U.S. media.

Ultimately, the campaign and the support it had helped raise had an impact. On January 27, the American and Soviet governments announced that the scheduled February Moscow summit was canceled. Officials in Washington said that the president was preoccupied with the Gulf War and could not leave Washington, but there was a better reason:"Leading Republicans in the House and Senate warned Mr. Bush last week that a trip to Moscow at this time would be widely opposed in Congress."[38] The next day, Soviet officials announced that Moscow was preparing to withdraw some troops from the Baltics, presumably those responsible for the killings in Vilnius and Riga.

The events in the Baltic and the behavior of the leaders of the world's two superpowers provided further evidence that American foreign policy could be profoundly influenced by domestic interests capable of capturing the media's attention and helping shape the content of its output on a given international issue. For years, political scientists taught their students that foreign policy matters were deemed "distant issues" by the American public. But now an international incident had become intimate and concrete to thoughtful people as visual images and audio messages leaped out of TV sets and radios into the living rooms of millions of Americans. As critiques of "talk radio" would indicate later, the electronic media were now proving to be as effective in influencing Washington officials as were traditional lobbying campaigns.

For months after Bloody Sunday, Landsbergis feared an assault on the parliament could not be discounted, and the killings in Riga a week after the massacre in Vilnius fed his fears. Consequently, he refused to remove the barriers that surrounded the building. Young men, many of whom had served in the Red Army, were recruited to defend it, and they remained there while the parliament was in session until after the failed August 1991 coup in the Soviet Union.

American-Lithuanian activists meanwhile continued to disseminate information about Bloody Sunday. For example, several weeks after the massacre, Ginte Damusis was visited in New York by a Mr. Stasys Kuprys, who had just arrived from Vilnius. He provided Ginte with film footage, given to him by an unnamed person in parliament, that provided further scenes of Bloody Sunday.

Ginte contacted Daiva Kezys, a Long Island realtor who had helped secure the seaman Kudirka's release in the 1970s. Daiva had done video work for the Lithuanian Information Center in the past. Like Bardzukas, she was an amateur activist who was devoting time to the Lithuanian cause. Daiva transposed the film from the European PAL/SECAM system to the NTSC system that is used in the United States. She edited the film—provided voice overs and music—and produced English and Lithuanian versions, which the LIC distributed throughout the United States.

The twenty-minute video *Bloody Sunday* is a powerful portrayal. It shows Soviet soldiers clubbing protesters with their rifles, people falling to gunfire, tanks roaring through the crowd, and other scenes depicted by American TV.

But it also shows horrible pictures of corpses in the morgue and the dying Loreta Asanaviciute, who expired in the hospital. At one point the camera zooms to her crushed pelvis, where one can clearly see the imprint of the tank treads that tore gaping wounds in her flesh. College viewers of the video often weep openly when the narrator repeats what Loreta asked her uncle as she was being driven to the hospital: "Uncle, are my legs too crushed to get married?"[39]

In the video's concluding frames, still photos of the people who were killed on Bloody Sunday are flashed across the screen as voices singing "My Precious Lithuania" are heard in the background. Typically all audiences, even one of tough marines at the Twenty-ninth Palm training base in the high desert of California, were deeply moved by the video. "Good psy-ops," a general who had lost an eye in Vietnam told me after seeing it.

Footage from *Bloody Sunday* was packaged by other filmmakers, and one film produced by students at Brown University was ultimately shown to a White House audience. It is not clear who provided all of the film, but many videos were made available immediately after Bloody Sunday, and in spite of efforts to prevent copies from being taken out of the country, many reached the West.

Sections of Daiva's video were used by ABC's *Nightline* because a producer of that show had her copy filched from her luggage when she left Lithuania. She discovered her loss after arriving in the United States; someone had sliced into her suitcase with a knife and removed the video. Clearly, KGB agents had been looking out for it and in this instance had been successful in their mission.[40]

In some cases, Lithuanian-Americans helped circulate details concerning Bloody Sunday, details that would later be used by journalists and others who would not let the story rest. For example, since I had written a number of op-ed pieces in defense of Lithuanian independence, I would occasionally receive unsolicited information from people I did not know personally. On one occasion, someone sent me a reprint of a fax from a college student in Lithuania to his cousin in Livingston, New Jersey. It provided an eyewitness account of Bloody Sunday.

January 15, 1991, 9:30 A.M.

Dear Vita, Vidmantai, and children:
    I've just finished my night watch at the University. [She was referring to Vytautas Magnus University, which had been established by émigré and Lithuanian professors in Kaunas.] This letter will be short because I have to give it to Prof. Kalvaitis.

I would like to describe what I, and Jonas and our friends, saw at the Vilnius television tower the night it was attacked. [Upon hearing Landsbergis's appeal, the students had traveled from Kaunas to Vilnius to show their support.]

We arrived at the tower around 1:30 A.M. There were still no tanks. In about 15–20 minutes, tanks arrived at point "1." [A crudely drawn map was provided with the letter.] People standing in front of trucks stopped the tanks. The tanks began to fire blanks from their guns. The noise shattered windowpanes. But the people continued to stand. The tanks aimed their searchlights at the crowd, fired over their heads, but everyone shouted "Freedom" and stood their ground. Some kind of gas was then released. The people wrapped their heads and faces, but still stood. I think many were afraid, at least I was, but no one ran. Then tanks appeared at point "2." They approached the trucks filled with sand. Men linked arms and stood in front of the trucks but the tanks did not stop. The men stepped aside, but two who were sitting on a tank perished under its tracks. They didn't even scream. My friend stood six feet from a man being crushed. The tanks rolled over a truck and two cars and stopped. Then it suddenly turned toward the hill and crushed a girl at point "3."

At that moment trucks and armored vehicles began to approach from point "4" toward the tower. They were filled with paratroopers. The tanks fired off some rounds and drove up the hill toward the tower. In other words they could have gone there without crushing either cars or people.

And then the slaughter began. People stood at the tower fence. The soldiers shot into the air and the ground, the ricocheting bullets hit some people. One soldier shot bursts right into the crowd. There could have been more, but one certainly did. A soldier who refused to shoot was in turn shot by an officer. I don't know what happened right at the tower, but there was shooting, and more shooting, and more shooting. Ambulances came, but the people did not run. The soldiers were already in the tower, they smashed and destroyed everything. No one knows how many people were left in the tower nor what happened to them. Sixty-four persons vanished without a trace, 14 were killed, over 100 were wounded, 20 of them critically. There are no words to describe what we saw or what we felt. I still cannot fathom the source of the courage displayed by those who fell under the tanks or stood before a firing machine gun. I was not fired upon and am still alive. It is hard for me to write, perhaps later I can write in more detail, I will ask Jonas and my friends to help me. But I am writing now so that America will learn of this. Lucija Baskauskaite has said that such facts are in short supply in America. You can tell the world that Ceslovas and Jonas Tallat-Kelpsa were witnesses and we will find many others who saw and will write what they saw. We plan to organize a letter writing and sending campaign at the University. Those who were at the tower and defended it with their lives are HEROES. And there are many such and blood will continue to be spilled if Bush needs more. Just try to imagine what it's like to stand in the cold two or three nights in a row and wait for the tanks to arrive and for the shooting to start, without knowing who will be shot: you, your brother, your friend, a women or a child. But NO ONE ran.

From there we drove to the Parliament and again waited. And everyone thought this would be it, but still waited. The Deputies made their last speeches. In the morning the tanks began to roll again but did not stop. And more people were there than ever before, though there was much less hope. Metal barricades were erected during the night. Heavy machinery was brought in to block the streets, while the number of people grew. Processions passed, Masses were said by the Poles and the Lithuanians. The Russian Orthodox church ringing its bells.

I now hear that Landsbergis has said that some people are still alive and hiding in the tower. Though Gorbachev promised to allow the Health Minister into the tower, he was permitted only on the first floor. There must be many bodies there. Soldiers are seen carrying out many large bags. They could be defenders.

The Kaunas television is operating now:

KAUNAS TV/RADIO
Telephone: 22-55-52
FAX (007) (0127) 22-85-00 or 22-36-34
TELEX 26-98-57 VYTUN SU

What Gorbachev is saying is a horrible filthy lie. The tower was surrounded by people who love Lithuania, no one fought, no one attacked, no one was armed, people stood and died.

Try to inform as many people as possible of this. Send any official reactions to the Kaunas TV station or the University. I'm including Lucija's card.

She asked me to send you her best wishes. Kristina could come here when things quiet down. We are already planning a "task force."

I'm ending because I have to hand this letter over.

We are all alive and well.

Cesius[41]

The Lucija Baskauskaite referred to in the fax is a Lithuanian-American anthropologist from California who encouraged witnesses to Bloody Sunday to commit their testimony to paper. Later the testimonials would be used to counter the propaganda from Moscow about who was responsible for the tragedy, and they might be used in war crime trials if the criminals are even brought to justice. "I sent boxes and boxes of such testimonials to Scandinavia," Lucija told me.[42]

Dr. Baskaukaite had fled Lithuania in the arms of her parents during World War II as Soviet troops advanced upon her home. Forty-six years later she left her post at California State University at Northridge and returned to Lithuania to serve as pro-rector of the Vytautas Magnus University, which was reestablished in 1989 by émigré Lithuanian academics and their Lithuanian counterparts to provide Lithuanian college students access to Western scholarship and English instruction. Soviet authorities had closed the school in 1950 and it reopened in Kaunas in 1989.

Lucija was visiting her husband, who was working in Vilnius, the weekend of Bloody Sunday, and when the couple and their children saw a tank roar across a median strip in the city's downtown they decided to leave for Kaunas. "Later, when the news reached us about the attack on the TV tower, I went to the Kaunas station and remained there for thirty-six hours to provide information about the developments in Vilnius." From that post she had organized the campaign to write and collect eyewitness accounts about Bloody Sunday and related developments. In this fashion she hoped to abort Soviet efforts to convince the world that the Lithuanians were to blame for the massacre.

Lithuanian-Americans who received information from Lithuania disseminated it throughout the United States with the assistance of activists in the diaspora. Although such efforts were often ad hoc and unorganized, the material was used by journalists and academics to inform news stories, op-ed pieces, and articles about the horrors and heroism of Bloody Sunday.

On February 1, Gorbachev proclaimed that he had appointed a delegation to negotiate with the three Baltic leaders. This was a lame attempt to parry Western accounts that had damaged his image, and events continued to work against him. For example, on February 10 the Lithuanians held a referendum that allowed voters to declare whether they favored or opposed Lithuanian independence. By close to a 90 percent margin, the Lithuanian electorate voted in favor of independence and thereby dealt a death blow to Gorbachev's charge that the March 11, 1990, declaration was simply a "palace coup d'etat" masterminded by Landsbergis and the ultranationalists in Sajudis. The referendum was a resounding vote of confidence in Landsbergis and a resolute rebuff to Gorbachev, who heard the results with grim foreboding, for he knew that the outcome of his struggle with Landsbergis could determine the survival of the USSR.

The Lithuanians' bid for independence and Moscow's attempt to crush it would facilitate an even greater threat to Soviet rule—the resurrection of the Russian democratic movement.

9 THE EMPIRE COLLAPSES

Vilnius was the last straw and our patience ran out. . . . Honestly, had it not been for Vilnius we would not have refused to storm the White House.

—*Colonel Sergei Goncharov on why his Alpha unit did not attack the Russian White House in August 1991*

On June 4, 1991, I had hired a car in Riga, arranged through Intourist, to drive to Vilnius. I was the only passenger, and the four-and-a-half-hour trip cost me the princely sum of twenty dollars. My Russian driver was so elated at his good fortune that he bought me a bottle of champagne even before I left him with a five-dollar tip.

The trip had begun as an outing. Two hours after leaving Riga, we stopped at a makeshift roadside stand and ate shashlik, barbecued pork, in the cool late-morning air. The highway stop was crowded with truck drivers and other travelers. I had observed that the food was only part of the attraction: most of the drivers also bought large plastic bottles of home-brewed beer. Here was a vivid example of private enterprise in operation and a show of confidence about prospects for the future. Bags of cement and concrete blocks were strewn around the small building, indicating that it was in the process of being expanded. The more optimistic Latvians, like their Estonian and Lithuanian cousins, were building in the expectation that the Baltic countries would acquire greater control over decisions previously made solely by Moscow. But only the romantics dreamed that true independence would soon become a reality.

The trip took on a more serious tone, however, when we stopped at the Latvia-Lithuania border and waited until a ceremony commemorating an assault on Lithuanian border guards had been concluded. A burned-out trailer was physical evidence of the attack, which Lithuanian authorities had attributed to the hated OMON (the special Soviet police unit) unit stationed in Riga. (While in Latvia's capital city I had witnessed its handiwork when I visited the park where several people had been killed the week after Bloody Sunday.) The ceremony was conducted with dignity, marked by a priest's blessings, several patriotic songs, and brief statements by local dignitaries. As was frequently the case during such occasions, a small number of Lithuanians from the diaspora were present in a show of solidarity with their former countrymen. The ceremony was especially moving because the day had grown warmer, the sun was bright, and the air smelled of freshly turned earth and newly budding trees and flowers.

Shootings, bombings, and other violent actions by Soviet security forces had become common throughout the Baltics, and the local population was convinced that neo-Stalinists in Moscow were preparing a coup. Some felt Gorbachev himself was at risk, others believed he would side with the hardliners, still others said it did not matter, the Lithuanians would be a target whoever was behind it. They were the first to bolt from the USSR and they had emboldened other separatists to follow their example. In June 1989, the Belorussian popular front movement had held its founding congress in Vilnius when it was impossible to do so in Minsk. During the January 1991, events, when the Lithuanian parliament was targeted by Gorbachev's agents, several volunteers from Ukraine, in traditional uniforms, joined the Lithuanian defenders in a show of solidarity with them.

After the abortive attempt to depose Landsbergis, the Old Bolsheviks were horrified to read reports that secession-minded nationalists from all parts of the Caucasus, Central Asia, and even Ukraine were traveling to Vilnius to consult with Sajudis activists. By his failure to crush the Lithuanian rebellion, Gorbachev had fanned the flames of nationalism throughout the USSR. The former air force general Dzhokhar M. Dudayev, who had been stationed in Estonia and had called for a sovereign Chechen republic in November 1990, had consulted with Landsbergis.

Equally disconcerting was evidence that some Communist leaders were following Brazauskas's example, i.e., lending their prestige and influence to independence drives. Nor did it escape the Russians in the CPSU, KGB, and ministries that some of their comrades, including "staunch Leninists," had begun to search for ways to escape the fate of their colleagues in Eastern Europe by making appeals to the most "primitive bourgeois impulses." For example, in Ukraine, Leonid Kravchuk was achieving popular support as he became more vocal in his nationalistic pronouncements.

For the neo-Stalinists, the Lithuanians had not only incited nationalist movements throughout the USSR, they also had demonstrated to Communist leaders that nationalism could fill the vacuum left by the collapse of Marxism-Leninism. For that they could never be forgiven.

In the summer of 1991, the Moscow press ran numerous stories about the "coming coup." For example, the *Moscow News,* a liberal newspaper published in English, carried stories along these lines. The previous fall, I had met with the newspaper's editors to discuss my becoming a contributor to its pages, but the events of January 1991 had severed the relationship. If the weather was any portent, the coup predictions were erroneous.

Upon arriving in Vilnius, I had registered at the Neringa Hotel, a Soviet-style establishment on Gedimino Street. Later I ate a quick meal at the Neringa restaurant next door to it. Sometimes the food there was good, sometimes awful. That night it was awful, and I left the restaurant experiencing the first pangs of indigestion. I walked through the ancient section of Vilnius and admired the city's impressive collection of seventeenth, eighteenth, and nineteenth century buildings. There were even a few from earlier centuries that remained in good condition. These architectural treasures could be fully restored to their old brilliance once the Lithuanians were successful in their independence campaign.

It was still light at ten o'clock. As I consulted my watch I turned a corner onto Pilies Street and came upon an ominous scene—several armed troops were being briefed by the captain who commanded them. They possessed a combat radio and automatic weapons and wore battle fatigues. In late December 1990, Defense Minister Yazov and Interior Minister Pugo had announced the formation of joint army-militia units that would be deployed in the USSR's larger cities to fight crime. But the Lithuanians interpreted the actual deployment of these units as further evidence that another attempt to deny them independence was imminent. There was a large contingent of soldiers stationed in the northern part of the city, only minutes away from the parliament building, which borders on the old section of Vilnius. Although the sight of troops was unsettling, I had not had much sleep since I had arrived in Riga, and I retired early.

At breakfast the next morning, I learned that the city was buzzing with reports that another attack was about to begin. I was told by Lithuanian friends that there had been troop movements, including armored vehicles, which had traversed the streets of Vilnius late the previous evening. Landsbergis had appeared on radio, and thousands of people responded to his plea to gather at Independence Square to protect the parliament and Lithuanian independence against a second Bloody Sunday.

The attack never came, but Lithuanian parliamentarians that I met the next day deemed the troop movements to be a dry run for a coup that could occur at any time. Some Western journalists I had spoken with dismissed the claim, believing instead that Landsbergis was ringing alarm bells to attract Western attention. Wishing to avoid another massacre, President Bush would compel Gorbachev to reach an accommodation with the Lithuanian government. I spoke with a young American diplomat, George Krol, who had been sent by the American legation in Leningrad to survey the scene. He indicated that there had been extensive troop movements the previous evening but all was quiet that day.

Ever since the "January events," Lithuanians from all parts of the country had made a pilgrimage to Vilnius, arriving by bus, train, and car as a gesture of support for their nation's independence. Daily, small crowds gathered on the square outside of parliament, where in January thousands of people had put their lives on the line for their country. Henceforth it would become hallowed ground for Lithuanian patriots. In one area there were people debating the latest developments in Moscow, while elsewhere senior citizens conducted vigils around wooden crucifixes and other homemade religious artifacts. Some intrepid pilgrims remained in the square all night and built small bonfires for warmth. Signs were placed on the barriers declaring "Free Lithuania!" and "Moscow Out!" and the like.

One proclaimed in English, "Mr. Nixon save us!" The former American president had visited Vilnius in March 1991, accompanied by his adviser on the Soviet Union, Dmitri Simes. As was always the case when a prominent Western statesman like Nixon visited Lithuania, his presence and the publicity it generated provided the Lithuanians with a safeguard against a further attack.

Among the various artistic depictions of Bloody Sunday, I found the work of schoolchildren most vivid and compelling. Immediately after the tragedy, students throughout Lithuania had been asked by their teachers to convey their feelings about the horrible but historic event that had taken place in their country's capital city. Typically tanks were colored in black crayon, as were the assaulting troops. Soviet power was portrayed by one child as a dragon breathing fire on a line of protesters. Traditional Lithuanian symbols, religious and otherwise, were a marked feature of the drawings, which indicated that they had been maintained by the older generation during the dark years of Soviet rule and surreptitiously passed on to the children.

Steel wire columns had been anchored to the parliament's roof to prevent helicopters from landing there with assault troops. In the foyer to Landsbergis's office, several young men in civilian suits stood guard with Uzi submachine guns to provide their president protection. Walking through the parliament's halls, I saw other defenders, armed often with old World War II bolt-action rifles, guarding the entrances, which were blocked with sandbags. Most of them were bivouacked in the bowels of the building and took their meals there. On one occasion I was searching for Mecys Laurinkus's office—he belonged to the council's presidium—when I entered a small hallway and smelled gasoline. The corridor was dark, so it took me a while to get accustomed to the dim light and I spot the source of the stench: several boxes of Molotov cocktails, which appeared to be freshly made, as their cotton fabric wicks were white and free of dust or soot.

I recalled reading about the popular misperception that the crude antitank weapon had its origin in brave partisan resistance to the Nazis' invasion of Russia during World War II. The weapon derived its name from Stalin's foreign minister, V. M. Molotov, but the term was coined by Finns who heroically resisted the Red Army when it invaded their country in 1939. Stalin, who otherwise had keen respect for the power of ethnonationalism, had been carried away by ideological zeal when he assumed that the Finnish proletariat would honor their commitment to Marxist dogma and ignore nationalist appeals to fight their "liberators." The outgunned but gutsy Finns crippled many tanks by igniting them with the crude but deadly weapon. The Russians defeated the smaller nation in that war, but as a result of the Red Army's poor showing, Hitler concluded that the Soviet Union would be an easy target for his Wehrmacht. The Soviet leaders in punishing a small country fifty years later were once again to pay a heavy price for their brutality.

Several military vehicles, with communications equipment, stood in the parliament's courtyard to provide the building with emergency means of sending and receiving messages. A TV truck also was located there. It had been driven to parliament on Bloody Sunday by an ethnic Russian to provide the independence government with a TV capability after Lithuanian authorities had lost control of the city's television complex. Since January 13, the pro-Soviet Lithuanian Communists dominated Lithuanian TV, but no one watched the programs produced by Lithuanian "Quislings."

Once in the parliament building, visitors were neither closely watched nor followed by the guards or deputies and their aides. The Lithuanians assigned to Parliament assumed everyone who was allowed in was a friend, someone who supported their cause. Visitors, therefore, were overwhelmed by a powerful sense of solidarity and shared vicariously the powerful emotions of the real independence fighters. The atmosphere was absolutely intoxicating.

Before leaving Lithuania, I asked Algimantas Cekuolis—whom the Lithuanian émigrés continued to distrust even though he had demonstrated in word and deed his support for Lithuanian independence—what he thought about the prospects for a coup. He did not hesitate in answering my question. "The Soviet system is so rotten, no one will fight to save it. If there is a coup, it will fail. I know lots of Soviet officers, and they hate Yazov."[1] Cekuolis was speaking of the Soviet defense minister, and there were lots of people in Washington as well as Vilnius who were concerned about the Red Army.

The Soviet military establishment was shocked when Gorbachev pulled the rug out from under the Communist regimes of Eastern Europe and then allowed East Germany to reunify with West Germany. It was horrified when it learned that he and Shevardnadze had acceded to Bush's demand that a reunified Germany remain in NATO. World War II had cost the Soviet Union 27 million dead, twice that number wounded, and the destruction of vast areas of the homeland in the Red Army's battles with the Germans. One of Stalin's major wartime goals was to secure a buffer zone to prevent a future German attack through weak and/or hostile countries in Eastern Europe. But in a flash, Gorbachev had surrendered the *cordon sanitaire* to the West and forced the Red Army to draw lines of defense back within the USSR itself.

Moreover, because of his mishandling of the economy, tens of thousands of Soviet officers and men and their families were returning home in the face of a severe housing shortage. An estimated 200,000 members of military families were homeless in the metropolitan area of Moscow alone. And many military families that found shelter lived in squalor. The wives and children of proud professional officers were confined to small apartments where several families shared bath and toilet facilities. And in contrast to housing they enjoyed in East Germany, the troops lived in tents or dilapidated billets on Soviet bases. Because funds were lacking, training suffered as tanks, trucks, and aircraft were kept in storage sheds or hangars for want of fuel. Over time, the space-age weapon systems that the military-industrial complex had produced at great cost to Soviet society became useless; spare parts were unavailable to keep them operative, or they rusted in depots because there was no fuel or transport to move them to the protection of military bases. Because of Gorbachev's failure to crack down on draft dodgers, many units were badly undermanned and officers were forced to unload freight cars, pull guard duty, and perform other demeaning tasks that previously had been performed by enlisted men. And commanders were appalled that a growing number of men who did answer the draft call had criminal records. Older officers, moreover, were discouraged to see the best and brightest youngsters among their ranks leaving the service because they believed there was no future in the once mighty Red Army.

What's more, it was not bad enough that Soviet troops were being withdrawn from Eastern Europe, the nationalists were demanding "Red Army Go Home!" in Estonia, Latvia, and Lithuania. With the forward lines of defense in Eastern Europe lost, the strategic importance of the Baltic republics had acquired even greater urgency. The Baltic republics were of special interest to the Red Army establishment because the Soviet military elite had always been stationed in the region; the Baltic fleet was located there, along with crack army units and critical air force wings. In addition to their strategic importance in providing forward defenses for St. Petersburg and Moscow, the Baltic republics were coveted as posts by army, navy, and air force personnel, because living standards there were far superior to those elsewhere in the USSR. Indeed, many former military personnel retired in Latvia and Estonia, in particular, where there were large Russian populations, and the thought that they could not spend their "golden years" in the Baltic region angered Soviet officers who had served there.

I left Lithuania with no clear idea what was to happen next, but I had an unsettling experience that indicated something was afoot. This was my third trip to Lithuania since I had been invited to witness the February 1990 elections. On previous occasions, I had detected no evidence that I was being watched. But two days before I was scheduled to leave Vilnius for Moscow, I discovered that I was being followed. I had left the parliament building, and as I walked casually down Gedimino Street toward the Neringa, I turned to look in the window of a bookstore and saw a man about twenty feet behind me stop and pivot as if something had caught his eye in a nearby shop. I walked another fifty feet and stopped suddenly when I noticed that a kiosk was selling German beer for rubles. Once again the man stopped and turned, looking toward a nearby building. Ten minutes later I was sitting on a park bench when I saw him walking in my direction with a female companion. They passed without incident, and I thought the entire affair a coincidence until two days later on an Aeroflot flight to Moscow, I spotted him at the Vilnius airport. He boarded my plane, and I last saw him in Moscow while waiting for my baggage. I observed him leaving the airport terminal without toting even a small handbag.

In Moscow, a number of dramatic events had occurred after the massacre in Lithuania. Gorbachev had attempted to deny the Soviet people the truth about events in Vilnius. The TV footage that I had observed, and commented upon at CNN's Washington headquarters, had originated from the television station in Kaunas, which never had been wrested from the Lithuanians. And from that Kaunas station, TV film depicting Bloody Sunday had been beamed to all of the Baltic countries, as well as Poland and Finland. But the signal only reached a small number of people in the Soviet Union. For several days, Moscow-produced Soviet TV broadcasts, like *Vremya,* provided a distorted picture of developments in Vilnius. Viewers were led to believe through selected film editing and voice-overs that the Lithuanians had been the first to resort to violence and that the Soviet forces had fought back in self-defense.

The most shameful distortion of developments in Vilnius was the work of Aleksandr Nevzorov, the man who produced, directed, and starred in the popular Leningrad TV program *600 Seconds.* The program had attracted an audience of eighty million viewers by virtue of its glitzy treatment of corruption, vice, and crime that afflicted all areas of the USSR. Nevzorov made no secret of the fact that he had close connections with the KGB, which he characterized as "incorruptible and not for sale." According to David Remnick:

> The day after the shootings, Nevzorov and his crew piled into one of those tuna-can-sized Ladas and raced from Leningrad to Vilnius, where thy quickly shot a ten-minute piece. Nevzorov called his film *Nashi*—"Ours," or "Our People," meaning . . . Russians. The idea was that the military was the defender of "Ours" and the Lithuanians an unruly—no, treasonous!—mob. Nevzorov called Landsbergis's pro-independence government "fascists" who had "declared war" on the state. In other words, the message was the same as Gorbachev's. . . . But it was the imagery that did it. With a Kalashnikov slung over his shoulder and snippets of *Das Rheingold* booming on the soundtrack, Nevzorov inspected the fierce and sturdy faces of the troops inside the television center. They were defenders of the faith, defenders of the holy airwaves. They would save us all against the hordes of ungrateful Lithuanian college professors.[2]

The campaign to deny Russian viewers accurate depictions of events in Vilnius, however, was foiled by the work of a thirty-two-year-old Lithuanian television correspondent, Ricardus Sartavicius. He had gathered footage taken by Lithuanian and foreign cameramen and, in Hedrick Smith's words, "took an overnight train to Leningrad and delivered . . . footage to Bella Kurkova, the feisty executive producer of *Fifth Wheel,* Leningrad's most audacious program."[3]

That evening an accurate account of the bloody assault on innocent civilians, who bravely stood their ground and defied the Red Army, was aired. Leningrad mayor Anatoly Sobchak appeared on the show, and his presence provided legitimacy to the Lithuanians' portrayal of the massacre. Smith writes,

"This was the first visual rebuttal of Moscow's version of events. The Kremlin's censors were caught off guard because the transmission came from Leningrad; as a result, the contraband film got relayed to much of the nation."[4]

The courage which the Lithuanians displayed in the face of tanks and armed troops had a deep and lasting impact upon the Russians who viewed TV broadcasts of Bloody Sunday. The visual footage and press accounts of developments in Vilnius, which followed for many weeks after January 13, helped restore the Russian democrats' morale. The Lithuanians' display of bravery not only inspired them, it provided them with several practical lessons.

The first lesson was that the hard-liners would not sit back and allow the Soviet system to be superseded by a "democracy" without a fight. The hard-liners' attempt to crush the most visible and successful independence movement in the USSR was abortive, but it was concrete proof that they would resort to force to retain power. They had lost one battle, but they were prepared to continue the conflict. This meant that the democrats had to be proactive—that is, to take the initiative and fight back.

Another lesson was that the people represented the most powerful weapon the democrats could bring to bear in their struggle with the forces of reaction. The Lithuanians had demonstrated that an army with nuclear weapons, and capable of launching blitzkrieg attacks against powerful neighbors, was useless in preventing a true people's revolution. If Landsbergis's call for popular demonstrations had gone unheeded, there is no question that he would have been removed from office and the rebellion crushed. Russian democrats could not expect to mobilize the same proportion of their population as the Lithuanian activists did. But the Lithuanians demonstrated that a relatively small number of people who were prepared to die for freedom constituted a potent weapon. What's more, television would give added velocity to their protest and force the authorities to the conclusion that they might be joined by opponents to Soviet rule in other parts of the USSR.

A third lesson concerned military morale. In the past, the Stalinists had resorted to brute force to keep the people cowed, but that option was predicated upon the loyalty of the military and security forces. Had Gorbachev given the order to move on the parliament and to arrest its occupants, undoubtedly the coup would have succeeded, but many commanders and their troops had refused to turn their weapons on innocent civilians. Lithuanians monitoring Soviet troop movements in Kaunas had observed on several occasions helicopters leaving a base near the city but, rather than flying to Vilnius, twenty minutes away by air, circling their base and returning to it without moving against the rebels. The Stalinists would have even greater reason to believe that in a future showdown with the Russian democrats both commanders and soldiers would resist orders to fire upon civilians. Such fears were bolstered when a group of pro-democracy Soviet officers—who had formed the Democratic Officers Movement (SHIELD)—traveled to Vilnius and issued a report disputing claims by the procurator's office in Moscow that the Lithuanians had started the violence and the troops had reacted in self-defense.

The SHIELD report was based upon information gleaned from messages sent by the tank commanders and vividly revealed the confusion that prevailed among the Soviet units:

> Such orders as were given by radio were in some cases to open fire, in others to show restraint. (As for the Soviet procuracy report alleging that Lithuanians had attacked the soldiers, this was one of the most disgraceful single episodes of Gorbachev's presidency.) "Shield" alleged that orders must have come directly from Gorbachev, but their only evidence was that according to the Soviet command structure, this was the procedure. As the attempted coup made apparent, however, the Soviet command structure had already begun to disintegrate.[5]

Then there was the reactionaries' morale. They were deeply demoralized, and many of them had lost their nerve; if the masses joined the reformers, the Soviet system was doomed. Doubts about the system's capacity to survive were reinforced as a growing number of people from the Soviet ruling elite joined the opposition. Fissures in the *nomenklatura's* ranks added to the democrats' capacity to mobilize the best and brightest elements in Soviet society against the neo-Stalinists.

The apparatchiks no doubt recalled the first Bloody Sunday of 1905, which had led to the 1917 Russian Revolution, and many feared the Bloody Sunday of 1991 might suggest that a second revolution was in the works. The first Bloody Sunday occurred in St. Petersburg when a Russian Orthodox priest, Father George Gapon, led a crowd of striking workers in a march on the Winter Palace to petition the czar and they were fired upon by the troops standing before them at Narva Gate. Forty of the strikers were killed. The strike failed, but in the words of Richard Pipes, "Bloody Sunday caused a wave of revulsion to sweep across the country: among the masses it damaged irreparably the image of the 'good tzar.'"[6] For many Russian reformers in 1991, Bloody Sunday destroyed their image of Mikhail Gorbachev as the heroic leader who had embarked upon pluralistic reforms and helped destroy communism in the "outer empire." He became the tzar who had resorted to force to save the "inner empire."

Still another lesson for the democrats was that they could not count on Gorbachev to lead them even if he reversed his course and realigned himself with them against the unrepentant Soviets. To this day it is unclear what role Gorbachev played in Bloody Sunday, but Landsbergis told me that he was responsible for the whole thing![7]

The day after the bloodletting, Gorbachev informed the Supreme Soviet that the Lithuanian authorities were at fault. He said a pro-Soviet delegation of twenty to thirty people had been "barred and beaten" on January 8 when they had gone to the Lithuanian parliament. Afterward they appealed to the local army commander for protection as they demonstrated at the TV station to "stop inflammatory broadcasts" that were emanating from it. When asked by a reporter whether he had authorized the use of force, he replied, "I . . . er . . . no, it was already morning when I found out."[8]

According to David Remnick, "Gorbachev waffled, and said the first he had heard of the assault was when he was wakened by his aides the next morning. Was he lying?" Remnick answers his own question: "It was hard to know which was worse: that he was telling the truth, and therefore not in control of the army and the KGB; or that he was lying, and at the head of a coup attempt against the Lithuanians." Afterward, Remnick asked Gorbachev's economic adviser, Nikolai Petrakov, about the report that Gorbachev had "slept through" Bloody Sunday. "Don't be naive," Petrakov responded.[9] He too would turn his back on Gorbachev after the incident.

While Gorbachev's role in the affair remains a mystery, what is clear is that it prompted many of his supporters to break with him. Sergei Stankevich, the baby-faced political scientist whose excellent command of English made him frequently welcome on American TV, told Remnick that he had joined the Communist Party because Gorbachev had promised to reform it. But standing on the street not far from the Kremlin on Bloody Sunday, he said, "Now, that's over. No more. I'm finished with Gorbachev. There are just so many times you can let yourself be deceived."

That same day, in a march on the central committee building in Moscow, Yuri Afanasyev, like Gorbachev a Communist apparatchik turned reformer, said to a crowd in Manezh Square fronting on the Kremlin, "The killings in Vilnius are the work of a dictatorship of reactionary circles—the generals, the KGB, the military-industrial complex, and the Communist Party chiefs."[10]

Bloody Sunday cost Gorbachev the support of talented, articulate men and women who had joined him in the struggle to introduce the principles of pluralism into all areas of Soviet life. "The failed coup attempt in Lithuania changed everything for the middle-aged intellectuals who had remained loyal to the idea of a reformed Communist Party," Remnick says.[11]

It was after Bloody Sunday that the disheartened Russian democrats turned to the Communist maverick Boris Yeltsin for leadership. Not many months before, many reformers would have hooted at the idea that he would replace Gorbachev as their champion.

In 1987, Gorbachev had Yeltsin expelled from the Politburo, and the next year he successfully blocked Yeltsin's bid to return to political power. But in 1989, Yeltsin demonstrated that he was a force to be reckoned with when he was elected to the Supreme Soviet of the Russian Republic by voters in his home city of Sverdlovsk. Since it is situated east of Moscow in the Ural Mountains, Yeltsin became known in the West as "the man from Siberia."

Like Gorbachev, Yeltsin realized the Soviet system was profoundly sick, but he seemed to know something Gorbachev was unable to accept, that it could not be preserved through tinkering but had to be scrapped altogether. Having successfully built a network of support among the reformers in the Russian parliament, Yeltsin was chosen chairman of that body on May 29, 1990. Fearful, and rightly so, that Yeltsin had successfully exploited Russian nationalism to fuel his political movement, Gorbachev had opposed Yeltsin's election to the post, from which he could challenge the Soviet president himself.

The reactionaries were even more appalled by Yeltsin's victory than Gorbachev, because they knew that he had an asset that Gorbachev lacked: the ability to arouse the common folk. Yeltsin's populist tendencies—exemplified by his two-fisted drinking, gruff talk, and physical bulk—indicated that unlike Gorbachev, he could mobilize mass support behind his political wagon. At the same time, he was a tough infighter who knew how to trade blows with the old apparatchiks. Should he replace Gorbachev as the leader of the "anti-Soviet" reform movement, he would be a dangerous opponent whom the neo-Stalinists both feared and loathed.

After he was appointed chairman of the Russian Supreme Soviet in May 1990, he became more heated in his criticism of Gorbachev. In July, he sent a chill of foreboding throughout the Communist establishment when he resigned from the CPSU, explaining, "In view of my great responsibilities toward the people of Russia and in connection with the move toward a multiparty system, I cannot fulfill only the instructions of the Communist Party. As the highest elected figure in the republic, I have to bow to the will of all the people."[12] The hard-liners knew that through his post as Russian "president," this former Soviet apparatchik was establishing an institutional base to oppose them, and alarm bells rang in party headquarters and Soviet ministries all across the empire.

The next day, the mayors of Moscow and Leningrad, Gavril K. Popov and Anatoly A. Sobchak, followed Yeltsin's example. When Yeltsin announced his resignation during the CPSU congress, TV cameras spanned the gathering and revealed an audience in shock. I recall one military officer shaking his head in disbelief—as his neighbors looked upon the podium stunned, silent, and frightened—while the tall, burly Yeltsin delivered his farewell address. Here was proof that the elite consensus that had enabled the Soviet leadership to cope with internal and external crises alike was collapsing.

One of the major elements of that consensus was Article 6 of the Soviet constitution, which gave the CPSU a political monopoly. Yeltsin's resignation was predicated on support for a multiparty system, and the Communist appartchiks witnessing his farewell speech had to ask themselves a pivotal question: did Yeltsin, Popov, and Sobchak know something they did not know, that a change in power was in the works? In the Soviet Union, serious conflict often was avoided because the antagonists joined the stronger faction rather than fight it. That is, they joined and did not oppose the bandwagon. This was consistent with their pragmatic nature and propensity to defer to power rather than oppose it.

After Gorbachev realized that he could not prevent his rival's victory, he adopted a familiar tactic and sought to nullify Yeltsin's success by joining forces with him. Yeltsin had achieved popular power and attained legitimacy from the people themselves—if not through direct elections, as he would when he won the Russian presidency in June 1991, at least indirectly by representing them in his struggle against a system the people knew was flawed and corrupt. Gorbachev hoped to prevent Yeltsin from using popular support against him while exploiting it as an asset to blunt the neo-Stalinists' attacks on perestroika. It was because he operated from such a precarious position that Gorbachev would lurch from left to right over the next year.

Although always suspicious of a powerful Russian leader, the Lithuanians I spoke to supported Yeltsin in his struggle with Gorbachev. Some of them close to Brazauskas, such as Matulionas, frequently mentioned "Yeltsin's populism," which to them meant that here was a dangerous demagogue who would manipulate Russian nationalism to achieve power and ultimately put the Lithuanians in their place. Perhaps what Matulionas believed, but did not state openly, was that he feared that Yeltsin might also cooperate with Landsbergis. Clearly at this time there was a symbiotic relationship between Yeltsin and the Balts, which would ultimately empower both sides. Yeltsin had supported Lithuanian independence and openly opposed Gorbachev's embargo against the government in Vilnius. Gorbachev's hard line toward the Balts had damaged his image in the eyes of many democrats, while Yeltsin's forthright stand on the "Baltic question" had won him their support and helped mute the attacks that Gorbachev's spin doctors were leveling against him in the West.

The day after Bloody Sunday, Yeltsin flew to Estonia and in a show of solidarity met with the Baltic independence leaders. This outraged the neo-Stalinists, and even worse, he addressed Red Army officers and their men and urged them not to fire upon defenseless civilians.

In a radio address to the troops on January 13, Yeltsin said:

> "I am addressing myself to you soldier . . . Dictatorship is arriving, and it is you who is bringing it, sitting with a submachine gun in a tank . . . Do you think you are a Rambo—a hero who defends law and order? No! You are again a pawn in a dirty game, a grain of sand in the Kremlin's building of an imperial sand castle.
>
> This year you will take off your uniform, demobilize and tell your girlfriend how 'we bashed those Lithuanians'. . . Those 'memories' will be the only security you will be able to give her . . . neither freedom nor a good life—for you have blocked that path with your tank . . . It is you who has killed your chances . . . to live like civilized people.
>
> At the very moment when you are 'ensuring order' in the Baltics, people in your native town . . . will also go out into the streets in the name of freedom. And to your counterpart, just as to you in the Baltics, it will be explained that he, too, is facing 'extremists.'"

Also at that time, Dainis Ivans, the Latvian leader, reported the 103rd Vitebsk Airborne Division had been ordered to enter Riga but the division's deputy commander refused to obey: "Enough blood. I was in Afghanistan and I will not take action against civilians."[13]

For the reactionaries, Yeltsin's words and actions amounted to treason pure and simple. They were not unmindful of the fact, however, that in Yeltsin the democrats had a leader who was as tough as they were, for he too had proved himself a brutal political infighter in the CPSU. Although he drank too much, had a short attention span, and often showed poor judgment, he was fearless and was at his best in a fight. He also possessed an asset that none of his opponents enjoyed—mass appeal. He gained the people's support through his enthusiastic attacks upon party hacks and their perks and revelations about the corruption that was endemic to the Soviet regime. He was the first major Russian Communist leader to leave the CPSU in 1990; and then a year later, in

July 1991, as the popularly elected president of Russia, he ordered all party cells to be disbanded in the military and in factories, government ministries, and collective farms throughout Russia.

In addition to personal courage and his boldness, he also demonstrated that he was a skillful political tactician. For example, when Gorbachev proposed a referendum to blunt Yeltsin's "union of four" proposal (which called for a new union organized by the presidents of Russia, Ukraine, Kazakhstan, and Belorussia), Yeltsin had a second question included in the referendum that provided for the direct and popular election of Russia's president. On June 12, 1991, he became the first popularly elected leader in Russia's thousand-year history when he secured a stunning first-round victory. Although he faced five opponents, he won 57 percent of the votes to get elected. And to the horror of the reactionaries in the Red Army, polling results indicated that in spite of Herculean efforts to tarnish Yeltsin's image, ordinary soldiers gave him most of their votes. Indeed, among young troopers he captured 75 percent of their ballots.[14]

Yeltsin helped himself with the armed forces by selecting Aleksandr Rutskoi, an air force general, as his vice-presidential running mate. But he also won many votes among the military because of his charisma and his capacity to enhance his image as a strong man, as the kind of man Russians loved to lead them, by rebounding from a series of political defeats. On July 9, Russian TV viewers watched riveted when Yeltsin was sworn in as Russia's president and received the blessing of Patriarch Aleksei II, the head of the Russian Orthodox Church. Like a Sergei Eisenstein movie epic, the ceremony projected an image of might, mystery, and unyielding power.

But the campaign to unseat Gorbachev began several months earlier when in March, Yeltsin supporters, numbering 100,000, took to the streets of Moscow in a massive anti-Gorbachev demonstration. Among the demands the protesters made was that Gorbachev step down and be replaced by a collective executive of republic leaders; another was that Soviet troops withdraw from Lithuania. In response, Boris Pugo, the ethnic Latvian Stalinist who headed the interior ministry, deployed fifty thousand troops to help bolster the city police, but they failed to intimidate the demonstrators and keep them at home. They chanted, "Yeltsin! Yeltsin!" and "Gorbachev, go away!" and, David Remnick reports, "within sight of the extraordinary cordon of military vehicles, water cannon, and troops in riot gear, the throng demonstrated the embattled Soviet President's inability to suppress the growing shift of allegiance to Mr. Yeltsin, the President of the Russian republic."[15]

The Yeltsinites had scored an impressive victory on the streets of Moscow that day, but they also defeated hard-liners in the Russian parliament. Neo-Stalinists in that body had tried to censor Yeltsin but were soundly defeated by the legislators. And in February 1991, Yeltsin, via TV, made a personal appeal that Gorbachev resign because he was leading the country toward a dictatorship.

That spring, Gorbachev watched with dismay as he came under attack from all sides, and he suffered a further blow when strikes, conducted by coal miners demanding his resignation, spread throughout the country. He could not be unmindful of the fact that Yeltsin had captured the imagination of the masses and that the democrats were now infused with a new sense of confidence while the hard-liners were clearly in disarray. Apparently fearing that the democrats could mobilize the disgruntled masses into a truly powerful force against his rule, and realizing that the reactionaries were divided and demoralized, Gorbachev lurched back toward the democrats and aligned himself with the rising star of Boris Yeltsin. Perhaps, as in the past, this was only a tactical ploy. Later, after he deemed his political situation strengthened, he would once again turn against Yeltsin.

The aides of both men, fearing a civil war, had urged them to join hands against the forces of reaction that were gathering around them. It was against this backdrop that they agreed to collaborate and forge a new union. Recall that in November 1990, Gorbachev had proposed a new union, but it did not provide the republics real autonomy. Then Yeltsin had championed what became known as the "union of four" idea, a union of Russia, Belorussia, Ukraine, and Kazakhstan. This prompted Gorbachev to hold a referendum on March 17 to secure a vote of confidence in preserving the existing USSR. The Baltic countries, along with Armenia, Georgia, and Moldavia, boycotted the referendum, but it was endorsed by a majority of those who voted.

Still, leaders of the largest republics, including Yeltsin in Russia, Kravchuk in Ukraine, and Nazerbayev in Khazkhstan, wanted a union that would provide them with sovereign power at the expense of the Center, Moscow. Bending before the pressure of these men and weakened by the abortive coup in Lithuania, Gorbachev negotiated the "nine plus one" accord with Yeltsin and Nazerbayev in April 1991. It involved nine republic leaders, plus the Soviet president, and created a new union, one that would dramatically reduce the Moscow's powers.

The accord, arranged in Gorbachev's private residence in Novo-Ogaryova outside Moscow, was greeted by the hard-liners with grave forboding. If the nine plus one accord was enacted as scheduled in late August 1991, the power of the CPSU, the KGB, and other Soviet institutions they dominated would suffer a dramatic diminution. Moreover, the monopolistic powers Moscow always had enjoyed at the expense of the republics would be dramatically attenuated as power flowed away from Moscow toward the vast hinterland of the USSR. Among other things, Gorbachev had acceded to Yeltsin's demand that Russian, not Soviet, authorities henceforth would control the Russian Federation's vast vital resources. Finally, the agreement seemed to provide for the secession of the Baltic states and the three other republics that had not been a party to the accord.

Faced with their imminent political demise, the neo-Stalinists became desperate. The day after the nine plus one announcement, April 24, the plenum of the central committee of the CPSU convened and Gorbachev was assaulted by the neo-Stalinists. In response, he offered to resign, and other reformers threatened they would leave the party with him. Fearful that his departure would spell the demise of the CPSU and no doubt wary that he was setting them up, the hard-liners did not accept his resignation.

But they continued to press him. On June 17, Vice-President Valentin Pavlov failed in a clumsy attempt to seize power when he asked parliament to give him many of Gorbachev's duties on the flimsy pretext that Pavlov wished to lighten the Soviet president's awesome workload. Once again Gorbachev skillfully parried the ham-handed attempt of the far right to derail him. Upon leaving the scene of the confrontation, Gorbachev proclaimed to the press with a smile, "The coup is over."

But he was wrong! On June 20, Jack Matlock invited several recently elected reformers to lunch with him at Spasso House. That very morning in Washington, Boris Yeltsin had a scheduled meeting with President Bush. Matlock received a call from the office of Gavril Popov the mayor of Moscow. Popov could not attend the luncheon but he requested a meeting with the American ambassador an hour beforehand. Once the men were alone and had exchanged pleasantries, Popov—mindful of the resourcefulness of the KGB—scribbled a note which proclaimed in Russian: "A coup is being organized to remove Gorbachev. We must get word to Boris Nikolayevich."

Matlock, who both writes and speaks Russian, responded in kind.

"I'll send a message. But who is behind this?" Popov responded: "Pavlov, Kryuchkov, Yazov, Lukyanov."[16]

The plotters were respectively the prime minister of the USSR, the heads of the KGB and ministry of defense, and the chairman of the Soviet parliament. Matlock contacted Washington but said that President Bush should not reveal either the source of the alarming news or the people involved, since there had been no other independent confirmation of the coup. But that day while the foreign ministers of the United States and the Soviet Union were meeting in Berlin, Secretary of State Baker received a message. Soon afterward, Aleksandr Bessmertnykh received a call from his counterpart, James Baker. The American secretary of state urged the Russian to meet him at once but avoid detection by the press. Upon his arrival, Baker told Bessmertnykh, "I've just received a report from Washington. I understand it may come from intelligence sources. It seems that there may be an attempt to depose Gorbachev." [17]

Later in a telephone conversation, President Bush, in the process of informing Gorbachev that Yeltsin had not been disloyal to the Soviet president, revealed that Popov was the source of the coup alarm. Gorbachev handled the matter without any visible sign of conflict. But Matlock in his memoirs would chastise both Baker and Bush for their mishandling of the incident: "While Baker's reaction was thoughtless, President Bush's was reckless." Referring to the president, Matlock observed: "I would not have expected this from a former head of the CIA, who prided himself on professionalism and was quick to condemn any leak of the most trivial information, but it was a measure of how deep his infatuation with Gorbachev had gone." [18]

In spite of such attempts to emasculate his political power, and perhaps because he handled them with so little effort, Gorbachev turned a deaf ear to old comrades like Aleksandr Yakovlev. The latter had warned that the neo-Stalinists Gorbachev had gathered around him to protect his presidency were in fact bent on toppling him. His hubris would prove to be his undoing. As the day approached when the nine plus one agreement would become law, the plotters, fearful but angry and desperate, decided to force him from power. On July 29, in a meeting with Yeltsin and the Kazakhstan president, Nursultan Nazerbayev, Gorbachev burned his bridges with the hard-liners by agreeing to remove from their posts Kryuchkov, Pugo, and Pavlov soon after the union treaty was signed in late August.

That same day, President Bush arrived in Moscow to conduct a summit with Gorbachev. The Soviet leader had attended the June G-7 economic summit in London, but he got a cold shoulder from the world's leading capitalist countries when he presented them with a reform plan that they deemed so flawed they could not justify the economic aid Gorbachev was requesting. Under the plan the money would go to the outmoded state enterprises that were the source of the Soviet Union's economic malaise. Gorbachev hoped that Bush might be more forthcoming in their Moscow summit.

But Bush learned of Gorbachev's declining authority when he was informed by an American source (before Gorbachev knew of this incident) that six

Lithuanian border guards had been brutally murdered in a raid on their post at Medininkai, on the Belorussian border. They had been shot in the back of the head, gangland style. The killers were not identified, but everyone knew that the hated OMON, the special units under Boris Pugo's ministry of interior, were responsible for the killings.[19] Similar attacks on border posts had occurred in other parts of the Baltics, and the message was clear in each case: "Your borders are not secure and under your control. The Soviet state reins supreme!"

The murders also were an obvious attempt to embarrass Gorbachev and convey the message that the Soviet president was not in command of the USSR. Bush left Moscow lamenting that his partner's authority was in decline.

On Saturday, 17 August 1991, Kryuchkov contacted Yazov, Pavlov, and Gorbachev's chief of staff, Valery Boldin, and urged them to join him at a posh KGB operated bathhouse. The men agreed that the country was on the brink of chaos and that a state of national emergency had to be proclaimed. They would confront Gorbachev and ask him to support the move. If he refused to cooperate, they would declare him incapacitated and replace him with his vice-president Gennady Yanayev. The vice-president had not been previously consulted, and when he was informed, he balked, asserting that he did not have the experience to run the country. But the day after the bathhouse meeting, August 18, he gave his consent.[20]

On Monday morning, August 19, 1991, TASS issued a terse announcement that shocked early-morning commuters in Moscow. President Mikhail Gorbachev, "hampered by ill health" and incapable of discharging his duties, had been replaced by Vice-President Gennady Yanayev. At the time, Gorbachev was vacationing in the Crimea, in his opulent dacha at Foros on the Black Sea. TASS said that under the Soviet constitution, Vice-President Yanayev was Gorbachev's lawful replacement, and that for an interim period he would govern the country with the help of the "State Committee for the State of Emergency." There was no provision for the committee in the constitution, but all of its self-selected members were high-level officials that Gorbachev had appointed when he spurned his reformist allies the previous fall and lurched toward the right. In addition to Yanayev, the committee included Prime Minister Valentin Pavlov, Interior Minister Boris Pugo, KGB Chief Vladimir Kryuchkov, Defense Minister Dmitri Yazov, and several civilian members of the military-industrial complex. Later it was learned that Gorbachev's old law school chum and deputy, Anatoly Lukyanov, and his chief of staff, Valery Boldin, had supported the coup. In a second statement that day, TASS announced that the committee had imposed a six-month state of emergency throughout the USSR.

According to Gorbachev's account of events, Boldin had led a delegation of government and party officials to the Cape Foros compound on Sunday, August 18. Surprised when he learned of the motorcade's approach, Gorbachev "picked up the telephone but it wasn't working. I picked up a second, a third, a fourth, but none of them worked." When he tried an internal phone and discovered it, too, was dead, "I then realized that this mission was not the sort of mission with which we ordinarily had to deal. . . . I saw that this was a very serious situation. I thought that they were going to try to blackmail me or force me or compel me to do something. Anything was possible." When the delegation entered the compound, Gorbachev said, they "didn't stand on ceremony. With Chief of Staff Boldin at the head, they gave me an ultimatum, to transfer power to the vice-president."[21]

On August 18, Boris Yeltsin was in Kazakhstan consulting with Nazerbayev, and he returned to Moscow that same day. Kryuchkov had reversed an earlier plan to have him arrested upon his arrival: instead he would be placed under surveillance. The first Yeltsin had heard about the coup was over the radio at 7:00 A.M. on August 19 while he was in his dacha in Arkhangelskoye, a village fifteen miles outside Moscow. His daughter, Tanya, had waked him when the radio said an important announcement was imminent. Yeltsin was soon joined in his dacha by other reformers, and after composing a statement of protest they agreed to meet at the White House, where Yeltsin had an office. According to one report, a KGB squad assigned to arrest him (presumably their boss had changed his mind) failed because they had first gone to his apartment in Moscow. By the time they arrived in Arkhangelskoye, he had left for the Kremlin. Upon his arrival there, he was refused entry by the guards; they had not received orders to arrest him, so they allowed him to leave for the White House, where he would begin to organize opposition to the coup. Without Yeltsin to lead them, the democrats probably would not have mustered the strength to oppose and ultimately smash the coup. As was true in Lithuania under Landsbergis in January, one brave man made an enormous difference in Russia in August 1991.

Meanwhile, the Bush White House was confused and at first reacted as if the coup were a fait accompli. Jack Matlock is scathing in his assessment of how Bush and his aides handled the crisis. Brent Scowcroft, the head of the National Security Council, receives the brunt of the attack. He dismissed a CIA assessment that the coup was poorly organized and might not succeed. He said, "That's all just speculation at this point, no doubt with some wishful thinking mixed in." Scowcroft had advised that Bush not burn his bridges with the plotters by attacking them. Matlock asserts this was a monumental blunder. "Therefore, when the president made his first statement to the press, he sounded as if he thought the coup had been successful and he intended to deal with the emergency committee." For example, Bush "spoke of Gorbachev in the past tense, expressed the expectation that the coup leaders would carry out the Soviet Union's international obligations, and described their obviously illegal action as merely 'extraconstitutional.'"[22] This accepting attitude was especially damaging because the coup leaders would cite it for several days even after Bush issued a tougher statement later that day in which he condemned the coup. Matlock clearly deems this blunder consistent with what he sees as the Bush administration's failure to adopt a coherent and firm policy toward the USSR. Most specifically, he says that Bush and his advisers did not understand that the United States could influence events in the Soviet Union. Reagan knew this and acted accordingly. "Bush, on the other hand, was uncomfortable with change. Even when it was for the better, he had difficulty recognizing the improvement at first. He always seemed just a step behind—not so much that he endangered anything vital but enough to miss opportunities Reagan would have seized."[23]

The man who saved the day, of course, was Boris Yeltsin. His finest moment occurred on August 19 when he mounted a T-72 tank outside the White House and defied the coup forces. "Citizens of Russia. The legally elected president of the country has been removed from power. . . . We are dealing with a right-wing, reactionary, anti-constitutional coup d'état. . . . Accordingly, we proclaim all decisions and decrees of this committee to be illegal."[24] Yeltsin's supporters adopted the identical tactics the Lithuanians had employed in protecting their parliament building. They built a barricade circling the building with pavement stones, construction equipment, steel girders, and any other materials available that would help protect the White House. Its occupants reasoned that they could demonstrate an attack would not be cost-free (though it would be successful if the coup leaders could apply all of the military might they possessed). They hoped divisions in the plotters' ranks and in the military and support from the people would save the day for them.

For the millions in Russia who witnessed this dramatic scene and opposed the coup, here was evidence that it might not succeed and that they had a formidable man in the person of Boris Yeltsin to lead them against the neo-Stalinists. Simultaneously, Yeltsin's bravery and defiance disheartened the Old Bolsheviks; with memories of Bloody Sunday and the courageous and successful resistance of the Lithuanians fresh in their minds, they too realized that the coup was not completed.

One of the first signs that the coup might be abortive occurred when its leaders held a press conference on Monday, August 19, with the intent of demonstrating that they had nothing to hide but were moving in accord with Soviet law. It was a monumental blunder. Through satellite transmission, a global television audience witnessed the trembling hands of its spokesman, Gennady Yanayev, and the obvious discomfort of his fellow plotters. These men hardly looked confident, decisive, and resolute. Their bearing was rather one of defeat and confusion, that of men who had reached far beyond their grasp and now did not know how to resolve the crisis they had precipitated. It was revealing that Soviet reporters seemed to sense their weakness, because they asked the haggard and solemn conspirators pointed and impertinent questions. A twenty-four-year-old reporter from *Nezavisimayha Gazeta,* Tatyana Malkina, asked Yanayev, numbed with alcohol, "Tell me, please, do you realize that you have carried out a state coup?" The irreverent paper, which had predicted the coup, had been midwifed by Gorbachev's liberalization campaign, and like many Soviet young adults, Tatyana did not quake before Soviet power.[25]

The news conference did not rally the country around the coup leaders. On the contrary, it encouraged Muscovites to rush to the White House, where Yeltsin was organizing resistance. His news conference, conducted from the top of the tank, was beamed via TV for millions of people to witness both within and outside the borders of the USSR. Afterward, viewers in Moscow and other major Russian cities took to the streets in open displays of support for Yeltsin. His courageous stand produced additional political dividends because it encouraged leaders in the non-Russian republics—such as Kazakhstan's president, Nursultan Nazerbayev—to refrain from supporting the neo-Stalinists while prompting foreign governments to deny them diplomatic recognition. By Tuesday, August 20, it was clear that the plotters had lost their nerve, as several of them got blind drunk and others began to disassociate themselves from the action. On Wednesday, August 21, a group led by Rutskoi, but including several members of the coup, flew to Cape Foros to negotiate with Gorbachev. But this was only a ploy that Yeltsin had orchestrated. Upon their arrival in the Crimea the plotters were arrested, and the coup was over!

Upon first hearing news of the coup, many commentators in the Soviet Union and abroad clucked, "I told you so!" They recalled that in October 1964, Nikita Khrushchev was vacationing in his Crimean dacha when he was deposed. His fate was sealed because like Gorbachev, he had tried to recast Soviet society by reducing the Communist Party's power and denying Moscow a monopoly on major policy decisions at the expense of the constituent republics. Khrushchev's reforms, adopted during the "thaw period," were frequently likened to those associated with perestroika. From the outset, many Soviet and Western commentators had proclaimed that party hard-liners would sabotage perestroika. Well, they had been right!

Not quite. The Soviet Union in 1991 had changed dramatically since 1964. One of the major differences was that the Communist apparatchiks were badly demoralized and divided. Although many apparatchiks opposed Gorbachev's reformist policies from the very outset, others were prepared to go along with him because they had no alternative program of reform. Included in this category were men like Arkady Volsky, a leader of the powerful group of men who ran the massive industrial enterprises that Stalin had deemed the basis for Soviet economic might. Although they later had reservations about reforms, about the "rapid pace" of reform in particular, they remained convinced that the Soviet Union was doomed unless fundamental changes in all aspects of Soviet society were embraced. At the same time, by withholding support for bold changes like the Shatalin Plan, they both undermined Gorbachev politically and prevented the adoption of free-market principles that ultimately could set the economy on a new course. What they guaranteed were half measures that only made things worse. And like many of the unrepentant apparats, they blamed reforms as such for the economy's slide into ruin and decline and not the basic flaws of the command economy. Nonetheless, they were not prepared to join the coup leaders in crushing Gorbachev, Yeltsin, and the activists who supported them.

The demoralization of the hard-liners explained why many old guard apparatchiks, while agreeing with the coup leaders that the country was moving over an abyss toward its ultimate destruction, lacked the will to join the coup. It also accounted for the failure of the Putschists to act with resolve and storm the White House, kill Yeltsin, and crush secessionist movements in the Baltics and thereby save the empire.

Another reason the coup failed was that not all members of the Soviet military opposed reform. For many men who had served and fought bravely in Afghanistan, it was clear that the coup leaders were trying to revive a system that was unsalvageable. Also, they recalled that it was the Brezhnevites who had led them into the war and then refused to allow them to take the measures necessary to win it. Like their American counterparts who has tasted defeat in Vietnam, they blamed the politicians for the humiliation they and their men had suffered in a distant land.

Musings along these lines helped explain why Rutskoi could lead the resistance campaign and induce his old military comrades to keep their troops in the barracks while others refused outright to follow orders to attack the

White House. Pavel Grachev, who would become the Russian minister of defense, had at first condoned the coup but then told Yeltsin that he and his men would support the brave people in the White House who opposed the coup. The commander of Soviet air power, Yevgeni Shaposhnikov, threatened to use his planes against the forces loyal to the coup plotters. The KGB Alpha unit, which had been used with deadly force in Vilnius, refused to storm the building, while some members of the KGB denounced the coup and provided Yeltsin's people with a printing press to publish their leaflets of defiance.

On August 21, faced with the prospect of a civil war, Yazov, the Soviet defense minister, accepted the vote of his officers that the troops be returned to their barracks. Yazov said: "I will not be another Pinochet. . . . I'm sorry I ever got mixed up in this business."[26]

A third major reason for the coup's failure was that there were sufficient numbers of Russians who were prepared to risk their lives to oppose the hated Soviet system. Fortunately, only three were killed, but tens of thousands of others were ready to die. When Gorbachev returned from Cape Foros, dazed, disoriented, and exhausted, he shocked the world in his first news conference when he proclaimed he still was a Communist and the party was not responsible for the coup. He thanked and praised Yeltsin but acted as if he and the Russian president were equal partners who would work together in reforming the Soviet Union. Of course, he was wrong on both counts as Yeltsin would soon disband the CPSU and thereby demonstrate conclusively that he now was the premier leader of the Soviet Union.

It became clearer over the next several days that Gorbachev did not understand that a great transformation had taken place in the USSR since he first took power in 1985. Gradually, over the years of perestroika, millions of Soviet citizens had responded to his efforts to empower them at the grassroots. Through elections in 1989, 1990, and 1991 for the Congress of People's Deputies, the historical election in Lithuania, and Yeltsin's election to the Russian presidency, the political landscape of the USSR was transformed. And as is always the case when there is a shift in the political balance of power, it reflected a change in the consciousness of millions of people.

In postmortems of the failed coup, pundits observed that only a small number of people had taken to the streets in open support of Gorbachev and in opposition to the neo-Stalinists. But those who openly defied the coup, and had demonstrated support for a democratic society from the very outset of perestroika, were strategically placed in Soviet society. It did not escape the attention of many influential elites in the party, military, ministries, and industrial complex that these people represented the most talented and energetic element of society. Their quality, not their numbers, had a profound impact upon the elites who harbored grave doubts about democracy and free-market reforms. They represented a burgeoning middle class that had evolved after World War II as a result of new educational opportunities that led to employment as managers, technicians, researchers, and media workers, i.e., positions that are integral to an advanced industrial society. Although grudgingly, the party elites had to allow a growing number of citizens to acquire the educational skills necessary to keep the Soviet Union in the race with the West. They did so reluctantly, because they knew the Soviet middle class—like its counterparts in the West—would demand a greater voice in matters which were previously controlled by the party and its minions. But as Gorbachev realized, they could not be denied, since they possessed the talent, energy, and expertise that were needed to prevent the Soviet Union from falling farther behind the West and even the newly industrial countries of Asia.

Since elites throughout the Soviet hierarchy were Moscow-centered, street demonstrations in the capital dramatically increased the importance of the resistance in the minds of commanders who had the means to crush them. And via television, their numbers and influence were magnified throughout much of the USSR, where both elites and ordinary citizens watched as bystanders. The most perceptive among the Communist ruling elite lost their will to resist the inevitable when they realized that the democrats had history on their side.

Only the most dim-witted among them believed that the democratic revolution, which was sweeping advanced societies, could be checked at the borders of the Soviet empire. The Soviet elite had maintained power after World War II at the cost of economic underdevelopment and ultimately a decline in national power. Furthermore, it was impossible to educate people—and place them in positions where they had to use their minds to build sophisticated weapons systems, manage large enterprises, provide professional services, and perform all the other duties associated with a post-industrial society—without their making demands for a voice in decisions that affected their lives.

And even the most obtuse among the hard-liners could not be unmindful of the fact that many of their own children had joined the forces of democracy. Others, the more liberal-minded but still unrepentant Leninists among them in the party, KGB, military, and other Soviet power centers, could not ignore an alarming fact: Western-style democratic capitalism represented the road to national power and wealth.

After the failed coup, Yeltsin declared the CPSU an outlaw organization, and it was disbanded. Lithuania—which along with Estonia and Latvia had been targeted by the coup leaders because it was expected that their peoples would openly resist the coup—became a free and independent state on September 6, 1991, by a decree of the Soviet parliament. In spite of efforts to keep the USSR whole, Gorbachev had to accept the inevitable, and on Christmas Day 1991, the Soviet Union faded into the mist of history.

The Soviet empire was doomed. If it had not imploded in 1991 it probably would have been consumed in a serious cataclysmic civil war sometime later. But the empire broke up without a great loss of human life.

The Lithuanians played a vital role in the Soviet Union's benign collapse by restoring their independence in March 1990. Citizens of the empire knew that by boldly challenging Soviet might, the Lithuanians had driven a stake into the heart of the Soviet leviathan. Unlike Georgian and Azeri separatists, the Lithuanians had conducted a peaceful campaign that was predicated upon the rule of law. Their bold rebuff of Russian imperialism and brave stand in January 1991 encouraged other republics to follow their lead.

The Lithuanian rebellion and the failure of the Soviet monolith to crush it was a catalyst in the demise of the Leninist regime and Soviet empire. In the summer of 1992, Colonel Sergei Goncharov, the commander of the Alpha unit that had not attacked the RSFSR parliament building in August 1991, explained why his unit had refused to move. "Vilnius was the last straw and our patience ran out. . . . Honestly, had it not been for Vilnius we would not have refused to storm the White House."[27]

10 AN UNCERTAIN FUTURE

We will be back!
> —*Sign on Russian army truck leaving Lithuania*
> *in August 1993*

Our rockets are rusty but they still work!
> —*General Aleksandr Lebed, elected to the Russian duma*
> *in December 1995*

In June 1992, I spent a month in Lithuania as a new phase in its post-Soviet period was about to begin. Landsbergis and parliament had three years left to their terms of office, but both favored early elections in the fall, because the government was paralyzed. After Lithuania achieved international recognition as an independent state, the Sajudis faction did not work together in a coherent and disciplined fashion, and Landsbergis and his allies believed that a new parliament with a fresh mandate would break the logjam.

Arvydas Juozaitis, who accused Landsbergis of "authoritarian tendencies," stated categorically: "Landsbergis and Sajudis are mistaken if they think elections are good for them. They control the parliament now and they are responsible for political paralysis in Lithuania. Brazauskas and the LDLP [Lithuanian Democratic Labor Party] will win the election."[1] The reform Communists in Lithuania had chosen that name late in 1990 to indicate that they no longer were Marxist-Leninists.

Andrius Kubilius, who had become Sajudis's national chairman, disagreed. He was confident the election would produce a result favorable to Landsbergis and his conservative supporters in Sajudis. He conceded that there were divisions in the ranks of the former Sajudis block but predicted that those "obstructionists" would be defeated and their replacements would work together effectively. Moreover, a weak presidency was the primary source of political gridlock, and it could be broken if the powers of the chief executive were expanded. Under the stewardship of a strong president, the country's daunting economic and social problems would be addressed.[2]

Kubilius's optimism was based upon the results of a spring referendum proposing a new constitution that would greatly enhance presidential powers. It received a 70 percent favorable vote, but the referendum was not legally binding, since a majority of the eligible voters had not participated as mandated under the electoral law. Nonetheless, given the favorable outcome, Landsbergis was optimistic about winning the fall elections.

On this score, Landsbergis was badly mistaken. By the summer of 1992 there were strong signals that he was in trouble, although his most steadfast supporters in Lithuania and the émigré community ignored them. This myopia was understandable, given the monumental role that Landsbergis had played in Lithuania's drive for independence. Even his critics conceded that he had displayed great political acumen and personal courage in leading his people out of the empire. Had he resigned his office in the face of Gorbachev's threats, any replacement would have had difficulty sustaining the independence drive. The Kaunas radicals had neither the stature nor the nationwide political support to put someone in his shoes. Perhaps Ozolas, who enjoyed great popularity in 1990–91, could have filled them, but many of his colleagues, witnessing Landsbergis demise, would have lost their nerve. Under steady pressure from Moscow, and without unity, Ozolas could not have moved with the same vigor that Landsbergis did. Brazauskas was unacceptable to the Sajudis activists, and even if he somehow won without their support, he at best would have adopted a step-by-step strategy, delaying independence for many years. Indeed, it is probable that he would have accepted sovereign status—i.e., control over Lithuanian affairs—and stopped short of independence.

Landsbergis's leadership was both heroic and pivotal in the restoration of an independent Lithuania. The calm and steady stewardship he provided during the dangerous months of 1991 helped maintain the morale and determination of the Lithuanians in what was perhaps their finest hour as a people. His pivotal role in the rebellion's success provided compelling evidence that leaders shape the course of history and are not merely pawns of larger forces. Macroeconomic, social, cultural, and political trends provided the framework for revolutionary change in the USSR, but if Landsbergis had been forced from the stage or assassinated, Lithuania's bolt from the union probably would have been aborted. Ultimately, the primary forces responsible for the Soviet societal crisis would have eroded the foundations of that empire and destroyed it, but it might have endured into the twenty-first century.

If the Lithuanian rebellion had been crushed in early 1991, it is almost certain that separatists in other parts of the empire would have discontinued their breakaway campaigns and surrendered to the might of the Soviet Leviathan. Like the canary in the coal mine, the health of the Lithuanian rebellion was being closely monitored by those who were about to bolt from the USSR.

What we know for a fact is that a meek music scholar acquired the courage to stand firm in the face of the KGB and the Soviet military and his people emerged victorious. Their triumph in turn precipitated the series of events that ultimately destroyed the Soviet empire.

By 1992 the nationalist phase of Lithuania's post-Soviet period had ended. Unlike Estonia and Latvia, where the presence of large Russian populations fueled nationalist passions, Lithuania faced no equivalent internal threat to its sovereignty or culture. Lithuanians were preoccupied with mundane economic problems that Landsbergis and his allies were unable to resolve. Many Sajudis activists, who had been his close associates during the fateful years of 1990 and 1991, were critical of Landsbergis too.

Some lamented that he had become a victim of his own success, a casualty of hubris fed by his having been right and his critics wrong about critical decisions in the past. These included the March 11 restoration of Lithuanian independence and his refusal to bow to Soviet pressure and rescind that declaration.

Landsbergis surrounded himself with young people who had neither the expertise nor the stature to challenge his decisions. Confident that he knew what was best for Lithuania, he ignored advice from older, more experienced colleagues.

Others said Landsbergis's vision of Lithuania was flawed. He remained wedded to romanticized notions about restoring the country to its pre-Soviet status; a devout population celebrating Lithuanian folkways would shed the culture of Homo Sovieticus. But Soviet values and mores that encouraged people to lie and cheat without shame and to achieve personal economic gain at any price would not soon fade from Lithuanian society. And in contrast to the independence era, Lithuania was no longer a predominantly pastoral society in which most people worked the fields and lived in small villages. Lithuania had entered the urban industrial world and had become subject to all of the uncertainties of modern life.

Still others charged that Landsbergis was naive in thinking that the country could made a clean break with Russia on all fronts. Lithuania had important economic ties with Russia and depended, in particular, upon importing oil and gas from that source. Moreover, Landsbergis's reliance upon the West—gaining quick access to Western economic, political and security organizations—clashed with his own skepticism about the Western powers' indifference toward small countries and their infatuation with large ones. After all, Bush had stated very clearly that relations with the Soviet Union were more important than close ties with tiny Lithuania.

Landsbergis's political adversaries were even more pointed in their remarks. Brazauskas told me in January 1992: "Landsbergis is unrealistic. For a long time we will depend upon close economic relations with Russia. We cannot rely upon the West to buy our products. We need good economic relations with Russia, which is our natural trading partner.[3] This was the view of many Lithuanians now that they were free of the Soviet yoke. Their primary concerns were economic: job security, a living wage, pensions, and the costs of moving from a command economy to one based upon free-market principles, which few of them had ever experienced.

Finally, even an old ally like Romuoldas Ozolas concluded that Landsbergis had run out of ideas. "Landsbergis could act when the people lifted him up on a wave of national resistance," Ozolas said early in 1993. "But when the wave receded and he had to govern reasonably, he couldn't do that. He had no constructive ideas."[4]

The major reason why Landsbergis's stature had diminished in the eyes of many Lithuanians was economic hard times. Sajudis had been created to protest Soviet rule and to celebrate the Lithuanian national idea, but now that the Soviets no longer controlled the country and Lithuanians were in charge, the most pressing problems were economic. From the outset, Lithuania's economy had been stricken by Moscow's withholding petroleum exports, then reneging on trade agreements for energy, and still later reducing overall commercial relations with Vilnius.[5]

In 1991 and 1992, shortages of petroleum and natural gas were accompanied by soaring prices and declining economic output in both industrial and agricultural enterprises. These shortfalls had turned the voters against the government led by Prime Minister Abisala. In 1992 there was a 37.7 percent decline in gross domestic product (GDP), and a year later a 27.1 percent decline. Consequently most Lithuanians suffered a serious dip in living standards as inflation surged to over 1,000 percent in 1992 and fears about job security and pensions soared. One labor leader estimated that the real unemployment figure was close to 20 percent, not 10 percent as government statistics claimed.[6] The ineptitude of parliament or Landsbergis aside, there was little any Lithuanian government could have done to prevent the economic chaos that occurred as the country made the daunting transformation from a command to a free-market economy. Neither the university professors in

Sajudis nor their opponents, the reform Communists, understood the workings of a free-market economy. How could they, since few of them had ever experienced a capitalist society as adults? No one knew how to accomplish the Herculean task of building capitalism without spawning social and political unrest that sabotaged the drive for democracy. The Harvard professors and International Monetary Fund experts who were urging the Lithuanians to follow the Poles' policy of shock therapy ignored important differences between the two countries. During the Communist era, not all of Polish agriculture had been collectivized, many private entrepreneurs had continued to operate in the cities, and the Catholic Church retained considerable autonomy. In short, a civil society existed in Poland during the Soviet era. Lithuania had been a part of the Soviet Union, and the Lithuanians had to start from scratch.

Under Soviet occupation, all forms of private associational life were destroyed in Lithuania, and the people there were as dependent upon the state as were inhabitants of other parts of the former Soviet Union. After independence their lives were shattered as the old-style Stalinist enterprises were targeted for the junk heap. Like their counterparts in Russia, Lithuanians employed in the once mighty military-industrial complex suffered most severely. In the old days they had earned higher wages than other workers.

The collective farm system, moreover, had been dismantled without providing credits and other forms of assistance to the smaller agricultural enterprises that replaced them. Peasants, who had fared relatively well under the old economy, experienced declining living standards as prices for fuel, fertilizer, and equipment escalated. Brazauskas argued that without access to capital, privatization of agriculture would hurt, not enhance, the well-being of Lithuanian agricultural workers. Furthermore, farm income was suffering because Lithuanian agricultural products had been excluded from Western markets, while Western food products—even though more expensive than local alternatives—had become popular in Lithuania because of their cachet. And attempts to protect the poor and elderly from hardships, such as price controls on bread, resulted in insane anomalies. In 1992, bread was so cheap in Lithuania that Latvian farmers bought it by the truck loads to feed their livestock.

Intellectuals and other liberal professionals, who had enjoyed prestige and comparatively good salaries under the old economy, suffered as well. Doctors and nurses, researchers, writers, artists, and educators found their salaries had become subpar. With the termination of government subsidies there was no money available for their institutes, theaters, or schools. To make ends meet, many had to toil at two jobs or left their positions for more lucrative opportunities in the burgeoning private sector. Unfortunately, many in the last category were among the best in their fields. People who had been dismissed in reductions in force had to enter new fields or seek work abroad.

All but the most affluent households were struggling to keep pace with rising prices for food, shelter, clothing, and entertainment. And among ordinary folks, a sense of economic deprivation had grown in proportion to the soaring economic good fortune of those who were successfully exploiting the new economic opportunities. Meanwhile, the approximately one-fifth of the population living on pensions were discouraged as inflation robbed them of the security that they had assumed awaited them in their "golden years." What outraged all Lithuanians was seeing members of the Mafiya and the old Communist *nomenklatura* flaunt their new wealth.

Against this backdrop of declining economic security, voters turned from Sajudis two years after the March 11 declaration of independence. In the October 25 and November 15, 1992, parliamentary elections, the Lithuanian Democratic Labor Party (LDLP) won 73 out of 141 seats. Not many incumbents survived the election, although Landsbergis did, perhaps because his name was on a party list and he did not run in a head-to-head contest for his seat.

Widespread discontent with the economy was not the only reason the electorate turned against the right. Sajudis's leaders had opposed transforming the organization from an inchoate mass movement into a full-blown political party with branches and cadre operating throughout the country—at the outset presumably to assuage Moscow's fears about their true intentions, and later because they lacked the experience or inclination to do so. Had Sajudis made an effort to build a party network covering all segments of the population, perhaps its leaders would have acquired insight into what factory workers and collective farmers were thinking. Such interaction was crucial, because the intellectuals and academics in Sajudis—in contrast to many activists in the LDLP—did not have much contact with ordinary Lithuanians. Meanwhile, in parliament, the deputies joined factions, not parties, and deserted the factions as easily as they had joined them.[7]

The LDLP was a real party, with branches in every part of the country, often administrated by full-time cadre. Its members controlled most local governments, large industrial enterprises, and collective farms (and the cooperatives that replaced many of them with privatization), and were influential in the liberal professions. For Lithuanians, whose living standards were plunging, it made sense to turn to Brazauskas and a party with widespread governmental experience. Voters responded favorably to his observation "We have the people in charge with common sense who do not rely on fairy tales or fantasies to govern."[8]

There was an assumption that Brazauskas retained good relations with his former colleagues in Moscow and could negotiate deals with them that Landsbergis neither sought nor could achieve even if he tried. Most voters agreed with Brazauskas that it was sensible to maintain close economic relations with Russia and other former Soviet republics. Indeed, because of his reputed capacity to negotiate effectively with the Russians, Brazauskas was capable of exploiting issues that should have worked in Landsbergis's favor.

For example, Landsbergis and Sajudis continued to exploit nationalist sentiment fed by the Soviet troop issue. In January 1992, Landsbergis claimed that seventy thousand Soviet troops, now under the control of the Russian defense ministry, remained in Lithuania in violation of international law. "I have good relations with Yeltsin," Landsbergis said, but he feared Russian chauvinists might replace Yeltsin and try to reannex Lithuania. "If a large number of foreign troops were located not far from the White House," he asked me, "how would your president feel?"[9]

Brazauskas charged Landsbergis with inflating the numbers to attract fearful voters to his side. Brazauskas estimated that thirty thousand foreign troops remained in the country and that there was no reason to fear Russian aggression against Lithuania.[10] The people, however, wanted the former Soviet troops to leave, and in a June 1992 referendum they voted overwhelmingly for their withdrawal. But many voters who supported the referendum presumably believed that Brazauskas, not Landsbergis, was best qualified to negotiate their exodus.

The 1992, Seimas (as the parliament henceforth was called) elections also worked in Brazauskas's favor when voters endorsed a constitutional revision providing for a new presidency. Realizing that he had no chance of gaining victory, Landsbergis chose not to run, but leaders of the Christian Democratic Party and the Center Party persuaded Lozoraitis to made a bid for the post. The diplomat had never sought public office and was reluctant to accept the invitation, but knowing that there was no one else available and believing that a competitive election would enhance Lithuanian democracy, he threw his hat into the ring.

Lozoraitis received overwhelming support from the diaspora, but in Lithuania his opponents charged that as ambassador to the United States he was corrupt and ineffective. An émigré American physician, Kazys Bobelis (the last president of VLIK, the Supreme Committee for the Liberation of Lithuania), who had returned to Lithuania after independence and was elected to parliament and selected by Brazauskas to head the parliament's foreign relations committee, led the attack. In the process, Bobelis, whose father had been a commandant of Kaunas under Nazi rule, earned the enmity of many activists in the émigré community, such as Asta Banionis, who accused him of engaging in cynical political expediency. Bobelis, she said, "had attacked Sajudis when it was first established for being a Communist front" and now was aligning himself with people whom many in the diaspora deemed unrepentant Communists.[11]

Brazauskas won 60 percent of the votes in the February 14, 1993, election, but considering Lozoraitis's liabilities—he was a political neophyte, he entered the race late, and he did not have a national network—he could take satisfaction in his performance. The only areas where he got more votes than Brazauskas were the city of Kaunas and the raion (county) of Kaunas. He did not expect a victory, but he won one of sorts: by making the race competitive and challenging his opponent's policies, he advanced the cause of democracy in Lithuania.

After the election, Brazauskas removed him from his post in Washington but gave him the ambassadorship to Rome. Later, Brazauskas conceded that he had made a mistake in not allowing Lozoraitis to remain in Washington for a while longer. By replacing the diplomat Brazauskas had only earned the enmity of the diaspora. Lozoraitis died in Washington on June 12, 1994, and left behind a legacy of decency, dignity, and patriotism. The people he had represented during the long dark days of Soviet rule owed him a huge debt of gratitude for his lifetime commitment to a free and democratic Lithuania.

The back-to-back defeats of Landsbergis and Lozoraitis shocked the North American diaspora. Having struggled for almost fifty years to end Soviet rule in their old homeland, they were appalled that "the Communists" had been returned to power. In exile, they had sustained Lithuanian national life, waged a campaign against the brutal Soviet rule of their country, and given Sajudis critical support from abroad. It would be misleading, of course, to exaggerate the political influence of the Lithuanian diaspora. Had 800,000 persons of Lithuanian heritage lived in a country other than the United States, their ability to influence events in the Soviet Union would have been markedly reduced—perhaps it would have been nil. Lithuania's "special status" would not have existed and Gorbachev's "Baltic problem" would have been much less threatening to his regime. But the Lithuanians in America were a vital asset to the struggle, because they were citizens of the world's most powerful country, a place where influential allies in the media and government could be enlisted in the cause of Lithuanian independence.

Clearly, the knowledge on all sides that Gorbachev desperately needed close and friendly relations with Washington worked in the Lithuanians' behalf. It is reasonable to believe that without the diaspora in America, the Lithuanian independence movement would have been dismantled by force, that the attack on the parliament would have proceeded, and that Landsbergis would have been imprisoned or even killed. After Victor Nakas resigned as the Lithuanian embassy's political officer to protest Lozoraitis's dismissal, he said: "Without the diaspora, Lithuania would have been another Georgia. No one in the United States would have cared if the independence movement had been crushed!"[12]

Although the émigrés were shocked by the "return of the Communists" in their old homeland, the Lithuanian electorate did not favor the LDLP because they wanted a return to the Soviet system. Their behavior was predicated on several factors.

First, it was clear that no post-independence government could long survive the economic chaos and plunge in living standards that the transition from a command to a free-market economy dictated. Whoever was in charge at the time would be discredited.

Second, unlike the diaspora, many Lithuanians deemed Brazauskas a patriot who had played a pivotal role in ending Soviet rule. Also, still others believed that his step-by-step approach to independence was less dangerous and more prudent than the go-for-broke approach of Landsbergis and Sajudis. And as polls have indicated since the late 1980s, Brazauskas was well-liked by Lithuanians.

Third, while the vast majority of Lithuanians opposed a system that denied them national independence—and many complained about economic conditions—most Lithuanians were not altogether disenchanted with their lives under socialism. This became even more evident to them after they were exposed to the harsh realities of capitalism. "We didn't make much money under the old system but our jobs were safe; we didn't work hard and we had lots of free time." This is what one often heard when asking people about the past.

Finally, it is noteworthy that in contrast to Estonians and Latvians, Lithuanians after independence were more inclined to speak of the Soviet system in positive terms. In seeking an explanation for this finding, the pollster Vladys Gadys has observed, "Lithuanians are conservative and do not like change. It probably has something to do with their Catholic faith."[13]

Of course, those Lithuanians who look with favor upon the old Soviet economy forget that their plight today is rooted in the fact that the command economy was doomed and is the source of their present economic malaise. At any rate, by 1995 hopes that Brazauskas and his Democratic Labor Party would resurrect the best of the old world were dashed. Most Lithuanians were unhappy with Labor's rule, and about two-thirds indicated that they had little faith in government or politicians. About the same number of people indicated that their living standards continued to take a downward path, and they expressed outrage that corruption and crime had intensified under Labor's stewardship.

Official corruption was hardly surprising. "The apparats never learned to work under communism—why does anyone think they will under capitalism?" Egle Taurinskaite told me in a wry aside. Most of them had joined the Communist Party in search of political perks and economic advantages, not out of ideological zeal. Under the old system, party membership was a prerequisite to improved living standards and facilitated greater educational opportunities for one's children. Consequently, the most entrepreneurial and materialistic segments of society—and even many of the most gifted —gravitated toward the party and sought high posts in government. Under democratic government and an emerging free-market economy, they continue to see political office and governmental access as a legitimate way to improve one's economic situation. Like their counterparts in other areas of the former Soviet Union, they used their political contacts to gain economic favor through privatization. After all, they provided and interpreted the rules for privatization, knew the people who ran the enterprises and property being privatized, and could secure funding—if necessary—from Mafiya members or other enterprising individuals, including foreign partners, to buy into the capitalist dream. Meanwhile their idealistic opponents, who had refused to play ball with the old system, lacked the contacts, know-how, and single-mindedness to exploit free-market opportunities.

Political corruption had thrived under the rule of the Sajudis activists from 1990 to 1992, but largely because the old Communists controlled the national bureaucracies, local governments, and Soviet-era enterprises. From the very outset of independence, the appropriate official had to be bribed if one wanted to privatize property, rent a building, or engage in a commercial enterprise. Frequently, officials at all levels had to get a piece of the action to secure a license or other document that was provided routinely in the West.

In my summer visit to Lithuania in 1995, I found the press and public alike asserting that the prime minister, Aldolfas Slezevicius, was up to his eyeballs in corrupt activities. One account I heard on more than one occasion contended that frequently when meeting with foreign businessmen interested in doing business in Lithuania, the prime minister's practice was not to ask for a bribe outright. His approach was more subtle. At an appropriate moment in the conversation, he would write a figure on a sheet of paper, say $25,000. That's how much it would cost to operate in the country. In such a corrupt business environment, foreign entrepreneurs frequently have decided to invest their money and share their expertise in other countries.

Even four years after independence, travelers and truckers reported waiting as long as two days to cross Lithuania's main border checkpoint with Poland. The bottleneck was caused by illegal payoffs and deal-making of all kinds, which cost the Lithuanian government substantial revenues. Lithuania had become a pathway for the transfer of wealth looted from Russia, such as metals that fetch high prices in the West. In 1995, the American television program *60 Minutes* revealed that nuclear materials had been found in the safe of one of Lithuania's largest banks. No one has claimed them and they remain in the bank vault to this day.

Both organized criminal gangs and enterprising young men have moved a vast amount of smuggled goods from resource-rich areas of the former Soviet Union to Western buyers. Today, these "metalists" can be seen driving Western cars throughout Lithuania, and they are the ones who freely spend money in the new shops, restaurants, and bars that have appeared in the cities. Western law enforcement agencies like the FBI fear that these people will provide the manpower to smuggle drugs from the former Soviet Union to Western markets.

During the Soviet era, many ordinary, otherwise honest people were involved in stealing from the system, because that was the only way working people could survive. But no one thought of the practice as stealing, since all property "belonged to the people." The most ambitious rip-offs, however, were perpetrated by the party apparatchiks, since they had access to resources on a massive scale and the contacts to steal on a large scale without fear of being punished. They had friends in both law enforcement and the courts who protected them for a piece of the action. At the same time, they engaged in joint ventures with criminals who functioned throughout the Soviet era.

The ability of criminals to operate freely was restricted by the state, but because of the collapse of Soviet authority and the vast storehouse of state-owned wealth made available with privatization, organized criminal gangs have flourished and systematic corruption has scaled new heights. The Mafiya has grown in size and influence, and Lithuanians believe there are few significant enterprises that do not have mob connections. The profits earned from the massive smuggling of goods and commodities from Russia has provided mobsters with the capital to buy into the newly created capitalist market and to provide funds, enabling old Communist apparatchiks to exploit the privatization of enterprises, property, and land.

Extortion is a thriving business in the new capitalist economy, and mobsters have bombed establishments where their owners have refused to provide protection money. In 1993, there were 150 reports of bombings in Lithuania, thirty-one in Vilnius alone.[14]

Even more disturbing than property damage are the numerous murders that have been perpetrated by the Mafiya, mostly in places where the criminals have clashed over turf—in Vilnius, Kaunas, Klaipeda, and the Baltic resort city of Palanga. In the last case, a popular restaurant was struck by an antitank shell in a gangland attack. Since automatic weapons and antitank ordnance are widely available, the mobsters have the means to engage in bloody Rambo-like firefights. In other cases, businesspeople who refused to pay for protection and journalists who wrote about the Mafiya have been killed. For example, an editor for the newspaper *Respublica,* Vitas Lingys, was shot dead in broad daylight outside his apartment in 1993 because his paper had refused to stop publishing articles about the mob. It has been alleged that he was murdered because he linked gangs in Vilnius to a Russian mob operating in New York City's Little Odessa. His killer was Igor Achremov, a member of the Vilnius Brigade, a Georgian-Jewish gang reputedly led by Boris Dekanidze.[15] After being found guilty of ordering the murder, Dekanidze was executed by a firing squad in July 1995.

The evil deeds of organized crime are a source of national outrage, but violent assaults, robberies, and other forms of street crime figure far more importantly in the lives of average citizens. Unemployment, shrinking salaries, and the shredding of the country's social fabric have contributed to expanding criminal behavior, and underdeveloped law enforcement agencies have proved incapable of dealing with it. And what worries many Lithuanian parents even more than the prospects of having their homes burgled (muggings are still rare in Lithuania) is the fear that their children are being reared in a moral wasteland. Young people have become enthralled by the abundance that capitalism dangles before them, and their elders fear that the nihilism of Soviet culture will be replaced by a crude, mindless quest for material possessions in the new economy. Pornography, drugs, and sexual license all existed under the Soviet system, but they were kept in the shadows of society, not the forefront. Soviet ideologues preached self-sacrifice for the good of the community, but the gurus of the free market celebrate self-indulgence. At least, this is how many older Lithuanians assess the two systems. "I fought the Soviets, but at least we knew where our kids were then," I heard someone say at a party in Vilnius.

In two visits to Lithuania in 1995, I also witnessed a new assault on Lithuania's free press. The country's leading daily, *Lietuvos Rytas,* joined *Respublica* in producing a series of articles about political corruption and organized crime and the linkages between the two. In addition to providing space for charges leveled with special zeal by Romualdas Ozolas about the indiscretions of Prime Minister Slezevicius, the paper revealed that the minister of interior, Romasis Vaitekunas, was driving a Mercedes-Benz 600 SL that had been stolen from a German citizen earlier in 1995. Another story revealed that in a prison one hundred kilometers from Vilnius, a select group of prisoners were living as if in a luxury hotel. *Lietuvos Rytas* included front-page photos of the prisoners partying in their cushy refuge. Such shameful incidents, the paper proclaimed, could not have existed without the complicity of public officials. The officials under attack accused the press of publishing untruths, while the Mafiya decided to respond with force.

At 11:40 P.M. on the evening of November 16, 1995, a huge bomb seriously damaged an annex to the editorial offices of *Lietuvos Rytas,* which is located just off Gedimino Street, the major street in downtown Vilnius. There were no casualties, but the damage was so extensive that structural engineers said the building was unsafe and had to be torn down. The following weekend, *Lietuvos Rytas* and its two major competitors, *Respublica* and *Lietuvos Aides,* ran similar front-page stories attacking government corruption and blaming the bombing on the refusal of the government to get tough with criminal elements operating in the country.

Several weeks later, charges of widespread corruption and economic mismanagement were given added legitimacy when two of Lithuania's largest banks, Innovation and Litimpeks, were forced to close their doors in a banking moratorium. The heads of both banks were imprisoned, and the central bank board chairman resigned. The opposition in the parliament demanded that Prime Minister Slezevicius resign his post as well, but he refused to do so. In January, Foreign Minister Povilas Gylys and Defense Minister Linas Linkevicius submitted their resignations to protest the scandal, although President Brazauskas refused to accept them. In light of the banking crisis and growing disenchantment with the government, Landsbergis and his allies demanded the election date be moved up from the fall to the summer of 1996.

Public outrage soared when it was learned that the prime minister and the minister of interior had both withdrawn money from their accounts several days before the banks closed their doors. Brazauskas asked for their resignations, but Slezevicius vowed he would remain in office. He believed that he could rally the Labor deputies in the Seimas around him. But he was wrong. On February 8, 1996, he received a vote of no confidence; all of the opposition and most of his own party deputies voted for his removal.

Growing disenchantment with the ruling party had surfaced earlier in the year when Labor candidates suffered a serious setback in spring municipal elections. Landsbergis's Homeland Union captured 29.1 percent, of the votes and the Christian Democrats 16.9 percent, to the LDLP's 19.1 percent. It is premature to predict the LDLP's political demise in the national political arena, but it is likely that Labor will be turned out of power soon.[16]

But whatever happens politically in the short term, the specter of Homo Sovieticus—"Soviet Man," Soviet culture—will loom over Lithuanian society for many years to come. During the Soviet era—an entire lifetime for most Lithuanians—people were forced to lie, cheat, and steal to survive economic hardship and protect their families from arbitrary punishment at the hands of the authorities. In his commentary on the prospects for civil society in the former Soviet Union, the late Ernest Gellner has observed, "Far from creating a new social man, one freed from egotistic greed, commodity fetishism and competitiveness . . . the system created isolated, amoral, cynical individualists—without opportunity, skilled at doubletalk and trimming within the system, but incapable of effective enterprise."[17]

Every member of Lithuanian society was inculcated with "Soviet norms" of behavior, even those who opposed the system. The Soviet legacy accounts for the tendency of politicians to engage in personal attacks upon their opponents and make vicious, groundless charges about their rivals' motives. Allegations about real or alleged ties with the KGB have been a common practice. Such unsavory behavior exists in the West, but it is the norm not the exception throughout the former Soviet Union and is especially pernicious in content. Homo Sovieticus explains why those in power make decisions in secret, dictate terms, and deem compromise a sign of weakness and not a prudent attempt to advance a political program in a pluralistic society.

When all is said and done, however, the greatest problem facing Lithuania is associated with the disruptions that will continue as it makes the tortuous transition from communism to capitalism. That daunting process presents the country with a pivotal question that remains to be answered: what fallout can be expected from the hardships that will occur as the old Soviet enterprises are closed and workers lose jobs, salaries, and subsidies that had previously cushioned the transition? The total privatization of agriculture has shredded the economic life and social fabric of many agricultural communities. The dismal life that many older rural Lithuanians must endure is reflected in the encounter a resident of Vilnius reputedly had with an old woman in a village. "What do you do here, mother?" The woman answers, "We sing and the men drink!"

Notwithstanding existing difficulties and those that will plague Lithuania for many years, there are positive indicators suggesting the Lithuanians will succeed in building a democratic society and viable free-market economy.

Daryll Johnson, the first American ambassador to Lithuania after it received diplomatic recognition from Washington, acknowledges that Lithuanian has lagged behind Estonia and Latvia in developing a viable economy. But he notes that Lithuanians have moved with greater speed than their Baltic cousins in the massive privatization of apartments; about 90 percent are now privately owned. Lithuania also has met all the requirements demanded by the International Monetary Fund to receive assistance, most specifically keeping strict reins on spending and monetary policy. And in contrast to Russia, Lithuania has experienced great success in its war against inflation. The Lithuanian currency, the litas, is convertible, pegged to the dollar, and stable.[18] Now upscale restaurants like Stikliai no longer have a two-tiered pricing systems—dollars for scarce or imported products and the local currency for plentiful domestic ones. The litas is used to purchase everything.

New private shops and restaurants have mushroomed throughout Vilnius and other cities, and the gray drabness of the Soviet era has been replaced by a brighter, more congenial ambiance on the streets and in the shops. Members of the older generation will continue to experience economic hard times, but the prospects for younger people are hopeful. It is among the country's youth that one is most likely to find successful entrepreneurs or men and women who have found employment in the newly privatized enterprises. And it is expected that the country's GDP will show a gain of 3 percent to 5 percent in 1995.[19]

Lithuania has conducted several free and open elections and power has been transferred without violence. Johnson says that this peaceful transfer of power is a "tremendously important event" and Lithuania has done "far better on this score than Russia or Ukraine."[20] Moreover, in spite of conflict between public authorities and the infant private media, Lithuania enjoys a free press that is bravely fighting corruption and crime.

Finally, the Lithuanians have taken concrete steps to resolve old disputes and address national blemishes. Lithuania has adopted the most liberal citizenship law in the Baltics, and all Russians, Poles, and other minority peoples who have desired Lithuanian citizenship have received it. There are Polish deputies in the national parliament, and candidates running under a Polish party label did well in the municipal elections of 1995, even in some areas where Poles were a minority of the electorate.

Lithuania's relations with Poland are warm. In the spring of 1994, against the opposition of Landsbergis and Ozolas, the Lithuanian government signed a treaty of friendship with Poland. Among other things, the treaty recognized existing boundaries, and in it Warsaw acknowledged that Vilnius is Lithuania's capital. Later, Lithuania signed a similar treaty with Belarus.

The Russians have been less inclined to organize into parties, although at least one is in development, and Russians in Lithuania have not complained about their status in the country. And while not free of friction, Lithuanian-Russian relations are better than those between Tallinn and Riga respectively and Moscow. Lithuania was the first of the Baltic states to arrange the withdrawal of former Soviet troops from its soil, in August 1993, and Vilnius and Moscow have reached an agreement on the transit of Russian troops through Lithuania to Kaliningrad.

Finally, on September 22, 1994, the Lithuanian government made a public declaration asking the Jewish people's forgiveness for Lithuania's role in the Holocaust: "The government of the Republic of Lithuania assumes the responsibility for the persecution of those who took part in the killings, and will pursue this consistently, honestly and publicly." Simonas Alperavicius, the president of the Jewish Community of Lithuania, responded: "This is a very much awaited announcement, and it is very good that what had to be said was said in the strongest way."[21]

Lithuania is now a member of the Council of Europe and enjoys associate status in the West European Union. Through the Partnership for Peace Program, Lithuanian military units have been involved in joint exercises with Nordic, American, and other democratic military establishments. A small unit of Lithuanians is serving alongside American units in Bosnia as part of the NATO Implementation Force assigned to keep the peace there. The Lithuanians expect that over time such involvement will help build a defense establishment that adheres to democratic civil-military relations and sheds Soviet military practices. Ultimately they hope to become a full member of NATO.

The Lithuanians wish to rejoin Europe because they deem themselves part of the community of Euro-Atlantic democracies. But their desire for membership in NATO specifically has its roots in two nightmares that haunt all of the Baltic peoples. The first has its source in the chaos that exists in Russia and may produce a resurgent, imperial Russian state, led by a coalition of neo-

Soviets and ultranationalists. The second is the specter of the West denying the Baltics access to the European Union and NATO. Isolated, the Baltic countries, like Georgia and other former Soviet republics, will become Finlandized and one day be forced to join a Russian-dominated Commonwealth of Independent States. Under these oppressive circumstances they may lose both their independence and democracy.

In August 1993, as units of the former Soviet army left Lithuania, some soldiers dangled crudely written signs from their trucks proclaiming: "We will be back!" Many Lithuanians deem this a threat to be taken seriously, not merely an angry outburst of humiliated men who faced a clouded future back home. Russian defense analysts have made no secret of the fact that they deem the Baltics crucial to defending Russia. That is why even liberals like Andrei Kozarev, the former Russian foreign minister, have openly opposed extending NATO eastward. The Lithuanians can cite a series of disturbing developments that support fears about being reincorporated into a new Russian empire.

In September 1990, Soviet apparatchiks and Russian army officers established the "Dniester Soviet Socialist Republic" to forestall the creation of an independent Moldovan state (formerly called Moldavia). Later, when Russians on the left bank of the Dniester River began an insurgency against Moldovan police and defense forces they formed a "Dniester guard," which received weapons from the district's Fourteenth Army arsenal. Cossacks from Russia joined the guard, and in the summer of 1992 troops from the Fourteenth Army helped it overwhelm the Moldovan resisters.[22] The commander of the unit was General Aleksandr Lebed, who was elected to the duma in December 1995 and was a candidate for the Russian presidency in the summer of 1996. (In an interview with an American newspaper he warned the West, "Our rockets are rusty but they work!") Many non-Russians from all parts of the former Soviet Union see the trans-Dniester incident as the model for Russia resurrecting its empire.

I was given other examples by members of the Lithuanian defense ministry in a summer 1994 visit to Lithuania. They cited Georgia as evidence that the trans-Dniester scenario was being implemented in other areas of the former Soviet Union. Russian military leaders and old apparatchiks had manipulated the Abkhazian and Ossetian secessionist movements to destabilize Georgia and in the process forced Eduard Shevardnadze to accept Russian bases on his territory and to join the Commonwealth of Independent States (CIS).[23]

The brutal attack and devastation of Grosny, the capital of Chechnya, beginning in the winter of 1994–1995, and the subsequent brutal assault on the Russian village of Pervomayskoye to expel Chechen rebels there testify to the fact that even a reputed liberal government in Moscow prefers force, not peaceful negotiations, to settle disputes.

The impressive Communist showing in the 1995 duma elections under the stewardship of Gennady Zyuganov—who supported the August 1991 coup—and the utter failure of the democrats to attract significant support presages the Red-Brown (neo-Soviet and ultranationalist) coalition that many Lithuanians fear. And equally disquieting, Yeltsin's replacement of the last remaining democrats in his inner circle with hard-liners indicates that the center of gravity has moved toward the forces of reaction in Russia. Although Washington in its official pronouncements suggests that the political situation has not changed all that much and Zyuganov is a pragmatist, in fact American analysts foresee a marked deterioration in relations between Washington and Moscow. And what must concern everyone who fears a return to autocracy in Russia is the prospect that the Communists and their allies will renationalize much of their country's enterprises in an attempt to reduce the economic pain the masses are suffering. Of course, such a move would be disastrous, because it would only plunge the Russian economy into a deeper funk.

When I made a brief visit to Lithuania in the winter of 1995–1996, I expected Lithuanian leaders would be upset over the Communist victory in the recent Russian elections and worried about a highly publicized document written by defense analysts in Moscow that called for military occupation of the Baltic states if any attempt was made to include them in NATO. To my surprise, I found that they were less concerned about the threat from Russia than, in the words of Andrius Kubilius, the fact "that the West has turned its back on us!" Kubilius is the faction leader of the conservative Homeland Union. His concern that Lithuania would become isolated by the West was also expressed by Emmanuelis Zingeris, the Lithuanian Jewish leader and member of the Seimas's committee on foreign relations.[24]

They had good reason to be despondent. Earlier in 1995, Washington pundits had predicted that by the year's end Poland and perhaps the Czech Republic and Hungary would be given membership in NATO. This would be the first expansion of the alliance eastward, and the Baltics anticipated that they would be included in a later phase of the process. Both President Clinton and Vice-President Al Gore continued to proclaim that the Balts were future candidates for membership.

But earlier in the year, such prominent former officials such as Paul Nitze, who has once served the Truman administration and finished his public service as Ronald Reagan's arms control adviser, and Jack Matlock, the former

American ambassador to the Soviet Union, had expressed their opposition to enlarging NATO. In a letter to Secretary of State Warren Christopher, they warned this would feed Russian fears of being isolated and, as Boris Yeltsin had said, would draw a new Iron Curtain across Europe.[25]

The administration persisted, however; for example, Strobe Talbott, second in charge at the State Department and the administration's expert on the former Soviet Union, wrote an article favoring NATO expansion in the *New York Review of Books* in August 1995. But several months later the administration seemed to have given in: the opposition of prominent American Cold Warriors and Russian reformers, the requirement of having good relations with Moscow as the United States prepared to send twenty thousand peacekeepers to Bosnia, fears about nuclear proliferation, the Communists' victory in the 1995 duma elections, and uncertainty about who would become president after the summer 1996 Russian presidential elections all ultimately convinced President Clinton that prudence demanded a freeze on NATO's enlargement. In January 1996, Clinton renewed his pledge to enlarge NATO, but since no final decision would be made until after the November presidential elections, many pundits interpreted this move as merely an attempt to win votes from Americans of East and Central European descent.

What troubled the Lithuanians even more than their perception that Washington was backtracking on NATO's expansion was the conclusion that the West Europeans were dragging their feet on Baltic membership in the European Union. They had assumed membership in the EU was fully accepted. Zingeris cited Helmut Kohl's opposition to Baltic membership in EU (at a December 1995 meeting in Madrid) because the Balts had not achieved the economic advances required for membership in the organization.[26]

Both Zingeris and Kubilius feared that the combination of serious problems at home, because of the transition to capitalism, and international isolation might result in Lithuania's becoming Finlandized. "We would remain independent, but Moscow would dominate our foreign relations," Kubilius said.[27] They did not fear an open military attack but rather a campaign of subversion. The chauvinists in Moscow would exploit Lithuania's economic difficulties and manipulate political discord and social upheaval to force it into the CIS.

Lithuanian opposition leaders shared these fears with friends in the U.S. Congress. They, in turn, urged President Clinton to speak out against Russian threats to the Balts' security. On December 15, 1995, Clinton wrote in a letter to Dick Durbin (Dem., Illinois): "The United States has a direct and material interest in the security, independence, sovereignty and territorial integrity of the Baltic States." Then, addressing the Russian defense paper in particular, Clinton added, "While the paper appears to have no official standing, we utterly reject its irresponsible political prescriptions. Such threats by Moscow would be inconsistent with Russian obligations under international law and OSCE [Organization for Security And Cooperation in Europe]."[28]

That is a start, but similar statements from all the leaders of the Western alliance could be directed toward Moscow. Of course, words are not enough. Lithuania's independence and perhaps its democracy will remain at risk if the West does not take concrete measures to safeguard the zone of democracy that has been created in Europe with the collapse of communism. If membership in NATO is out of the question, the Western democracies must take other overt measures to safeguard the security of the Baltic countries. Whatever action is taken, no one in Moscow should doubt U.S. resolve on this issue.

The American people and their leaders should not forget that the United States suffered 100,000 killed and three times that number wounded during the Cold War, at a cost of several trillion dollars. Lithuanian resolve in the showdown over independence led directly to the breakup of the Soviet Union and to freedom for the other republics. Lithuanian independence also led to the right-wing coup against Gorbachev and to its failure. The Baltic peoples played a pivotal part in ridding Europe of the scourge of Communism. To allow them to fall prey to a new Russian imperial power would mean those American lives were lost in vain and that the world was again moving toward a disastrous cold war.

NOTES

Chapter 1: Showdown

1. For a discussion of the August 1991 coup, see Stuart Loory and Ann Imse, *CNN Report: Seven Days That Shook The World* (Atlanta: Turner Publishing, 1991). For two excellent accounts of the events leading up to and including the coup see Hedrick Smith, *The New Russians* (New York: Avon Books, 1991), pp. 555–647; also, David Remnick, *Lenin's Tomb* (New York: Vintage Books, 1994), pp. 433–90.

Chapter 2: A Turbulent History

1. For a discussion of the Memel question, see David M. Crowe, *The Baltic States and The Great Powers* (Boulder, Colo.: Westview Press, 1993), pp. 1–54.
2. For histories of Lithuania, see Alfred Erich Senn, *The Emergence of Modern Lithuania* (New York: Columbia University Press, 1959); Jack Stukas, *Awakening Lithuania* (Madison, N.J.: Florham Park Press, 1963); Antanas J. Van Reenan, *Lithuanian Diaspora: Konigsberg to Chicago* (Lanham, N.Y.: University Press of America, 1990).
3. Alfred Eric Senn, *Jonas Basanavicius* (Newton, Mass.: Oriental Research Partners, 1980).
4. For an informative discussion of the Lithuanian language, see Algirdis Sabaliauskas, *We the Balts* (Vilnius: Science and Encyclopedia Publishing, 1993).
5. These estimates are taken from Stukas, *Awakening Lithuania,* and are deemed inflated by Victor Nakas (interview, spring 1994), who formerly worked for the Lithuanian Information Center in Washington.
6. These estimates regarding the return of Lithuanian-Americans to their homeland between the wars were made by Nakas in an interview in the spring of 1994.
7. Ezra Mendelsohn, *The Jews of East Central Europe Between the World Wars* (Bloomington: Indiana University Press, 1983).
8. Istvan Deak, "Surviving the Holocaust: The Kovno Ghetto Diary," *New York Review of Books,* November 8, 1990, p. 54.
9. For a historical survey of Lithuanian-Polish relations, see Stephen R. Burant, "Polish-Lithuanian Relations: Past, Present, and Future," *Problems of Communism,* May–June 1991.

10. Anatol Lieven, *The Baltic Revolution* (New Haven, Conn.: Yale University Press, 1994), p. 66.

11. Anthony Reed and David Fisher, *The Deadly Embrace* (New York: W. W. Norton, 1988), p. 346.

12. Ibid., p. 367.

13. Crowe, *Baltic States and the Great Powers,* p. 104.

14. Romuald J. Misiunas and Rein Taagerpera, *The Baltic States: Years of Dependence 1940–1990* (Berkeley: University of California Press, 1993).

15. Crowe, *Baltic States and the Great Powers,* p. 156.

16. Ibid., p. 157.

17. Reed and Fisher, *Deadly Embrace,* p. 467.

18. Misiunas and Taagerpera, *Baltic Statese,* p. 25.

19. Ibid., p. 47.

20. Ibid.

21. Daniel Jonah Goldhagen, *Hitler's Willing Executioners* (New York: Knopf, 1996), p. 423.

22. Mendelsohn, *Jews of East Central Europe,* pp. 238–39.

23. Lieven, *Baltic Revolution,* p. 150.

24. Aleksandras Shtromas, address at Lithuanian embassy in Washington, September 23, 1994.

25. Aleksandras Shtromas, "The Jewish and Gentile Experience of the Holocaust: A Personal Perspective," Assumption College Eleventh Annual Rabbi Joseph Klein Lecture, April 10, 1989, p. 18.

26. Ibid., p. 19.

27. Misiunas and Taagerpera, *Baltic States,* p. 68.

28. Ibid., p. 63.

29. Interview, Ausra Jurasas, the writer and literary critic married to Jonas Jurasas, spring 1979.

30. Danuate Bialiauskas, statement made at conference on ethnic conflict in Lithuania at Kaunas University in the spring of 1992.

31. Yuri Urbanovich—a product of a Lithuanian-Armenian marriage born and raised in Georgia, and a member of the faculty of the Soviet foreign ministry's Diplomatic Academy—lived in Klaipeda in the 1970s. He was told by his superiors that he should not be surprised to observe displays of nationalism among the Lithuanians because the "bourgeois impulse" remained strong in the Baltic republics. Interview, spring 1994. As a consequence, authorities in Moscow were reluctant to allow foreigners to travel to the region.

32. For a comprehensive discussion of Marxist thinking about ethnonationalism, see Walker Connor, *The National Question in Marxist-Leninist Theory and Strategy* (Princeton, N. J.: Princeton University Press, 1984).

33. For a discussion of Stalin's views on ethnonationalism, see Bohdan Nahaylo and Victor Swoboda, *Soviet Disunion* (New York: Free Press, 1989), pp. 61–62.

34. Ibid., p. 95.

35. Ibid., p. 110.

36. Ibid., p. 111.

37. Amy Knight, *Beria: Stalin's Lieutenant* (Princeton, N. J.: Princeton University Press, 1993), pp. 189–90.

38. For a discussion of Shelest's removal, see Nahaylo and Swoboda, *Soviet Disunion,* pp. 177–79.

39. Ibid., pp. 183–85.

40. See, for example, Brian Silver, "Levels of Sociocultural Development Among Soviet Nationalisties: A Partial Test of the Equalization Hypothesis," *American Political Science Review,* December 1974, pp. 618–47.

41. Rasma Karklins, *Ethnic Relations in the USSR* (Boston: Unwin Hyman, 1986), p. 93. Karklins provides a detailed account of Soviet nationalities policy in practice.

42. Barbara Anderson and Brian Silver, "Some Factors in the Linguistic and Ethnic Russification of Soviet Nationalities," in Lubomyr Hajda and Mark Beissinger, eds., *The Nationalities Factor in Soviet Politics and Society* (Boulder, Colo.: Westview Press, 1990), p. 119.

43. See Gertrude E. Schroeder, "Nationalities and the Soviet Economy," and Romuald J. Misiunas, "The Baltic Republics," both in Hajda and Beissinger, *Nationalities Factor,* pp. 43–71, 206.

44. Aleksandras Shtromas, "The Baltic States as Soviet Republics," in Graham Smith, ed., *The Baltic States* (New York: St. Martin's Press, 1994), p. 100.

45. Ibid., p. 101.

46. Misiunis, "Baltic Republics," p. 209.

47. Interview, Algimantas Cekuolis, June 1991.

48. Interview of Vytautas Landsbergis in *Lithuanian Review,* May 11, 1990.

49. Interview, Algirdas Degutis, January 1991.

Chapter 3: Lithuanian Nationalism Endures

1. Van Reenan, *Lithuanian Diaspora,* p. 69.

2. Ibid., p. 70.

3. Ibid.

4. Ibid.

5. Interview, Stasys Lozoraitis, fall 1993.

6. For Baroni's biography, see Lawrence M. O'Rourke, *Geno: The Life and Mission of Geno Baroni* (Mahwah, N. J.: Paulist Press, 1991).

7. This resulted in my book *The Superpowers in Crisis* (New York: Pergamon-Brassey's, 1987). I concluded: "Since 1917 Russians have adopted myriad strategies to destroy values and loyalities to which the USSR's ethnic minorities cling. They have failed. If anything, the non-Russians in the USSR have become even bolder in resisting both attempts on the part of their 'elder brothers' to inculcate

them with a Soviet (read 'Russian') consciousness and a massive KGB campaign to crush ethnic civil rights activists. At times the KGB will enjoy victories, but the nationality question will continue to be a divisive force in Soviet society. In the face of austerity, relations between the Russians and the ethnic minorities will get worse" (p. 56).

8. Zbigniew Brzezinski was one of the first scholars to foresee the USSR's ultimate demise. See his "The Soviet Political System: Transformation of Degeneration," in Z. Brzezinski, ed., *Dilemmas of Change in Soviet Politics* (New York: Columbia University Press, 1960), pp. 1–24. But most mainstream experts ignored the nationalities question altogether. See, for example, Stephen F. Cohen, *Rethinking the Soviet Experience* (New York: Oxford University Press, 1985).

9. See statement provided Father Casimer Pugevicius from Father Sigitas Tamkevicius, "Chronicle of Courage," undated memo, p. 5.

10. Richard J. Krickus, "Faith and State in Lithuania," Outlook, *Washington Post*, January 11, 1976.

11. Interview, Simas Kudirka, summer 1979.

12. Simas Kudirka and Larry Eichel, *For Those Still at Sea* (New York: Dial Press, 1978), p. 9.

13. Ibid., p. 94.

14. Tomas Venclova, *Lithuanian Literature: A Survey* (New York: Lithuanian National Foundation, 1979), pp. 12–14.

15. Andrei Sakharov, *Memoirs* (New York: Alfred A. Knopf, 1990), pp. 436–38.

16. For a comprehensive discussion of the Catholic civil rights activists and their samizdat, see V. Standly Vardys, *The Catholic Church, Dissent and Nationality in Soviet Lithuania* (New York: Columbia University Press, 1978).

17. Alvydas Dargis, "The Children of the Fountain," *Lithuania in the World* (Vilnius), Vol. 3, No. 3 (1995), pp. 8–12.

18. See Tamkevicius, "Chronicle of Courage."

19. For his complete letter, see Venclova, *Lithuanian Literature,* p. 20.

20. Interview, Jonas Jurasas, summer 1979.

21. V. Stanley Vardys, "Lithuanian National Politics," *Problems of Communism,* July–August 1989, pp. 54–55.

22. Krickus, *Superpowers in Crisis,* pp. 44–47.

Chapter 4: Popular Front Revolutionaries

1. Jan A. Trapans, "The Sources of Latvia's Popular Movement," in Trapans, ed., *Toward Independence: The Baltic Popular Front Movements* (Boulder, Colo: Westview Press, 1991), p. 27. For a comprehensive treatment of the three Baltic popular front movements, see Walter C. Clemens, Jr., *Baltic Independence and Russian Empire* (New York: St. Martin's Press, 1991).

2. Lieven, *Baltic Revolution,* p. 220.

3. Rein Taagepera, *Estonia: Return to Independence* (Boulder, Colo: Westview Press, 1993), pp. 128–30.

4. Interview, Mecys Laurinkus, June 1994.

5. Ibid.

6. Interview, Algirdas Degutis, January 1992.

7. Lieven, *Baltic Rrevolution,* p. 226.

8. Interview, Asta Banionis, spring 1994.

9. Interview, Charles Krause, February 1990.

10. Interview, Victor Nakas, spring 1994.

11. Alfred Erich Senn, *Lithuania Awakening* (Berkeley, Calif.: University of California Press, 1990), p. 172.

12. Interview, Linas Kojelis, October 1994.

13. Interview, Viktoras Petkus, February 1990.

14. V. Stanley Vardys, "Lithuanian National Politics," *Problems of Communism,* July–August 1989, pp. 54–55.

15. Interview, Arvydas Juozaitis, summer 1992.

16. Remnick, *Lenin's Tomb,* p. 292.

17. Ibid., p. 295.

18. Ibid.

19. Aleksandr Yakovlev, *The October Revolution and Perestroika* (Moscow: Novosti Press Agency Publishing House, 1989), p. 62.

20. Ibid., p. 64.

21. Vardys, "Lithuanian National Politics," p. 64.

22. Ibid., p. 62.

23. Inteview, Algirdas Brazauskas, January 1992.

24. Vardys, "Lithuanian National Politics," p. 64.

25. Interview, Mecys Laurinkus, June 1994.

26. Alfred Erich Senn, "Toward Lithuanian Independence: Algirdas Brazauskas and the CPL," *Problems of Communism,* March–April 1990, p. 21.

27. Interview, Victor Nakas, spring 1994.

28. Senn, "Toward Lithuanian Independence," p. 26.

29. Ibid., p. 27.

30. Alfred Erich Senn, *Gorbachev's Failure in Lithuania* (New York: St. Martin's Press, 1995), p. 56.

31. Ibid., p. 63.

32. Ibid., p. 64.

33. Ibid., p. 65.

34. Ibid., p. 67.

35. Ibid., p. 72.

36. Ibid.

37. Ibid., p. 73.

38. Senn, "Toward Lithuanian Independence," p. 26.

39. Ibid.

40. Ibid., p. 27.

41. Ibid., p. 26.

42. Interview, Algirdas Brazauksas, January 1992.

43. Gordon Head and Raza Alishauskiene, "Overwhelming Support by Lithuanians for Government's Declaration of Independence" (London and Vilnius: *Galllup* Spring 1990). See table 5 in this report.

44. Anonymous.

45. Interview, Algirdas Degutis, January 1992.

46. Interview, Ambassador Daryll Johnson, summer 1994.

47. Lieven, *Baltic Revolution,* p. 232.

Chapter 5: Free Elections

1. I saw Zukas's documentary in the summer of 1994. It is a powerful indictment of the Soviet military practice of subjecting young recruits to brutal physical punishment at the hands of their officers and peers. Perhaps I could not have viewed the film dispassionately, because the previous day I had toured the basement cells of the KGB headquarters building in Vilnius. After a brief visit I left depressed and physically drained.

2. I was told this by a number of people I interviewed such as Nikolai Medvedev, a deputy in the Lithuanian parliament, in the fall of 1990.

3. During my visit to Moscow that fall I had the opportunity to talk with Lionginas at length and discovered that he had sound political instincts acquired in part because he had what we called in Newark "street smarts."

4. Smith, *New Russians,* pp. 354–55.

5. Arydas Zygas, speech delivered at Cathedral Square on Independence Day, February 16, 1990.

6. Interview, Stasys Lozoraitis, fall 1993.

7. In subsequent visits to Lithuania, I spoke with Cekuolis on several occasions and he proved to be well informed and an adroit analyst of political affairs in the USSR.

Chapter 6: Independence

1. Michael R. Beschloss and Strobe Talbott, *At the Highest Levels* (Boston: Little, Brown, 1993), p. 173.

2. Interview, Laima Pangonyte, summer 1994.

3. *New York Times,* January 12, 1990.

4. Beschloss and Talbott, *At the Highest Levels,* p. 174.

5. Ibid., pp. 173–74.

6. Senn, *Gorbachev's Failure in Lithuania,* p. 82.

7. Interview, Victor Nakas, spring 1992, and Aleksandras Abisala, January 1992.

8. Lieven, *Baltic Revolution,* p. 239.

9. Speech by author, "Perestroika and Gorbachev: The View from America," delivered in Vilnius, February 20, 1990.

10. Lieven, *Baltic Revolution,* p. 233.

11. Ibid., pp. 233–34.
12. Ibid., p. 236.
13. Interview, Stasys Lorzoraitis, fall 1992.
14. Jack Matlock, *Autopsy on an Empire* (New York: Random House, 1995), p. 229.
15. Ibid., p. 230.
16. Ibid., p. 323.
17. Ibid., p. 325.
18. Interview, Vytautas Landsbergis, June 1994.
19. Algirdas J. Silas, ed., *Lithuanian Independence: The U.S. Government Response 1990-1991* (Chicago: Ethnic Community Services, 1991), pp. 2–9.
20. *Washington Post,* March 27, 1990.
21. *New York Times,* April 1, 1990.
22. Smith, *New Russians,* pp. 537–38.
23. *New York Times,* April 8, 1990.
24. Interview, Vytautas Landsbergis, June 1994.
25. Senn, *Gorbachev's Failure in Lithuania,* pp. 113.
26. Ibid., p. 119.
27. Ibid.
28. Smith, *New Russians,* p. 601.
29. Senn, *Gorbachev's Failure in Lithuania,* p. 121.
30. Ibid., p. 122
31. Senn, *Lithuania Awakening,* pp. 240–41.
32. Vardys, "Lithuanian National Politics," p. 59.
33. Smith, *New Russians,* p. 372.
34. For more on relations between Poles and Lithuanians in Lithuania, see Richard J. Krickus, "Lithuania's Polish Question," *Report on the USSR,* November 29, 1991, pp. 20–23.
35. Timothy Garton Ash, *The Magic Lantern* (New York: Random House, 1990), p. 142.
36. Smith, *New Russians,* p. 348.

Chapter 7: America's Response

1. Beschloss and Talbott, *At the Highest Levels,* p. 164.
2. Ibid., p. 165.
3. Ibid.
4. Silas, ed., *Lithuanian Independence,* p. 3.
5. *New York Times,* March 29, 1990.
6. *Washington Times,* March 29, 1990.
7. Ibid., March 28, 1990.
8. *New York Times,* April 23 and 24, 1990.
9. Matlock, *Autopsy on an Empire,* p. 379.
10. Ibid., p. 380

11. Joe McGinnis, *The Selling of the President* (New York: Trident Press, 1968).
12. The Bush adminisration's adroit use of TV was overshadowed by the shameful exploitation of the race card as exemplified by the infamous Willy Horton spot.
13. Beschloss and Talbott, *At the Highest Levels,* p. 195.
14. This piece appeared in the *Atlanta Constitution,* March 29, 1990.
15. Marlin Fitzwater, *Call the Briefing* (New York: Times Books, 1995), p. 351.
16. Interview, Egidijus Bickauskas, October 1990.
17. Interview, Vytautas Landsbergis, summer 1994.
18. Interview with Polish leader Romuald Meczkowski in Vilnius, June 1994.

Chapter 8: Bloody Sunday

1. *Washington Post,* December 21, 1990.
2. Smith, *New Russians,* p. 602.
3. Memo from Mykolas Burokevicius to Gorbachev, dated January 7, 1991. I would like to thank my colleague Joe Bozicevic for translating the document from the original Russian.
4. Senn, *Gorbachev's Failure in Lithuania,* p. 128.
5. Lieven, *Baltic Revolution,* p. 246.
6. Senn, *Gorbachev's Failure in Lithuania,* p. 128.
7. Interview, Vytautas Landsbergis, June 1994.
8. Senn, *Gorbachev's Failure in Lithuania,* p. 130
9. Ibid., p. 131
10. Alfred Eric Senn, *Crisis in Lithuania,* January 1991 (Chicago: Publication of Akiraciai, 1991), p. 7.
11. Senn, *Gorbachev's Failure in Lithuania,* p. 130.
12. Interview, Arvydas Matulionas, June 1991.
13. Senn, *Crisis in Lithuania,* p. 8.
14. Ibid., p. 8.
15. Ibid., p. 11.
16. Ibid.
17. Vytautas Landsbergis, statement in Washington, D.C., before the Conference on Security and Cooperation in Europe (CSCE), Spring 1991.
18. Interview, Arvydas Matulionas, June 1991.
19. Interview, Rita Dapkus, January 1992.
20. Interview, Loreta Musanya, July 1995.
21. Interview, Ona Volungeviciute, July 1995.
22. Story related to me by a colleague at Mary Washington College, Paul Slayton.
23. Interview, Vytautas Landsbergis, June 1994. One person who publicly called for Landsbergis's resignation the Thursday before Bloody Sunday was Bronius Genzelis. See Senn, *Crisis in Lithuania,* p. 5.
24. Interview, Lowry and Barnabas Wyman, spring 1991.
25. Interview, Rita Dapkus, January 1992.

26. This and other statements made by Lithuanian schoolchildren were circulated in the winter of 1992–93 by the Lithuanian embassy when an art exhibit depicting Bloody Sunday was held at the Children's Art Museum in Washington, D.C.
27. Interview, Paul Goble, September 1994.
28. Interviews conducted in June 1994 with several members of the Lithuanian radio and TV staff in Vilnius.
29. Smith, *New Russians,* p. 612.
30. Ibid.
31. Beschloss and Talbott, *At the Highest Levels,* p. 216.
32. Ibid., p. 300.
33. Interview, Asta Banionis, summer 1994.
34. Ibid.
35. Ibid.
36. Beschloss and Talbott, *At the Highest Levels,* pp. 307–8.
37. Ibid., p. 318.
38. *New York Times,* January 28, 1991.
39. Excerpts from Daiva Kezys's film *Bloody Sunday.*
40. Interview, Daiva Kezys, summer 1994. Later a Canadian filmmaker, Zoe Dirse, produced a video for Canadian television, *Baltic Fire,* that covered the murder of five people in Riga, a week after Bloody Sunday.
41. Fax from anonymous source.
42. Interview, Lucija Baskauskaite, June 1994.

Chapter 9: The Empire Collapses
1. Interview, Algimantas Cekuolis, June 1991.
2. Remnick, *Lenin's Tomb,* pp. 394–96.
3. Smith, *New Russians,* p. 564.
4. Ibid.
5. Lieven, *Baltic Revolution,* p. 202.
6. Richard Pipes, *The Russian Revolution* (New York: Alfred A. Knopf, 1990), pp. 24–25.
7. Interview, Vytautas Landsbergis, January 1992.
8. Smith, *New Russians,* p. 605.
9. Remnick, *Lenin's Tomb,* p. 355. To this day Gorbachev claims that hard-liners ordered the attack without his knowledge. See *New York Times,* March 10, 1995.
10. Both quotes are from Remnick, *Lenin's Tomb,* p. 389.
11. Ibid., p. 351.
12. Smith, *New Russians,* p. 526.
13. For the Yeltsin address, see the *Washington Post,* August 26, 1996. For the Ivans quote, see Smith, op cit, p. 610.
14. See Matlock, *Autopsy on an Empire,* p. 522.
15. Remnick, *Lenin's Tomb,* p. 351.

16. Matlock, *Autopsy on an Empire,* p. 541.
17. Remnick, *Lenin's Tomb,* p. 436.
18. Matlock, *Autopsy on an Empire,* p. 545.
19. Ibid., p. 564.
20. Ibid., pp. 579–80.
21. Loory and Imse, *CNN Reports,* p. 51.
22. Matlock, *Autopsy on an Empire,* pp. 587–88.
23. Ibid., p. 591.
24. Loory and Imse, *CNN Reports,* p. 36.
25. Remnick, *Lenin's Tomb,* p. 471.
26. Ibid., p. 485.
27. Senn, *Gorbachev's Failure in Lithuania,* pp. 138–39.

Chapter 10: An Uncertain Future

1. Interview, Arvydas Juozaitis, summer 1992.
2. Interview, Andrius Kubilius, summer 1992.
3. Interview, Algimantas Brzauskas, January 1992.
4. *Philadelphia Inquirer,* February 14, 1993, p. 6.
5. For a comprehensive discussion of Soviet energy policy, see John M. Kramer, *The Energy Gap in Eastern Europe* (Lexington, Mass.: Lexington Books, 1990). See also Kramer, "'Energy Shock' from Russia Jolts Baltic States," *Radio Free Europe/Radio Liberty,* April 23, 1993, pp. 41–49.
6. Coopers and Lybrand, *Lithuania: A Business and Investment Guide* (Vilnius, 1995), pp. 1–2.
7. Salius Grinius, *Radio Free Europe/Radio Liberty,* December 6, 1993, p. 6.
8. *Philadelphia Inquirer,* February 14, 1993.
9. Interview, Vytautas Landsbergis, January 1992.
10. Interview, Algimantas Brazauskas, January 1992.
11. Interview, Asta Banionis, summer 1994.
12. Interview, Victor Nakas, summer 1995.
13. Interview, Vladys Gadys, summer 1995.
14. *Baltic Independent,* March 24–30, 1995, p. 5.
15. Sherry Ricchiardi, "Killing the Messenger," *American Journalism Review,* November 1995, p. 19.
16. For a discussion of the 1995 muncipal elections, see International Republican Institute, *Lithuania: Situation Update 1995 Municipal Election* (Washington, D.C.: April 5, 1995).
17. Ernest Gellner, *Conditions of Liberty* (London: Hamish Hamilton, 1994), p. 5.
18. Interview, Daryll Johnson, fall 1994.
19. Coopers and Lybrand, *Lithuania,* p. 2.
20. Interview, Daryll Johnson, fall 1994.
21. Press release, embassy of the Republic of Lithuania, September 22, 1994.

22. See Daria Fane, "Moldova: Breaking Lose from Moscow," in Ian Bremmer and Ray Taras, eds. *Nations and Politics in the Soviet Successor States* (Cambridge: Cambridge University Press, 1993), pp. 138–39.

23. Interview, Ignas Stankovicius, summer 1994.

24. Interviews with Andrius Kubilius and Emmanuelis Zingeris, January 1996.

25. See Strobe Talbott, "Why NATO Should Grow," *New York Review of Books,* August 10, 1995, pp. 27–30.

26. Interview, Emmanuelis Zingeris, January 1996.

27. Interview, Andrius Kubilius, January 1996.

28. *Baltic Independent,* January 12–18 1996.

APPENDIX 1: CHRONOLOGY OF MAJOR EVENTS

13th century   First Lithuanian state founded.

14th century   Lithuanian-Polish Union formed

1795   So-called third partition of Poland results in most of Lithuania being absorbed by Russian empire.

1830s and 1860s   Lithuanians join Poles in rebelling against the Russians.

1918   Independent Lithuanian state established on February 16.

1926   December coup ends democracy in Lithuania.

1939   Klaipeda (Memel) is seized by Germany from Lithuania.
Molotov-Ribbentrop Pact is signed and in secret protocol Lithuania is awarded to the USSR.
Lithuania is forced to signed defense pact with Soviet Union.
Vilnius is returned to Lithuania.

1940   Soviet Union occupies Lithuania.
Phony election is held and the USSR annexes Lithuania.
U.S. government refuses to recognize Soviet annexation of the Baltic countries.
Stalin begins to deport thousands of Lithuanians.

1941   Germans invade USSR and take control of Lithuania. As a result of the Holocaust there, 140,000 to 143,000 Jews are murdered.

1944   Thousands of Lithuanians flee their homeland as the Red Army approaches.

1945   Soviet Union reoccupies Lithuania and tens of thousands of Lithuanians are deported to the Soviet Union.
Lithuanian resistance movement opposes occupation until 1953, when it is crushed.

1972   First issue of the *Chronicle of the Catholic Church of Lithuania* appears.

1985   Mikhail Gorbachev is selected general secretary of the Communist Party of the Soviet Union by the Politburo.

1987   Old dissidents in all three Baltic countries conduct demonstrations in commemoration of the 1939 Molotov-Ribbentrop Pact.

1988   Liberty League demonstrates in Vilnius to commemorate the 1918 declaration of independence.
Sajudis is formed.
Demonstrations are conducted by Sajudis, which at this point characterizes itself as a perestroika movement.
Aleksandr Yakovlev visits Vilnius and scolds party hardliners for not working with Sajudis. He claims expressions of nationalism are not inconsistent with Lenin's teachings.
Millions of people link hands from Vilnius through Riga to Tallinn in a massive display of Baltic solidarity.
Lithuanian Communist reformer Algirdas Brazauskas is selected first secretary of the Lithuanian Communist Party.
Sajudis conducts its founding congress.

1989   Elections are held for the USSR Congress of People's
            Deputies (CPD) and Sajudis wins most of the
            Lithuanian seats.

            Brazauskas breaks with the CPSU and takes 80 percent
            of the Lithuanian Communist Party's membership
            with him.

1990   Gorbachev visits Lithuania in an unsuccessful attempt
            to persuade a majority of Lithuanian Communists to
            remain in the CPSU.

            Sajudis enjoys landslide victory in February-March
            elections for the Lithuanian Supreme Soviet.

            The newly named Lithuanian Supreme Council selects
            Vytautas Landsbergis as chairman ("president") and
            restores Lithuania's independence on March 11.

            The CPD elects Gorbachev president of the USSR, and
            he declares the March 11 Lithuanian declaration
            illegal.

            Gorbachev begins economic embargo on Lithuania in
            April after an early show of force fails to get Lands-
            bergis to rescind the declaration.

            Gorbachev conducts summit with President George
            Bush in Washington in late spring after the U.S. gov-
            ernment warns Gorbachev that he must lift the
            embargo.

            After Landsbergis agrees to "freeze" the declaration, the
            embargo is lifted on June 30 and plans for a negoti-
            ated settlement to the dispute are arranged. The talks
            never formerly take place because both sides disagree
            about ground rules.

            In the fall, Gorbachev begins to shed his reformist
            advisers and moves toward the hard-liners after a
            meeting with Red Army officers.

            Landsbergis meets with President Bush in the White
            House on December 10 and warns that Gorbachev
            is prepared to use force against the Lithuanian
            government.

            The Soviet foreign minister, Eduard Shevardnadze,
            warns that a "dictatorship is coming."

1991   After receiving an urgent message from Lithuanian neo-Stalinist Mykolas Burokevicius, Gorbachev warns Lithuanians that they must restore the "constitutional order" or face his imposition of presidential rule.

After several earlier demonstrations by the pro-Soviet Edinstvo group, which were conducted to provoke a crisis, Soviet troops occupy Lithuanian press building.

Early in the morning of January 13, Soviet paratroopers led by the infamous KGB Alpha unit occupy the TV tower in Vilnius and kill thirteen civilians. But the expected assault on parliament, where Landsbergis and sixty deputies plus staff have gathered, never occurs. Gorbachev later declares he did not order the attack, but no one, not even his former advisers, believes him. Widespread TV coverage of "Bloody Sunday" musters support from Lithuanians among American politicians, opinion-molders, and ordinary citizens.

A large pro-Yeltsin, anti-Gorbachev demonstration takes place in Moscow in late March.

On April 23, Gorbachev meets with republic leaders and they sign the "nine plus one" accord, which greatly diminishes the power of the Soviet ministries in favor of the republics.

A coup led by KGB head Vladimir Kryuchkov begins on August 18; Gorbachev is placed under house arrest at his Cape Foros compound in the Ukraine. Boris Yeltsin gathers his supporters at the Russian White House and declares the coup illegal. Adopting tactics the Lithuanians used in January of that year, the Russian democrats resist the coup.

After the coup leaders surrender on August 21, Gorbachev returns to Moscow. But Yeltsin henceforth becomes the supreme leader, and he disbands the CPSU.

Russia recognizes Lithuania's independence on September 6.

Gorbachev resigns on December 25 and the Soviet empire fades into history.

APPENDIX 2: BIOGRAPHICAL GUIDE

Abisala, Aleksandras. Scientist from Kaunas and Sajudis activist who was elected to the parliament in 1990. Later, between July and November 1992, he replaced Gediminas Vagnorious as prime minister.

Banionis, Asta. Executive director of the Lithuanian-American Community in Arlington, Virginia. She met with President George Bush soon after Bloody Sunday and urged him to impose sanctions upon the Soviet Union.

Bickauskas, Egidijus. An early Sajudis founder who was elected to the USSR Congress of People's Deputies in 1989 and later served as Lithuanian ambassador to Russia. A deputy since 1990, he is a leader in the Center Party today.

Brazauskas, Algirdas. Party reformer who became first secretary of the Lithuanian Communist Party in 1988 and broke with the CPSU in 1989. In 1990 he led the newly named Lithuanian Democratic Labor Party, which gained control of the Lithuanian government in the fall elections of 1992. In February 1993 he was elected president of Lithuania.

Buracas, Antanas. Economist and Sajudis leader, elected to the USSR Congress of People's Deputies in 1989.

Burokevicius, Mykolas. Professor of community history at Vilnius University who led the rump pro-Soviet Lithuanian Communist Party after Brazauskas broke with the CPSU in 1989. In January 1991, he urged Gorbachev to impose presidential rule upon Lithuania and expel the "bourgeois nationalists" who controlled the Lithuanian government.

Cekuolis, Algimantas. A diplomat and journalist during the Soviet era who became a founder of Sajudis.

Cepaitis, Virgilijus. English and Russian translator who was a leading Sajudis radical deputy until late 1991, when he resigned after it was revealed that he had been a KGB informer.

Damusis, Ginte. An activist in Ateitis, the Lithuanian Catholic organization, who worked for Father Casimer Pugevicius in the Lithuanian Information Center's Brooklyn office. After Lithuania was granted diplomatic recognition, she served at the Lithuanian UN legation in New York City.

Jermalavicius, Juozas. Head of ideology for the Lithuanian Communist Party who remained loyal to the CPSU and formed the State Committee for National Salvation, which encouraged Gorbachev to crush the Lithuanian government in January 1991. Jermalavicius and Burokevicius were be arrested in Belarus in 1994 and returned to Lithuania.

Juozaitis, Arvydas. Bronze medal Olympic swimmer, philosopher, and founder of Sajudis who later broke with Landsbergis and the Kaunas radicals.

Kojelis, Linas. Lithuanian youth activist who served in Reagan White House as liaison with U.S. white ethnic communities. As president of the U.S. Baltic Foundation, he has continued to design and implement programs to promote democracy and capitalism in all three Baltic countries.

Kubilius, Andrius. Sajudis activist who became its national director after the 1990 elections. Later he was elected to the Seimas and served as the faction leader of the Homeland Union, the conservative party Landsbergis leads today.

Landsbergis, Vytautas. Musicologist whose family played an active role in the Lithuanian national movement. He became Sajudis chairman in 1989, and after being selected chairman of the Lithuanian Supreme Council (parliament) in March 1990, he led the campaign to reclaim Lithuanian independence. Refusing to bow to pressure from Gorbachev and demonstrating great courage during the Bloody Sunday weekend, he became the principal leader of the Lithuanian rebellion. In 1992, most of his Sajudis associates were not reelected to the Seimas as the Lithuanian Democratic Labor Party swept the elections.

Laurinkus, Mecys. Philosopher from Vilnius University who encouraged Landsbergis to join Sajudis. He was elected to the parliament in 1990 and on Bloody Sunday he was the head of security at the parliament.

Lozoraitis, Stasys. The leading diplomat of the former independent Lithuanian government during the Cold War. After leaving his post as ambassador to the Vatican, he served in Washington in the late 1980s. He urged Landsbergis to declare independence in March 1990, and he became ambassador to the United States after Lithuania was granted recognition by Washington in the wake of the August coup. In February 1993, he ran an unsuccessful race for president against Brazauskas.

Nakas, Victor. An Ateitis activist who later worked for Father Pugevicius as the Washington representative of the Lithuanian Information Center. After Lithuania was granted recognition by the United States, he served as political officer in the Lithuanian embassy in Washington. He left after Brazauskas reassigned Lozoraitis to Rome in 1993.

Ozolas, Romualdas. A philosopher, Communist, and Sajudis founder who was elected to the parliament in 1990 and became one of two deputy prime ministers that year. He met with Jack Matlock, U.S. ambassador to Russia, three days before the March 11 declaration and refused to accept Matlock's statement that Washington would not recognize Lithuanian independence. Later he formed the Center Party, which he leads with Bickauskas today.

Petkus, Viktoras. Catholic civil rights activist who was imprisoned for "anti-Soviet" activities in the 1950s. Later he would help establish the Lithuanian Helsinki Watch Group with the poet Tomas Venclova, the priest Father Karolis Garuckas, and the Jewish scientist Eitananas Finkelsteinas.

Prunskiene, Kazimiera. An economist, Communist, and Sajudis founder, she was elected to the USSR Congress of People's Deputies in 1989. She was prime minister from March 1990 until January 1991, when she resigned in protest over the parliament's refusal to agree to price hikes she favored.

Pugevicius, Casimer. Roman Catholic priest who served as mentor for many young activists in the Lithuanian-American community. A journalist by training, he established the Lithuanian Information Center while serving as director of Lithuanian Catholic Religious Aid. At a time when few American journalists were writing about the Soviet occupation of Lithuania, Father Cas coaxed them to do so by providing English translations of the *Chronicles of the Catholic Church in Lithuania,* and other samizdats.

Sakadolskis, Romas. An Ateitis activist who served as the desk officer for Lithuania at the Voice of America. His broadcasts enjoyed a wide following in Lithuania.

Terleckas, Antanas. Leader of the Liberty League, which was founded secretly and led protests against Soviet rule years before Sajudis was established.

Zingeris, Emmanuelis. Young Jewish leader and prótegé of Landsbergis who was elected to the parliament in 1990. A member of the Homeland Union today, Zingeris refuted the charge of Soviet hard-liners in the late 1980s that Sajudis was led by racists.

INDEX

Abisala, Aleksandras (Lithuanian prime minister), 96, 226
Achremov, Igor (Vilnius Brigade member), 202
activism, 47–70. *See also* Ateitis; Bloody Sunday; Sajudis
    calendar demonstrations, 48
    by Catholics, 37–39, 42–45
    in Estonia, 49
    Green movement, 48–49, 50
    by intellectuals, 45–46, 48, 50, 51
    in Latvia, 48
    in Lithuania, 49–52, 54
    reactions to Bloody Sunday, 156–159, 160–161
Adomaitis, Regimantas (Lithuanian actor), 53
Afanasyev, Yuri (Russian democrat), 62, 175
AFL-CIO, 121
Alksnis, Viktor (Latvian Soyuz leader), 27
Alperavicius, Simonas (Jewish Community of Lithuania president), 206
American Latvian Association, 48
apparatchiks, Soviet. *See* Bolsheviks; CPSU; hard-liners, Soviet; neo-Stalinists
Armenia, 22
Artists' Union (Lithuania), 50
Asanaviciute, Loreta (Lithuanian patriot), 147, 161
Ash, Timothy Garton, 116
Ateitis movement ("Futurist" movement), 9, 33, 35
Ausra ("Dawn"), 8
Azerbaijan, 22, 73, 117
Azerbaijani Popular Front, 117

Bakatin, Vadim (head of Soviet ministry of interior), 112, 137
Baker, James, 118, 122, 130–131, 182
Baku (Azerbaijan), Red Army massacre in, 117
Baltic Fire (Dirse), 219n.40
Baltics. *See* Estonia; Latvia; Lithuania; Lithuania, history of; Lithuania, independent
Baltic-Soviet defense treaty, 14
Baltic Way demonstration (1989), 66
Baltic Workshop Group (U.S. State Department), 152
Banionis, Asta (Lithuanian-American lobbyist), 52–53, 156–157, 158, 159, 198, 226
Baroni, Geno (Italian-American priest), 34–35
Basanavicius, Jonas (Lithuanian publisher), 8
Baskauskaite, Lucija (Lithuanian-American anthropologist), 162, 163, 164
Bauer, Otto (Austrian Marxist), 21
Baukas, Vytautas and Rasa (Lithuanian patriots), 149
Belorussia, 22, 166
Beria, Lavrenti, 23–24
Beriozov, Vladimir (Russian secretary of LCP), 61
Berlin Wall, 115–116
Bernstein, Leonard, 116
Beschloss, Michael R., 155, 158–159
Bessmertnykh, Aleksandr (Soviet foreign minister), 182
Bickauskas, Egidijus (a Sajudis founder and CDP member), 131, 226
Bieliauskas, Danute (Lithuanian doctor), 19–20

Bieliauskas, Vytautas (World Lithuanian
   Community president), 62
Bloody Sunday, 1905 (St. Petersburg), 174
Bloody Sunday, 1991 (Vilnius), 136–164,
   219n.26
   American activism, 156–159, 160–161
   Bush reacts to, 153, 155
   casualties, 146, 147, 162
   children's drawings of, 168
   eyewitness accounts, 147, 149, 150–151,
      152, 161–164
   film smuggled out, 151–152, 160–161,
      172–173
   Fitzwater reacts to, 145
   Gorbachev reacts to, 147, 153–154
   Gorbachev's image destroyed by, 174–176
   Landsbergis and deputies gather in parlia-
      ment, 146, 149
   Landsbergis composed and steadfast, 150
   Landsbergis fears further attacks, 160
   Landsbergis mobilizes Lithuanian patriots,
      139, 140, 145
   Landsbergis tries to reach Gorbachev, 144
   Landsbergis urged to flee/resign, 150,
      218n.23
   LCP urges Gorbachev to use force,
      144–145
   Lithuanians, passive resistance by, 141, 147,
      150, 151
   Lithuanians stand fast, 146, 147, 149, 162
   Lithuanian TV/radio coverage of,
      141–142, 153, 169, 171–172
   parliament staff informs VOA, 148–149
   pro-Soviet demonstrations prior to,
      139–140
   singing by the defenders, 89, 141, 150, 152
   Soviet military attacks Lithuanians at TV
      station, 152–153
   Soviet military attacks Lithuanians at TV
      tower, 146–147, 149, 151
   Soviet military attacks parliament,
      149–151
   Soviet military morale, 173–174
   Soviet military presence in, 140
   Soviet military searches for arms and halts
      trains, 145
   Soviet military surrounds TV station prior
      to, 143
   U.S., public outcry in, 152
   Western media coverage of, 151–152,
      153–156
Bloody Sunday (video), 160–161

Bobelis, Kazys (VLIK president), 197–198
Boldin, Valery (Gorbachev's chief of staff),
   183–184, 186
Bolsheviks, 116. See also hard-liners, Soviet;
   neo-Stalinists
   attempt to thwart Sajudis, 64
   low morale of, 88, 116, 166, 185
   opposition to Lithuanian independence
      movement, 67
   troubled by open anti-Soviet sentiment,
      57, 60
   troubled by separatists, 95
Boruta, Father Jonas, 37
Brazauskas, Algirdas (LCP secretary), 226
   career of, 61–62
   criticizes Landsbergis, 194, 197
   denounces Soviet military, 145
   elected deputy-prime minister, 97–98
   facilitates LCP/CPSU split, 66, 67–69
   popularity of, 62, 69–70, 199
   relationship with Sajudis, 57, 63, 64
   replaces Lozoraitis, 198
   step-by-step independence urged by, 133,
      192
   suspected of plotting to block Lithuanian
      independence, 68
   urges Lithuanian sovereign authority to
      CPSU, 66–67
Brezhnev, Leonid, 25
Britain, 11
Brzezinski, Zbigniew (Carter Admin.
   national security adviser), 37, 56, 214n.8
Buracas, Antanas (a Sajudis founder), 51, 63,
   65, 76, 78–79, 226
Burokevicius, Mykolas (Lithuanian Bolshevik), 112, 137–138, 153, 226
Bush, George, 88
   on Baltic independence, 118
   Bloody Sunday, reaction to, 153, 155, 159
   coup, leaks information to Gorbachev
      about, 182
   coup, reaction to, 184
   criticized for Lithuanian position, 130,
      155, 158
   Gorbachev, political dependence on,
      101–102, 105, 119, 122, 124, 125, 155, 158
   and Hussein, 133
   Landsbergis meets with, 133–134, 137, 143
   Lithuanian independence not recognized
      by, 98, 99–100, 104, 119
   Malta summit, 118
   meets with Baltic leaders, 157–158, 159

Bush, George, *continued*
  Moscow summit attended by, 182
  Prunskiene meets with, 138
  reelection bid, 155, 158
  use of TV, 123, 218n.12
  Washington summit, 120, 122, 124
  Yeltsin meets with, 181
Byelorussia, 22, 166

capitalism, 189, 195, 199, 200, 202
Carter, Jimmy, 54, 56, 123
Cas, Father. *See* Pugevicius, Father Casimer
Catholic Church, Lithuanian
  paganism and, 9
  persecution by Stalin, 39
  Polish cast of, 9
  and Russification attempt, 8, 37–38
Catholicism
  activism by Catholics, 37–39, 42–45
  nationalism and, 9, 37–38
Cekuolis, Algimantas (Sajudis activist), 53,
    216n.7, 226
  on Lithuanian independence, 93
  on possibility of coup, 170
  on Soviet corruption, 28, 47
Center Party (Lithuania), 197
Cepaitis, Virgiljius (Sajudis leader), 105, 227
Chechnya (Chechen republic), 166, 207–208
Chicago, 10
Children's Art Museum (Washington, D.C.),
    219n.26
Christian Democratic Party (Lithuania), 197
Chronicle of Current Events, 41
Chronicle of the Catholic Church in Lithuania,
    37–39, 42–45, 223
Clinton, Bill, 208–210
Club for the Defense of the Environment
    (Vides Aizasardzibas Klubs, VAK;
    Latvia), 48–49
CNN, 123, 151–152
Cold War, 115–116, 121, 210
Committee for the Salvation of Lithuania,
    145
communism
  intellectuals' belief in, 28–29
  pollution and, 80
Communist leaders' belief in right to rule,
    116
Communist Party of the Soviet Union. *See*
    CPSU
Congregation of the Eucharist, 37
Congress of People's Deputies. *See* CPD

conservatives, U.S., 121–122
coup attempt against Gorbachev. *See* Soviet
    Union, collapse of
Cox, Charles (U.S. Congressman), 72
CPD (Congress of People's Deputies;
    USSR), 64, 104
  Lithuanian-Russian tensions in, 76
CPSU (Communist Party of the Soviet
    Union)
  and Article 6 of Soviet constitution, 67,
    177
  corruption in, 85
  criticizes Gorbachev, 181
  growth of, 27
  LCP separates from, 67–69
  loses power/credibility, 57
  tensions with LCP, 66–67

Dainis, Ivans (Latvian leader), 178
Damusis, Ginte (assistant of Father Cas
    Pugevicius), 53, 54, 160, 227
Dapkus, Rita (Lithuanian parliament's press
    secretary), 148, 150–151
Deak, Istvan, 11–12
Defense of Human Rights Helsinki–86
    (Latvia), 48
Degutis, Algirdas (Lithuanian libertarian),
    29, 51, 69
Dekanidze, Boris (Vilnius Brigade leader),
    202
Dekanozov, Vladimir Georgievich (NKVD
    foreign dept. head), 15
Democratic Officers Movement (SHIELD;
    Soviet Union), 174
demonstrations. *See* activism; Bloody Sunday
Desert Shield, 133
Desert Storm, 133
diaspora, Lithuanian, 198–199
  KGB and, 55
  Landsbergis popular with, 133
  Lithuanian Information Center, 35–36
  Lithuanian repatriation fought by, 32–33
  as nourishing Lithuanian independence,
    31–34
  rallies Congress and public opinion, 151,
    156, 159
  size of, 9–10, 211n.5
  underground publications of, 34, 37–39
Dirse, Zoe (Canadian filmmaker)
  Baltic Fire, 219n.40
Dissent, 121
Dniester guard, 207

Dniester Soviet Socialist Republic, 207
Dudayev, Dzhokhar M. (Soviet air force general), 166
Dukakis, Michael, 123
Durbin, Richard (U.S. Congressman), 72

Edinstvo ("Unity"; Socialist Movement for Perestroika in Lithuania), 113–114
demonstrations by, 139, 140–141
elections in Lithuania, 30, 71–93
attempts to thwart Sajudis candidates, 96
campaigning, 97
fraud and tampering, 89–90
Independence Day demonstrations, 50, 71–74, 79–83
Landsbergis elected chairman, 97
monitors of, 72, 84–85
nationalism as the heart of, 96–97
Sajudis success in, 97
Ellis, Rear Admiral William B., 40
émigrés. See diaspora, Lithuanian
Engels, Frederick, 20
Estonia
Baltic-Soviet defense treaty, 14
boycotts referendum to preserve Soviet Union, 180
economic conditions in, 73–74
European Union membership by, 209
Germans in, 7
Russification of, 73
strategic position of, 171
Estonian-American National Council, 158
ethnonationalism, 21, 22–23
European Economic Community, 154
European Union (EU), 209
Eustis, Ralph (Coast Guard commander), 39–40
Evans, Roland (American journalist), 120–121, 155
Extraordinary Congress of the Communist Party of Lithuania (1989; Vilnius), 67–68

Fifth Wheel, 172
Finkelsteinas, Eitanas (Jewish Lithuanian scientist), 42
Finland, 15, 169
Fitzwater, Marlin, 130, 145
Foley, Thomas S. (U.S. Speaker of the House), 119
forest brotherhood (Lithuanian resistance), 80, 88–89

Four-Man Proposal (1987; Latvia), 49
four plus three plan, 143–144
Freedom League (Lithuania), 52, 56–57, 61

Gapon, Father George (Russian Orthodox priest), 174
Garuckas, Father Karolis (Lithuanian priest), 42
Gates, Robert (CIA director), 158
Geda, Sigitas (Lithuanian writer), 53
Gediminas, Duke, 110
Gedimino Square demonstration (1988; Cathedral Square, Vilnius), 52, 57
Gellner, Ernest, 204
Geneva 1949 ruling on forced conscription, 71, 144
Genzelis, Bronius (a Sajudis leader), 51, 105, 132–133, 218n.23
Georgia, 22, 180
protest of Soviet rule, 73
Red Army massacre in, 117
Geremek, Bronislaw (a Solidarity leader), 114
Germany, reunified, 124–125, 170
Gimtasis Krastas, 53
Gingrich, Newt, 119
glasnost, 73, 141, 142
Goble, Paul (U.S. State Department official), 152, 156–157
Gompert, David (U.S. National Security Council member), 158
Goncharov, Sergei (KGB Alpha unit commander), 190
Gorbachev, Mikhail
anger toward Balts, 66, 118
anger toward hard-liners, 111–112
anger toward Sajudis, 64–66
authority declines, 182–183
Baker meets with, 122
Balts, grants economic freedom to, 74
Bloody Sunday, as destroying image of, 174–176
Bloody Sunday, reaction to, 147, 153–154, 164
Bloody Sunday, role in, 175, 219n.9
brutality by, 73, 117 (see also Bloody Sunday, 1991)
on the centralized state, 65
chastises party leadership, KGB, police, 50
Cold War allowed to end by, 115
communism in Eastern Europe ended by, 117
coup plotted against, 181–182, 183–186

Gorbachev, Mikhail, *continued*
  economy mishandled by, 170
  German reunification aided by, 170
  glasnost, 73
  Landsbergis, relationship with, 116
  Lithuania, imposes economic embargo on,
    109–110, 122
  Lithuania, proposes presidential rule for,
    137–138, 140, 142
  Lithuania, urged to use force against,
    144–145
  Lithuanian independence, opposed by, 74,
    94–95, 109
  Lithuanian referendum favored by, 143
  Malta summit, 118
  naive about TV's potential, 141–142
  Nazerbayev meets with, 182
  neo-Stalinists courted by, 136–137
  neo-Stalinists' criticism of, 181
  nine plus one accord, 180–181
  perestroika, 106–107, 119
  popularity in the West, 116–117
  Prunskiene meets with, 138
  reforms proposed at London summit, 182
  reforms reversed by, 136
  replaced by Yanayev, 183–184
  resignation urged, 179–180
  returns from Cape Foros retreat, 2, 184
  shock over LCP/CPSU split, 69
  skill at manipulating Western press, 72–73,
    117, 154
  use of force as anathema to perestroika,
    105, 118
  Washington summit, 120, 122, 124
  Western support, dependence on, 154
  Yakovlev, relationship with, 59
  Yeltsin, relationship with, 111, 176, 177,
    180, 188
Gore, Al, 208
Grachev, Pavel (Russian defense minister), 1,
  188
Grand Vilnius Congress (1905, Seimas), 10
Green movement, 48–49, 50
Grinius, Kestutis (Sajudis member), 84–86,
  91, 97
Griskevicius, Petras (LCP leader), 27, 50
Gulf War, 131, 133, 134, 155, 158
Gylys, Povilas (Lithuanian foreign minister),
  203

hard-liners, Soviet, 136. *See also* Bolsheviks;
  neo-Stalinists
  admiration for Americans, 87–88

criticize Gorbachev, 181
determination of, 173
dismay over reforms, 50–51, 187
worried about nine plus one accord,
  180–181
Harris, Cindy Jurciukonis (aide to Sen.
  Riegle), 81
Helms, Jesse, 120
Helsinki Accords, 42
Herder, Johann Gottfried, 7
Hitler, Adolf
  invades France, 14–15
  sees Soviet Union as weak, 169
  signs Molotov-Ribbentrop Pact, 13–14
  takes over Memel, 4–5, 13
Hitler-Stalin Pact. *See* Molotov-Ribbentrop
  Pact
Holocaust, 16–18, 206, 223
Homeland Union (Lithuania), 204
Hotel Lietuva (Vilnius), 72
Howe, Irving, 121
Hussein, Saddam. *See* Gulf War

Ignalina Atomic Energy plant (Lithuania),
  145
immigrants. *See* diaspora, Lithuanian
independence, Lithuanian (1990-1991), 3, 74,
  94–117. *See also* Bloody Sunday, 1991;
  elections in Lithuania
  Bolshevik opposition to, 67
  diaspora support of, 31–34
  Gorbachev imposes economic embargo,
    109–110, 122
  Gorbachev responds with force, 107–108
  Gorbachev's opposition to, 74, 94–95
  Landsbergis's push for, 64, 81
  Lithuanians expect U.S. recognition, 98,
    100, 104–105, 119
  Poland, negotiations with, 114–115
  republics' interest in, 83–84, 95, 129–130,
    166
  Soviet negotiations with, 110–111, 124,
    127, 128, 130–131
  Soviet parliament, decreed by, 189–190
  Soviet use of force feared, 105, 167–169
  step-by-step *vs.* immediate, 103–104
  treatment of non-Lithuanians, 113
  U.S. does not recognize, 98, 99–101, 104,
    106, 119, 125–127
  U.S. support of, 120, 124
Innovation, 203
interfronts, 113
Iron Wolf, 13

Jablonskis, Jonas (Lithuanian linguist), 8

Jadvyga, Princess (Polish heiress), 6

Jermalavicius, Juozas (Bolshevik LCP leader), 68, 145, 146, 153, 227

Jewish Scientific Institute (YIVO, New York City), 53

Jews in Lithuania, 11–12, 98–99
  Communist Party membership of, 17, 18
  Holocaust, 16–18, 223

Jogaila, Prince, 6

Johnson, Daryll (American ambassador to Lithuania), 205

John XXIII, Pope, 34

The Jungle (Sinclair), 10

Juozaitis, Arvydas (Sajudis founder), 49, 64, 227
  on Gorbachev's reforms, 50
  helps found Sajudis, 51
  hostility toward Landsbergis, 51
  on Sajudis and Landsbergis, 58, 191
  tours North America, 53

Jurasas, Ausra (Lithuanian literary critic; wife of Jonas), 19

Jurasas, Jonas (Lithuanian theater director), 19, 44–45

Kagan, Joseph (Jewish Lithuanian émigré), 98–99

Kalanta, Romas (Lithuanian worker and dissident), 43

Karkle, Tija (VAK volunteer), 49

Karklins, Rasma, 26

Kaunas Faction, 52, 104

Kaunas (Lithuania), 11, 12, 79
  anti-Soviet riot, 1960, 43
  Ninth Fort, 17
  pollution in, 80

Kazakhstan, 22

Kemp, Jack, 130

Kennedy-Nixon debates, 123

Kezys, Daiva (Lithuanian-American activist), 160–161

KGB, 132, 216n.1
  attempts to crush ethnic civil rights activists, 213–214n.7
  attempts to provoke violence in Lithuania, 140
  attempts to thwart underground publications, 37, 38
  Bloody Sunday massacre by, 146–147 (see also Bloody Sunday, 1991)
  harasses dissidents, 41–42, 44, 48

Lithuanian diaspora and, 55
  opposes coup, 188
  opposes perestroika, 137
  thwarts anti-Soviet demonstrations, 43

Khrisostom, Archbishop, 140

Khrushchev, Nikita, 158
  delivers indictment of Stalin, 58
  reforms by, 186–187
  releases Lithuanian deportees, 88
  treatment of non-Russians, 25

Kissinger, Henry, 56

Klaipeda (Lithuania), 4–5

Klopotowski, Tadeusz (a Polish senator), 114, 115

Knight, Amy, 24

Knights for Lithuania, 35

Kohl, Helmut, 110, 209

Kojelis, elder, 56

Kojelis, Linas (Lithuanian-American lobbyist), 56, 227

Kovalev, Sergei (Russian biologist), 41–42, 43

Kovno. See Kaunas

Krause, Charles, 54

Kravchuk, Leonid (Ukrainian leader), 166, 180

Kreve-Mickevicius, Vincas (Lithuanian prime minister), 15

Krickus, Richard J.
  The Superpowers in Crisis, 213–214n.7

Krol, George (American diplomat), 168

Kryuchkov, Vladimir A. (KGB chairman), 136, 137, 181, 182, 183, 186

Kubilius, Andrius (Sajudis office manager and Homeland Union leader), 91, 191–192, 208, 209, 227

Kudaba, Ceslovas (Lithuanian geographer), 53

Kudirka, Simas (Lithuanian would-be defector), 39–40

Kuklyte, Virginija (Lithuanian schoolgirl), 152

Kuprys, Stasys (Lithuanian patriot), 160

Kurkova, Bella (Soviet TV producer), 172

Kuron, Jacek (a Solidarity leader), 114

Kuwait. See Gulf War

Kuzmickas, Bronius (a Sajudis founder and Lithuanian deputy chairman), 51, 111

Kyrgyzstan, 22

Labor Party. See Lithuanian Democratic Labor Party

LAC (Lithuanian American Council), 32

La Guardia, Fiorello, 33
Landsbergis, Gabrielus (grandfather of
    Vytautas Landsbergis), 8
Landsbergis, Vytautas (Lithuanian president),
    28, 30, 203, 227
  Bush meets with, 133–134, 137, 143
  calls for Lithuanian independence, 64
  courage and determination of, 110,
    192–193
  criticism of, 139, 140, 191, 194, 197
  elected president, 97
  four plus three plan proposed by, 143–144
  Gorbachev blamed for Bloody Sunday by,
    175
  Gorbachev's relationship with, 116
  hostility toward Juozaitis, 51
  on independence, 101–102, 103
  independence, incautious push for, 81, 98,
    102–103, 106
  mobilizes Lithuanian patriots, 139, 140,
    145–146
  on nationalism, 62
  nationalists form the republics consult
    with, 166
  negotiations with Soviets, 110–111, 124,
    127, 128, 130–131
  participation in CPD, 65
  popularity of, 69, 70, 133
  presidency in trouble, 191–192, 193–194,
    197
  reacts to Soviet military force, 108–109
  reacts to Soviet military threats and price
    increases, 140, 143
  on Soviet troops in Lithuania, 197
  tours North America, 53
  urges U.S. to recognize Lithuanian inde-
    pendence, 109
Latvia. See also Riga
  activism in, 48
  Baltic-Soviet defense treaty, 14
  boycotts referendum to preserve Soviet
    Union, 180
  economic conditions in, 73–74
  European Union membership, 209
  Germans in, 7
  Russification of, 27, 73
  strategic position of, 171
Latvian language, 8
Laurinkus, Mecys (Lithuanian parliament
    member), 49, 51, 227
Lavut, Aleksandr (Russian democratic
    activist), 43–44

LCP. See Lithuanian Communist Party
LCRA (Lithuanian Catholic Religious Aid),
    35–36, 53–54, 160
LDLP. See Lithuanian Democratic Labor
    Party
Lebed, Aleksandr (Russian commander), 207
Lenin, Vladimir Ilyich
  on nationalism, 21
  signs treaty with Lithuania, 11
  treatment of non-Russians, 21–22
LIC (Lithuanian Information Center),
    35–36, 53–54, 160
Lietuvos Aides, 203
Lietuvos Rytas, 203
Lieven, Anatol, 17, 49, 103–104, 138
Ligachev, Yegor (Soviet hard-liner), 67, 125
Lingys, Vitas (Lithuanian newspaper editor),
    202
Linkevicius, Linas (Lithuanian defense min-
    ister), 203
Literatu Svetaine (Literary Café; Vilnius), 79
Lithuania
  activism in, 49–52, 54
  buildings in, 78–79, 90
  crime in, 201–202
  cuisine of, 89
  economic conditions in, 73–74
  formality of Lithuanians, 74
  Germans in, 12
  homogeneous population of, 26
  Poles and Russians in, 12, 67, 82, 113–115,
    134
  rural character of, 86
  Soviet reparations for occupation, 108
  Soviet troops in, 106, 107, 127, 140,
    167–168, 197
  status of women in, 84
Lithuania, history of, 4–29. See also Bloody
    Sunday, 1991; diaspora, Lithuania; elec-
    tions in Lithuania; independence,
    Lithuanian; Kaunas; Lithuania, indepen-
    dent; nationalism; Vilnius
  Ateitis movement, 9, 33, 35
  Baltic-Soviet defense treaty, 14
  boycotts referendum to preserve Soviet
    Union, 180
  Catholicism, 6, 9, 37–38
  chronology of major events, 222–225
  democracy ends, 222
  forest brotherhood, 80, 88–89
  German occupation, 16, 18–19
  Germans in Lithuania Minor, 7

Gorbachev imposes economic embargo, 109–110, 122
Hitler takes over Memel, 4–5, 13
Holocaust, 16–18, 223
independence established, 1200s, 5–6
independence established, 1918, 7, 11
independence established, 1990-1991, 74
Klaipeda occupation, 4–5
League of Nations membership, 11
Lenin renounces claims to Lithuania, 11
Lithuania Major absorbed by Russia, 7
Lithuanian border guards murdered, 165–166, 183
migration of Lithuanians, 20, 32, 33
military coup in 1926, 12
minority problems, 11–12
nationalism, 7–8, 27
Polish-Lithuanian Commonwealth, 6
Polish-Lithuanian relations strained, 12
referendum proposal rejected, 143
referendum upholds independence, 164
Russification, 8–9, 23, 24–27, 36–38, 73, 213–214n.7
Soviet annexation, 14–16, 131, 144 (*see also* Molotov-Ribbentrop Pact)
Soviet occupation, 14–16, 19–20
Stalin oppresses Lithuanians, 16, 19, 88
strategic location of Lithuania, 5, 6, 171
Taryba established, 11
United States recognizes Lithuania, 11
Lithuania, independent
agriculture, 195, 204–205
attitude toward Soviet system, 199–200, 202–203
banking crisis, 203
capitalism, 200, 202, 204
citizenship law, 205–206
Communists return to power, 197–198
corruption/crime, 200–204
economy, 193, 194–196, 205
elections, 203–204
European status, 206, 209
fear of abandonment by the West, 208
fear of Russian reincorporation/manipulation, 207–208, 209
free press, 203, 205
Holocaust, apology for role in, 206
Labor party, 191, 196–197, 200, 204
nationalist phase ends, 193
NATO, membership desired, 206–207, 208
Poland, relations with, 206

Russia, relations with, 193, 194, 197, 206
Soviet culture remaining, 193, 204
Soviet troops withdrawn, 206, 207
unemployment, 194
Lithuanian-American Community, 52–53, 157–159
Lithuanian American Council (LAC), 32
Lithuanian Catholic Religious Aid (LCRA), 35–36, 53–54, 160
Lithuanian Communist Party (LCP)
autonomy from Moscow, 27–28
and corruption, 200
and CPSU, 66–69
losses in Lithuanian elections, 97
night party, 68, 137, 139, 153
opposes Lithuanian independence, 144–145
relationship to Sajudis, 60–61, 64, 69
Lithuanian Democratic Labor Party (LDLP), 191, 196–197, 200, 204
Lithuanian embassy (Moscow), 128–129
Lithuanian Helsinki Watch Group, 42, 45–46
Lithuanian Independence Day demonstrations (1988), 50, 71–74, 79–83
Lithuanian Information Center (LIC), 35–36, 53–54, 160
Lithuanian language, 7, 8, 67
Lithuanian legation hotel (Moscow), 128–129
Lithuanian Supreme Council, 97, 139
Litimpeks, 203
Little Odessa (New York City), 202
London economic summit, 182
Lozoraitis, Stasys (elder; Lithuanian foreign minister), 33–34
Lozoraitis, Stasys (younger; Lithuanian ambassador), 34, 89, 104–105, 197, 198, 228
Lukyanov, Anatoly (Soviet parliament chairman), 181, 183, 186
Luxembourg, Rosa (Polish theorist), 21

Mafiya, 72, 85, 98, 196, 202, 203
Malkina, Tatyana (Soviet reporter), 186
Malta summit (1989), 118
Marx, Karl, 20
Matlock, Jack (U.S. ambassador to the Soviet Union), 105–106, 122
criticizes Bush, 181, 184–185
on NATO, 208–209

Matulionas, Arvydas (LCP Politburo member), 132–133, 137, 144–145, 177
Mazheikai oil refinery (Lithuania), 109
McGinnis, Joe
    The Selling of the President, 123
Medalinskas, Alvydas (a Sajudis founder), 131–133
media, power of, 123, 141–142, 153–156, 160, 218n.12
media coverage of Lithuania, 36, 54, 120–121, 122–123, 124
    Bloody Sunday covered by Lithuanian TV/radio, 141–142, 153, 169, 171–172
    Independence Day demonstrations, 71–73
Medvedev, Nikolai (Sajudis member), 113
Medvedev, Vadim (Soviet Politburo member), 67
Memel, 4–5
Mendelsohn, Ezra, 11, 17
Michnik, Adam (a Solidarity leader), 114
Miller, John (U.S. Congressman), 72
Mindaugas, King, 6
missiles, SS-18, 2
Mitkin, Nikolai (Russian secretary of LCP), 59–60, 61
Mitterrand, François, 110
Moldova (formerly Moldavia), 22, 180, 207
Molotov, Vyacheslav Mikhailovich, 15–16
Molotov cocktails, 169
Molotov-Ribbentrop Pact (1939), 12, 13–14, 144
    Balts request United Nations to condemn, 66
    illegality of, 58, 65–66, 131
    protested by Sakharov, 45–46
    protests of, 45–46, 48, 49–50, 60
Moscow News, 167
Moscow summits, 143, 157, 159–160, 182
Motieka, Kazimeras (a Sajudis leader), 141, 151
Musanya, Loretta (Lithuania patriot), 148

Nakas, Victor (Lithuanian Information Center official), 30, 123, 132, 228
    on Abisala, 96
    on the diaspora, 54, 199, 211n.5
    informs reporters about Lithuania, 53, 142
    KGB file on, 55
Natasha (Lithuanian counselor's secretary), 129
The Nation, 121
National Center for Urban Ethnic Affairs, 34–35

National Endowment for Democracy (U.S.), 53
National Heritage Society (Estonia), 49
nationalism, 7–8, 27, 30–46. *See also* diaspora, Lithuanian
    Catholicism and, 9, 37–38
    encouraged by Lithuanian independence, 166
    ethnic, 21, 22
    Lenin on, 21
    Marx on, 20
    and resistance to Soviet regime, 39–46
    Russification and, 8–9, 22–23, 24–27, 36–38, 73, 213–214n.7
    strengthened by 1988 Sajudis demonstrations, 62
    and underground publications, 34, 37–39, 41
National Salvation Committee (Lithuania), 145–146
NATO, 208–209
Nazerbayev, Nursultan (Khazkhstan president), 180, 182, 184
Nazi-Soviet Pact. *See* Molotov-Ribbentrop Pact
neo-Stalinists, 136–137, 166–167. *See also* Bolsheviks; hard-liners, Soviet
    criticize Gorbachev, 181
    demoralized, 174
    reaction to Yeltsin, 176, 181
Nevzorov, Aleksandr (Soviet TV newsman), 172
New York Times, 119
New Zealand, 15
Nezavisimayha Gazeta, 186
night party, 68, 137, 139, 153. *See also* Lithuanian Communist Party
nine plus one accord, 180–181
Ninth Fort (Kaunas, Lithuania), 17
Nitze, Paul (Reagan's arms control adviser), 208–209
Nixon, Richard, 123, 168
NKVD (predecessor of KGB), 17, 18
Novak, Robert (American journalist), 120–121, 155

Okinczyc, Czeslav (Polish Sajudis member), 114
Olis, Anthony (Chicago attorney), 31
OMON, 165–166, 183
On the Edge of the Abyss (Yakovlev), 59
OSCE (Organization for Security and Cooperation in Europe), 210

Ozolas, Romualdas (a Sajudis founder and
  Lithuanian deputy-prime minister), 97,
  115, 192, 228
  criticizes Landsbergis, 194
  criticizes Slezevicius, 203
  helps found Sajudis, 51
  meets with Matlock, 105
  warns of Soviet attack, 156

paganism, 9
Paleckis, Justas (elder; Lithuanian president),
  15, 66
Paleckis, Justas (younger; LCP chief of ideology), 66
Pangonyte, Laima (Sajudis filmmaker), 94
Pavlov, Valentin (Soviet prime minister), 137
  coup attempt, 181, 182, 183
perestroika, 46, 58, 106–107, 119, 187
  force as anathema to, 105, 118
  KGB opposes, 137
Petkevicius, Vytautas (Lithuanian writer),
  59–60
Petkus, Viktoras (Lithuanian dissident),
  41–42, 57, 228
Petrakov, Nikolai (Gorbachev's economic
  adviser), 175
Pipes, Richard, 174
Polabinskus, Aidas (Lithuanian-American
  student), 102
Poland
  under Communism, 195
  insurrections of 1830s and 1860s, 7–8
  support of Lithuania, 114
Poles in Lithuania, 12, 114–115
Polish-Lithuanian Commonwealth, 6
pollution, 80
Popov, Gavril K. (Moscow mayor), 177, 181
popular front. See activism
Pravda, 66
protests. See activism; Bloody Sunday
Prunskiene, Kazimiera (a Sajudis founder
  and Lithuanian prime minister), 75, 97,
  228
  Bush meets with, 138
  Gorbachev meets with, 110, 138
  helps found Sajudis, 51
  Landsbergis, relationship with, 111, 122,
  138
  Landsbergis ousts, 140
  price hikes proposed by, 139
Prussian language, 8
Pugevicius, Father Casimer, 34–36, 43, 54,
  228

Pugo, Boris (head of Soviet ministry of interior), 27, 112, 137, 167, 179, 182, 183
Putschists, 187

Reagan, Ronald, 104, 123, 185
Red Army, 169. See also Bloody Sunday, 1991
  brutality by, 71, 117, 216n.1
  demoralized and angry, 170–171, 177
  opposes coup, 187–188
  urged by Yeltsin not to fire on unarmed
  civilians, 178
Red-Brown coalition, 208
Remnick, David, 58, 175–176, 179
Republicans, U.S.
  TV manipulated by, 123
  on U.S.–Soviet relations, 119–120
resistance. See activism; Bloody Sunday
Respublica, 203
Ribbentrop, Joachim von, 5
Ribbentrop-Molotov Pact. See Molotov-
  Ribbentrop Pact
Rice, Condoleezza, 158, 159
Riegle, Senator Don, 81
Riga (Latvia), 166
  massacre in, 157, 160, 219n.40
Rikken, Mary Ann (American activist), 158
Roosevelt, Franklin, 20, 31, 32
Rosenberg, Alfred, 16
Rosenthal, Abe (American journalist), 121,
  155
Russia. See also Soviet Union
  and creation of Soviet Union, 21–22
  force used by, 207–208
  helps Lithuania break economic embargo,
  110
  Russification of Lithuania attempted by,
  8–9
  secessionist movements in, 207
  Yeltsin replaces democrats with hard-
  liners, 208
Russian democrats, 137, 159. See also Yeltsin,
  Boris
  morale of, 173
  relationship with Gorbachev, 175
  Yeltsin replaces with hard-liners, 208
Russian Helsinki Group (Moscow), 45
Russian Revolution, 1917, 174
Russian Soviet Federated Socialist Republics
  (RSFSR), 22
Rutskoi, Aleksandr (Russian vice-president),
  187
Ryzhkov, Nikolai (Soviet prime minister),
  111, 131, 137, 144

Sadunaite, Nijole (Lithuanian activist), 49–50

Safire, William (American journalist), 121, 155–156

Sajudis (Lietuvos Persitvakymo Sajudis; Lithuanian Reconstruction Movement), 30, 51–65
  composition of, 51–52
  decision to declare immediate independence, 103–104
  declares Lithuanian sovereignty, 63–64
  demonstration in Gedimino Square, 1988, 52, 57, 60–61, 62
  demonstration in Snieckus, 1988, 55, 62
  demonstration in Vingis Park, 1988, 60, 62
  diaspora's attitude toward, 52–54, 56
  election losses, 196
  formation of, 47, 51
  headquarters of, 92–93
  Independence Day demonstrations, 50, 71–74, 79–83
  lacks power in Lithuania, 65
  LCP, relationship to, 60–61, 64, 69
  Lithuanian Catholic attitude toward, 57, 63
  meets with Matlock to discuss independence, 105
  on Molotov-Ribbentrop Pact, 65–66
  motives of former Communists in, 77
  nationalist nature of, 58
  republics' interest in, 129–130
  Second Great Vilnius Seimas, 62–63
  wins seats on CPD, 64–65

Sakadolskis, Romas (Lithuanian-American activist), 55, 148–149, 228

Sakharov, Andrei
  protests Molotov-Ribbentrop Pact, 45–46
  released from prison, 57
  supports Lithuanian dissidents, 41–42

samizdats (underground publications), 34, 37–39, 41

Santara Sviesa (U.S.), 53

Sarpalius, Bill (U.S. Congressman), 72

Sartavicius, Ricardus (Lithuanian TV correspondent), 172–173

Schelest, Petro (Ukrainian Communist Party secretary), 25

Scowcroft, Brent (U.S. National Security Council director), 118–119, 155, 157–158, 184–185

Second Great Vilnius Seimas, 62–63

Selling of the President, The (McGinnis), 123

Senn, Alfred Erich, 112
  on Bloody Sunday, 140, 145
  on Brazauskas, 61, 64
  on Landsbergis, 111
  on LCP-CPSU tensions, 66

Shaposhnikov, Yevgeni, 1, 188

Shatalin Plan, 136

Shenin, Oleg (CPSU organizational secretary), 112

Sheremetyevo One airport (Moscow), 75–76

Shev, Vladislav (LCP and Lithuanian parliament member), 112, 137

Shevardnadze, Eduard (Soviet foreign minister), 106, 122, 130–131, 136, 207

SHIELD (Democratic Officers Movement; Soviet Union), 174

Shtromas, Aleksandras (Lithuanian Holocaust survivor), 17–18, 27

Simenas, Albertas (Lithuanian prime minister), 140

Simes, Dmitri (Nixon adviser), 168

Sinclair, Upton
  The Jungle, 10

SIOP (Single Integrated Operational Plan), 37

Siv, Sichan (White House Office of Public Affairs director), 157

600 Seconds, 172

60 Minutes, 201

Skabeikis, Marian (LIC worker), 53

Skindulas, Saulius (Lithuanian English teacher), 84, 90

Sladkevicius, Cardinal Vincentas (Lithuanian bishop), 79–80

Slezevicius, Aldolfas (Lithuanian prime minister), 200–201, 203–204

Smetona, Antanas (Lithuanian president), 12, 13, 15

Smith, Hedrick
  on Baku massacre, 117
  on Bloody Sunday, 154, 172–173
  on Communist Party, 76
  on embargo, 110
  on Russians in Lithuania, 114

Snieckus, Antanas (Lithuanian Communist leader), 24, 27

Sobchak, Anatoly A. (Leningrad mayor), 172, 177

socialism, Marxist, 20

Socialist Movement for Perestroika in Lithuania. See Edinstvo

social theory, Western, 20–21

Sokolauskas, Arturas (Lithuanian soldier), 71

Solidarity, 134
Songaila, Ringaudas (LCP leader), 50, 60, 61
Sovetskaya Litva, 39–40
Soviet-American Chautauqua conference
 (1986; Jurmala, Latvia), 48
Soviet culture, 91–92, 204
Soviet media
 censorship and distortions by, 55, 142, 163,
  171–172
 on Sajudis, 83
Soviet military. *See* Red Army
Soviet pluralism, 20, 25, 175–176
Soviet Union. *See also* CPSU; Soviet Union,
 collapse of; Stalin, Joseph
 buildings in, 90
 creation of, 21–22
 disinformation about Lithuania, 121, 123,
  134–135, 139
 economic sanctions against, 154
 favoritism toward Russians, 25–26
 food in, 128–129
 foreigners' travel restricted by, 20, 212n.31
 funding for civilian needs lacking, 74
 Gulf War exploited by, 133, 134
 invasion of Finland, 169
 Lithuania annexed by, 14–16
 Lithuania repatriation forced by, 32
 military strength of, 2
 nine plus one accord, 180–181
 presidential rule proposed for Lithuania,
  137–138, 140, 142
 red tape and inefficiency in, 75, 77–78
 referendum to preserve, 180
 Russification drive by, 8–9, 23, 24–27,
  36–38, 213–214n.7
 scope of change in, 188–189
 violence by security forces, 165–166
 West, dependence on, 77, 113, 154
Soviet Union, collapse of, 165–190
 coup, media coverage of, 1–2, 183, 186
 coup carried out, 183–184
 coup defeated/aborted, 185–189
 coup opposed by Soviet military, 187–188,
  190
 coup plotted, 181–182, 183–186, 189–190
 coup predicted, 166, 167, 170, 186
 neo-Stalinists demoralized, 174
 state of emergency imposed, 183–184
SS-18 missiles, 2
Stalin, Joseph
 on Bolsheviks and Lenin, 21
 oppression by, 16, 19, 88
 persecutes Catholic Church, 39

 Russification campaign of, 23
 signs Molotov-Ribbentrop Pact, 13–14
 on Snieckus, 27
Stankevich, Sergei (Soviet political scientist),
 175
State Committee for the State of Emergency
 (Soviet Union), 183–184
Sukys, Algirdas (Lithuanian patriot), 147
Sununu, John (White House chief of staff),
 159
Superpowers in Crisis, The (Krickus),
 213–214n.7
Supreme Committee for Liberation of
 Lithuania. *See* VLIK
Sweden, 15

Tajikistan, 22
Talbott, Strobe, 155, 158–159, 209
Tamkevicius, Father Sigitas, 37, 43
Tartars, 6
Taryba, 11
TASS, 183
Tatars, 6
Taurinskaite, Egle (assistant to Laurinkus),
 84, 200
Tautininkai, 12, 13
Tehran Conference (1943), 32
Terleckas, Antanas (Freedom League leader),
 49–50, 61, 229
Thatcher, Margaret, 116
Tiblisi (Georgia), Red Army massacre in, 117
Tiesa, 68
Transcaucasian Federation, 22
Trapans, Jan A., 48
Treaty of Lublin (1569), 6
Tripartite Alliance (1795), 6
Turkmenistan, 22
TV, power of, 123, 141–142
Twentieth Party Congress (1956; CPSU),
 59–60

Ukmerge (Lithuania), 86
Ukraine, 21–22, 166
underground publications (samizdats), 34,
 37–39, 41
union of four proposal, 179, 180
United States. *See also* diaspora, Lithuanian
 Balts' independence supported by,
  209–210
 ethnicity in, 34–35
 interest in Gorbachev's survival, 101–102,
  122

United States, *continued*
 Lithuanian nationalism and Catholicism
  in, 9
 Lithuania not recognized by, 98, 99–101,
  104, 106, 119, 125–127
 Lithuania recognized by, 11
 NATO expansion opposed by, 208–209
 outrage over massacre in Vilnius, 152
 on Russification of non-Russian Soviets,
  36–37
 Soviet annexation of Baltics not recognized by, 15, 20, 31, 56, 118, 119, 122
 Soviet dependence on, 77, 113
 Soviet goodwill needed by, 134
 as superpower, 77
 urges Soviet Union to respect Lithuanian
  independence, 119
Urbanovich, Yuri (Soviet Diplomatic Academy faculty member), 212n.31
Urbsys, Juozas (Lithuanian foreign minister),
  14, 60
Uskhochik, Vladimir N. (Soviet general), 151,
  154
USSR. *See* Soviet Union
Uzbekistan, 22, 110

Vaitekunas, Romasis (Lithuanian minister of
  interior), 203
VAK (Vides Aizsardzibas Klubs; Club for
  the Defense of the Environment;
  Latvia), 48–49
Van Reenan, Antanas J., 31, 32
Vardas, V. Stanley, 45, 60, 61
Varennikov, Valentin (a Soviet military com-
  mander), 146
Vasiliauskas, Lionginas (Sajudis member),
  74–75, 131, 216n.3
Velykanova, Tatiana (Russian democratic
  activist), 43–44
Venclova, Tomas (Lithuanian poet), 41, 42
Vigilant, 39–40
Vilkas, Eduardas (Sajudis deputy), 103–104
Vilnius Brigade, 202
Vilnius (Lithuania), 12, 61, 149. *See also*
  Bloody Sunday
 architecture of, 167
 crime in, 202
 Gedimino Square demonstration, 52, 57
 pilgrimages to, 168
VLIK (Vyriausias Lietuvos Islaisvinimo
  Komitetas), 55
 Lithuanian repatriation fought by, 32–33
Voice of America (VOA), 55, 148–149

Voldemaras, Augustinas, 12–13
Volsky, Arkady (Yeltsin opponent), 187
Volungeviciute, Ona (Lithuanian patriot),
  148, 149
Vremya, 145, 172
Vyriausias Lietuvos Islaisvinimo Komitetas.
  See VLIK
Vytautas Magnus University (Kaunas), 164

Warsaw Treaty Organization (WTO), 36–37
Washington Post, 119
Washington summit (1990), 120, 122, 124
Wells, Sumner (acting Secretary of State), 31
World Lithuanian Community, 62
WTO (Warsaw Treaty Organization), 36–37
Wujek, Henryk (a Polish leader), 114, 115
Wyman, Lowry and Barnabas (American
  lawyer and husband), 150

Yakovlev, Aleksandr (Soviet Politburo member), 58–59, 112
 On the Edge of the Abyss, 59
 on Lithuanian independence, 63, 95
 on nationalism, 59–60
 on reform, 59
 warns Gorbachev, 182
Yalta Conference (1945), 32
Yanayev, Gennady (Soviet vice-president), 1,
  137, 183, 186
Yankunin, Gleb (Russian orthodox priest),
  43–44
Yazov, Dimitri T. (Soviet defense minister),
  167, 170
 coup attempt, 181, 183, 186, 188
 reports Soviet threats, 125, 136
Yeltsin, Boris, 96, 159
 becomes chairman of Russian Supreme
  Soviet, 111, 176
 Bush meets with, 181
 character of, 178–179
 coup, arouses opposition to, 184
 coup, learns of, 184
 coup denounced by, 1
 coup forces defied by, 185, 186
 CPSU cells disbanded by, 179
 CPSU outlawed by, 1, 189
 elected president of Russia, 179
 Gorbachev, relationship with, 111, 176,
  177, 180, 188
 Gorbachev criticized by, 145, 176
 Gorbachev urged to resign by, 180
 meets with Baltic leaders, 178

nine plus one accord, 180–181
popular support for, 176, 177, 178, 179
replaces democrats with hard-liners, 208
resigns from CPSU, 176–177
supports Lithuania, 111, 177–178
union of four proposal, 179, 180
urges soldiers not to fire on unarmed
    civilians, 178
YIVO (Jewish Scientific Institute, New York
    City), 53
Youth Lithuania, 13

Zaleckas, Kestutis (Lithuanian CPD mem-
    ber), 64
Zeligowski, Lucijian (Polish general), 11, 12
Zingeris, Emmanuelis (Jewish Lithuanian
    leader), 53, 208, 209, 229
Zukas, Algimantas (Lithuanian filmmaker),
    71, 216n.1
Zygas, Arydas (American chemistry profes-
    sor), 83
Zyuganov, Gennady (Russian Communist
    leader), 208

ABOUT THE AUTHOR

Richard J. Krickus is Distinguished Professor of Political Science at Mary Washington College. His bachelor's, master's, and doctoral degrees are from the College of William and Mary, the University of Massachusetts, and Georgetown University, respectively. Cofounder of the National Center for Urban Ethnic Affairs, he has been a national security analyst for the Hudson Institute, and he held the H. L. Oppenheimer Chair for Warfighting Strategy at the U.S. Marine Corps University. Since serving as an international monitor to the 1990 Lithuanian elections, he has visited the Baltic countries on numerous occasions. Dr. Krickus' writing has appeared in the *Washington Post,* the *Wall Street Journal,* and the *Christian Science Monitor,* and he often appears on television to discuss changes in the former Soviet Union, the breakup of which he predicted in a previous book *Superpowers in Crisis: Implications of Domestic Discord* (Brassey's, 1987). Dr. Krickus lives in Oakton, Virginia.

DATE DUE

GAYLORD			PRINTED IN U.S.A.